ROOMS OFF
THE CORRIDOR

This book is dedicated, with her permission,

to

Elizabeth, Lady Brunner

who, in 1943,
proposed that the WI should have its own college,
and whose vision is one of the central threads
that run through the book.

ROOMS OFF THE CORRIDOR

Education in the WI and
50 years of Denman College
1948 – 1998

Anne Stamper

Copyright © National Federation of Women's Institutes
First published 1998 by WI Books
104 New Kings Road, London SW6 4LY

in association with Stable Ltd
Glebe House, Church Street
Crediton, Devon EX17 2AF

R.G. Smethurst, who has written the Preface, is President of the National Institute of
Adult Continuing Education. NIACE has a broad remit to promote lifelong learning
opportunities for adults. NIACE works to develop increased participation in education
and training for those who do not have easy access because of barriers of class, gender,
age, race, language and culture, learning difficulties or disabilities, or insufficient
financial resources. NIACE is a registered charity, number 1002775.
Address: NIACE, 21 De Montfort Street, Leicester LE1 7GE.

British Library Cataloguing in Publication Data.
A CIP catalogue record for this book is available from the British Library.

ISBN   0 947990 42 9

Printed and bound in Great Britain
by Short Run Press Ltd, Exeter, Devon

Back cover photograph:
Lady Brunner and Anne Stamper in front of Denman College.

Photographs from the archives of the National Federation of Women's Institutes and
Denman College. In addition (1) from *50 Years of Achievement*, Walker & Hood, Federated
WIs of Ontario, 1948; (4) *Grace Hadow*, Deneke, OUP, 1946; (10) photo by Elizabeth
Harvey; (14) from 'Housewife', article on Denman College by Janet Moss, May, 1949;
(15) photo by Joyce Cormack.

CONTENTS

List of Tables

List of Figures

PREFACE

Both in theory and in practice good adult education is deceptively simple. What is required is a shift in viewpoint – in the jargon, the substitution of consumer-led provision for producer-led provision, and of education as a life-long process for the notion that it should all be concentrated in the early years of life. An education system geared to life-long learning would ensure that provision is available to suit the wishes of the individual learner, covering the topics required in a style, and at a level, time and place, of his or her own choosing.

From its beginnings a century ago in Canada, through its somewhat surprising landfall in Britain in Anglesey in 1915, and its important work in both World Wars, to its widespread activities today, the Women's Institute movement has always been intimately concerned with education. At first, in Canada, this meant spreading knowledge of domestic science, and when the movement came to wartime Britain the first committee meeting of the first WI, at Llanfairpwll, agreed "that the food supply of the country be the special subject of discussion". But the concerns quickly spread to wider social issues, so that by 1919 the Constitution provided that the Women's Institutes had power to provide for the fuller education of countrywomen in citizenship, in public questions both national and international, and in music, drama and other cultural subjects as well as to secure instruction and training in all branches of handcrafts, domestic science, health and social welfare.

This book traces the way in which those early educational aims came to fruition not just in the programmes of the individual institutes but especially in the establishment of Denman College; in Lady Brunner's words "our own WI College – a place ... homely and welcoming, where, in the pleasantest of possible surroundings, away from the responsibilities and distractions of our usual lives ... we should be free to experiment along our own lines in the kind of courses we think would suit our members best".

Anne Stamper chronicles the attempts to fulfil this vision with sometimes painful honesty. It is the story of powerful, well-connected women like Trudie Denman, the young wife of a former Governor-General of Australia, Grace Hadow, Principal of what later became St Anne's College, Oxford, and Lady Brunner, grand-daughter of Henry Irving. But it is also the story of thousands of ordinary members of WIs who have come to Denman and had their lives transformed.

Starting where the student is, providing what the student wants, helping to encourage the anxious with excellently-qualified but ever-supportive tutors: my only concern is that in another fifty years Denman will seem just as innovative in promoting true life-long learning as it does today. Adult educators should read this account for inspiration, and WI members with pride.

R.G. Smethurst
Provost of Worcester College, Oxford
President, National Institute of Adult Continuing Education

ACKNOWLEDGEMENTS

I am indebted to many people who have helped me to write this book. I cannot begin to mention them all, but in particular I would like to record my thanks to:

The *NFWI Executive Committee* for commissioning the book, the *Denman Management Committee* for suggesting it in the first place, and for encouragement and interest in its progress and in the findings of the survey.

Dick Smethurst for the support and advice he has given to NFWI over the years, for allowing me to quote from his Livingstone Lecture, and for writing the preface to this book.

Elizabeth Lady Brunner, who talked to me at her home at Greys Court for several hours in September 1996. Hearing her talk about the founding of the college gave me some understanding of what mattered to WI members in the 1940s. It was a great privilege to hear her reflect on the growth and development of the college over 50 years.

Walter Drews, whose thesis saved me months of research time. Discussions with him provided me with a clearer picture of how Denman compared with other short-stay residential colleges.

Hilda Jones, who invited me to spend a day with her at her home and whose clear recollections of 20 years at the college provided me with a picture of its evolution that no one else could have given me.

Lady Anglesey, who met me at Denman to discuss the educational work of the NFWI and the part played in it by the college.

Staff at NFWI and Denman College who provided information and answered my often urgent questions, especially *Jean Brewer* and *Cheryl Summers* at NFWI HQ, and *Jeanette Booth, Diana Kearley, Rosemary Lynn, Tracy Strain* and *Kathy Tiernan* at Denman College, and   particularly *Graham Jones* who has always been willing to discuss ideas and produce statistics.

The Denman representatives of the Federations who distributed the questionnaires, and collected and returned them at a very busy time of year, and the 700-plus members who completed them.

Tutors at Denman who answered my questions and were always prepared to talk to me over meals and at other times snatched from their busy tutoring timetable.

Numerous students at Denman who talked to me over meals, or coffee or drinks, happy to share their experiences and to tell me what Denman and the WI had done for them.

Those members who replied to my letter in *Home and Country*, those who donated copies of the books I asked for, and those who wrote of their personal experiences, some of whom sent photographs and other memorabilia, all of which are now in the Denman archives.

Susan Stockley and *Anne Ballard,* who are working on the NFWI archives and who sorted out files for me that related to the educational work of the organisation.

Caroline Pike, who looks after the Denman archive of photographs, for helping me to select suitable illustrations for the book.

Meg Nellist, who tutored me on a calligraphy course, and who subsequently agreed to design the cover for the book.

Past Chairmen of the Denman College Management who have shared their experiences with me, by completing questionnaires or by talking to me.

Several people who remember the college in its early days, including *Margaret Palmer* the first secretary at Denman, *Mary Clarke*, the first gardener at the college, and *Elisabeth Harvey,* who worked at Home Acres.

Jean Baxter, one of the volunteer librarians at the college, who was tutored by Grace Hadow, and who passed on some documents found by Jan Bateson's daughter after her mother died. These are now in the college archives.

Lyndsay Hacket Pain, chairman of the 1985 Appeal Committee, who recalled that traumatic time in discussions with me.

Members of my own WI, *Ringmer Evening*, and the *East Sussex Federation*, who helped me in the development of the questionnaire.

WI Books Ltd for publishing and *Simon Goodenough* for editing a book that is somewhat different to the books usually on their list.

NIACE for help with the marketing of the book, and especially to *Sheila Carlton* for her support.

My family:

My daughter *Joanna*, who came with me to a 'Mothers and Daughters Weekend' during the time that I was writing the book, and helped me to see the college through other eyes. My son *Paul,* who gave professional advice on the design and analysis of the questionnaires. Above all, my husband *John,* who has been my data processing manager and computer consultant, has read every chapter in draft and made penetrating and useful comment, has checked the references and brought a logic to the endnotes. Not only this, he has cooked a lot of meals as well!

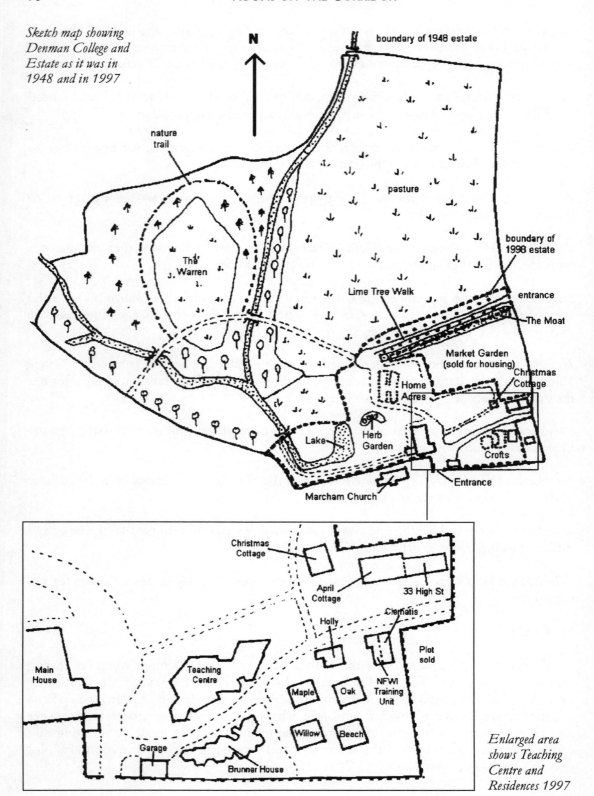

Sketch map showing Denman College and Estate as it was in 1948 and in 1997

N

boundary of 1948 estate

nature trail

pasture

The Warren

boundary of 1998 estate

Lime Tree Walk

entrance

The Moat

Market Garden (sold for housing)

Christmas Cottage

Home Acres

Crofts

Lake

Herb Garden

Entrance

Marcham Church

Christmas Cottage

April Cottage

33 High St

Holly

Clematis

Plot sold

Main House

Teaching Centre

Maple

Oak

NFWI Training Unit

Willow

Beech

Garage

Brunner House

Enlarged area shows Teaching Centre and Residences 1997

Sir Richard Livingstone opening Denman College in 1948

PART I

EDUCATING COUNTRYWOMEN

INTRODUCTION

On Friday 24th September 1948 Sir Richard Livingstone declared Denman College open. The opening ceremony took place on the day after the Annual General Meeting of the National Federation of Women's Institutes in London. As a result, WI members from all over the country were able to attend the official opening of *their* college. Those who were travelling from London came to Marcham, nine miles outside Oxford, in fleets of buses. In all, 250 people gathered for the occasion, not only WI members but also representatives of the Press and the BBC, and advisers and supporters from the academic world. After they had all been welcomed by the National Chairman, the Countess of Albermarle, Sir Richard Livingstone, President of Corpus Christi College, Oxford, gave the following address:

"On this great occasion I should like to say a few words about the importance of this college, whose name records the work of a great leader and figure in your movement. For all people life is a mixture of achievements and missed opportunities. It is like a corridor off which rooms open; each filled with treasures – history, art, music, literature, science, handicrafts and much more, all the infinite wealth of human nature and the world. But how many people walk down the corridor and enter few of the rooms?

"It is the business of education to help them to enter. Education is not schools or schooling; its purpose is to assist us to do the things we want to do, and cannot do without help – to read books, enjoy music and art, grow flowers or vegetables well, decorate a house, do needlework, bring up children, understand engines or the stars, or the laws of health, and much else.

"Schools, early education, are not enough for these purposes. Many people don't or won't, or can't learn at school; anyhow we discover new interests and needs in later life and want help to pursue them. That is where a place like Denman College comes in. It gives women the chance of learning and thinking about things which when young they could not study or did not think about studying. One can't do that sort of thing at home. One needs a place like this where one can get away from household duties and worries, and give one's whole time to the business in hand, get the best lecturers and teachers, meet and talk with other people.

"You may think that one can't do much in a week or a weekend. One can't, of course, go deeply into a subject, but one can make the most difficult step in all study – a beginning, and carry on study at home. One can widen one's horizon and let light into one's mind.

"What sort of things can you study here? Everything. I saw some of your suggested syllabuses, and in them were subjects such as Methods of Reading, Use of Leisure, Needlework, School and Home, Victorian Food and Fashions, etc, etc. These are some of the rooms off the corridor which this college can open.

And it isn't only the individuals who come here that will benefit. They will go back to their homes and villages richer human beings. The influence of the college will radiate beyond its walls. That is one of the advantages of the WI having such a place. Its members will take home to their Institutes what they have got here; and their homes and Institutes and villages will gain.

"And that has a wider importance still – an importance to the nation. We are apt to be more aware of our difficulties in life than our opportunities. The difficulties are real. But so are the opportunities. We are seeing the sun of one epoch of our history set. But sunset is followed by sunrise and we can create a better England – better because we give all its inhabitants the chance of a fuller, richer, more intelligent life. This chance your college brings to the members of Institutes which have created it.

"The college is the work of private enterprise. The State has not created or helped it. It has been created by the imagination, the faith, the enterprise and energy, patience and perseverance of those to whom the idea came and who have carried it out. We are conscious of the great debt which we owe to them. But though necessarily most of this labour has fallen mainly on a few people, the college is not only their creation; it is also the creation of the WIs all over the country, who have given subscriptions and gifts to make it what it is. It is a great co-operative work. This spirit, the spirit of imagination, of faith, of enterprise, of perseverance, of co-operation, has brought Denman College into being. That is a great tradition for those who come here to be inspired by and to maintain." [1]

The reply to this speech was given by Lady Denman who had been the first national chairman of the National Federation, and had led the organisation for 30 years; now she was to be honoured by having the college named after her. Sir Richard declared the college open by cutting a ribbon tied across the front door. As the photograph (Frontispiece, opposite p 11) shows, he cut it as close to one side as he could. Later he told people how "magnificent" the ribbon was, and how his Scots blood rebelled at the thought of having to destroy so much magnificence. He cut the ribbon as near to the end as possible so that it might be used again. [2]

****

The opening of Denman College was a great day for the Women's Institutes. It was the culmination of three years' hard work and fundraising by WIs in villages all over England and Wales, and it represented the importance of education in the life of the organisation. After the official opening ceremony was over, 43 members from 43 different WI County Federations stayed on for a conference to consider the educational work of WIs and how to make the best use of the new college.

In the first part of this book I shall endeavour to explain why, in the dark days in the middle of the Second World War, the WI had the vision and courage to decide to acquire their own short-term residential college. It will explore the adult education provision that was already well established in the WI and it will also consider how the WI leaders were influenced by other adult educators, especially by Sir Richard Livingstone.

In the second part, I shall describe how the college has developed over the succeeding fifty years, curriculum, tutors, facilities and patterns of learning. This part includes some of the results of a survey of members who have attended courses at the college recently. We shall see what part the college has played in the lives of those WI members, and discover how closely this matches with the vision of the founders.

CHAPTER ONE

THE WI STARTS IN CANADA

The opening of Denman College was the culmination of the educational policy and work of the early years of the Women's Institutes. In order to understand the educational nature of the organisation we must go back to its origins in Canada. The first WI in the world was formed on 19th February 1897 at Stoney Creek in Ontario and the inspiration behind its formation was a remarkable woman, Adelaide Hoodless, who was described by her biographer as a "domestic crusader". [1]

Adelaide Hoodless – leader and educationalist

Adelaide Hunter was born in 1857, the tenth child in the family. Her father had died several months earlier and, as the youngest of such a large one-parent family, her formal education had been minimal. Some of her brothers went to college, but she attended a local community school. Education, however, was something her family valued – "there was an atmosphere of intellectual curiosity in the household and the encouragement to explore the world of literature through books." [2]

In 1881 she married John Hoodless, who came from a prosperous business family in Hamilton. They had four children, two boys and two girls, but sadly the youngest boy, John Harold, died at the age of 14 months in August 1889. The cause of death seems to have been an intestinal infection caused by drinking contaminated milk. In Hamilton in those days milk was delivered in open containers, accessible to flies and other disease carriers. Adelaide seems to have blamed herself for the baby's death, and for the rest of her life she was particularly concerned with issues of domestic hygiene. As the wife of a well-to-do Hamilton business man she was involved in the local community and in the church. John Hoodless was a member of the local Board of Education, and became its chairman. He frequently visited schools in the city, and Adelaide often accompanied him, which gave her a considerable insight into the education system. She subsequently wrote:

> Education for education's sake is very beautiful in theory, but when we come down to facts, I venture to say that 90% of those who attend our schools seek education for its practical benefits. [3]

As a result of her visits to schools she came to think that the education of girls ought to be extended to include the practical skills that they would require when they grew up and ran homes and looked after families.

In 1889 Adelaide was one of the group of Hamilton women who founded the Hamilton branch of the Young Women's Christian Association (YWCA) to provide accommodation for young working women in the city. Many of these women were immigrants, single women seeking work, and the majority of them were unskilled. At the beginning the YWCA just provided somewhere for them to stay, but under the leadership of Adelaide (who was the President) classes in book-keeping, short hand and dressmaking were soon started. Later cookery classes were added which were attended not only by the women who lived in the hostel, but also by others from outside. In a speech which she gave much later, Adelaide explained her convictions in this way:

> I associated with girls chiefly from the commercial class, such as typewriters, office workers, shop girls – the majority of the girls of the YWCA belong to the commercial class – that was where I got my first inspiration in domestic science – I found, after this association with these girls for a great many years, that they were being commercialised; we had typewriters provided in our schools; we were offering everything to enable them to fill commercial occupations, and we were trying to draft (sic) masculine tendencies on feminine stock, and that has been the tendency of our system of education for some years. [4]

Domestic Science was a fairly new concept in North America, so sometimes Adelaide's audiences wanted to know exactly what it meant. This is a definition she gave:

> Domestic Science is the application of scientific principles to the management of the home. It teaches the value of pure air, proper food, systematic management, economy, care of children, domestic and civil sanitation and the prevention of disease. It calls for higher and higher ideals of home life and more respect for domestic occupations. In short, it is a direct education for women as homemakers. The management of the home has more to do with the moulding of character than any other influence, owing to the large place it fills in the life of the individual during the most plastic stage of development. We are therefore justified in an effort to secure a place for home economics or domestic science, in the education institutions of this country. [5]

Adelaide Hoodless was a woman of vision, with courage and ability to fight for a broader education for women. She regarded the promotion of home economics as a means of elevating women's work to the level of a profession and putting it on a par with a man's work.

In 1893, Adelaide was one of the Canadian delegation to the International Congress of Women at the Chicago World's Fair. It was here that Canadian women first learned about the International Council of Women, which had been founded in 1888 to provide a world-wide association for women's organisations. The members of the delegation became convinced that the women's organisations in Canada should be linked in a similar way, across the Provinces, as a National Council of Women, affiliated to the International Council. In this way they could work together to represent the views of women to the Government, for at that time it was quite common practice for women to draw up a petition but to get a man to present it, as they had so little power. On their return from Chicago, Adelaide and the others worked actively to set up such a Canadian National Council of Women. They succeeded in doing this; the inaugural meeting was held in Toronto in October 1893 with 1,500 women present. Adelaide Hoodless was elected the first Treasurer. Lady Aberdeen, the wife of the Governor General, was elected President.

Adelaide persuaded the National Council of Women to back her campaign for the introduction of Domestic Science into the school curriculum. At their National Council in 1894 she proposed:

> that the National Council of Women do all in its power to further the introduction of industrial (or manual) training for girls in the public school system in Canada, believing that such training will greatly conduce to the general welfare of Canadian homes, and that copies of this resolution be sent to the ministers of education of each provincial government. [6]

It was a long hard battle, but Adelaide was nothing if not determined. She spoke on the subject all over Ontario. In December 1896 she was invited to speak to a conference of the Farmer's Institute at the Ontario Agricultural College in Guelph. Her subject was 'The relation of Domestic Science to the Agricultural Population' and she began:

> When asked by your secretary to give an outline of the course in Domestic science suitable for an agricultural population, I felt somewhat puzzled at first to know where to make a distinction between life in a country house and in that of a city home... [7]

After referring to one expert who claimed that poor food, overwork and monotony were contributing factors in the high rate of insanity among rural people, she outlined her suggestions:

> ... the causes are easily preventable ... by scientific knowledge of the various articles of food and their nutritive value, and ... by the introduction of schools of domestic science in the rural districts, with lecture courses and clubs for farmers wives, where better methods for producing good results in butter making, poultry raising, bee culture, house decoration, cookery etc. may be intelligently discussed, thereby providing the best class of recreation, which is pleasure and profit combined...

> Farmers are beginning to realise the importance of scientific knowledge... Is it of greater importance that a farmer should know more about the scientific care of his sheep and cattle, than that a farmer's wife should know how to care for her family, or that his barns should have every labor saving contrivance, while she toils and drudges on the same old treadmill instituted by her grandmother, perhaps even to carrying water from a spring, a quarter of a mile from the house, which I know has been done... ?

That call for continuing education for women living in rural areas had immediate results. Erland Lee, secretary of the Farmer's Institute of Wentworth County was in the audience and he invited her to come to speak at the next 'Ladies night' of his Institute.

Formation of the first WI

Erland Lee came from Stoney Creek; both he and his wife Janet had been school teachers before he took a certificate in agriculture and became a farmer. Adelaide Hoodless accepted his invitation to speak at the meeting at Wentworth County Farmer's Institute, at which there were 35 wives present as guests. Her talk was about the importance of women's education in all branches of domestic science and homecraft.

Towards the end of her address she suggested that, just as the men had a Farmer's Institute, so the women should have their own organisation. The women present were enthusiastic about this idea, and fixed a meeting for the following week to discuss it further. They planned to invite other women to join them, and they asked Adelaide to come back again and speak.

It must have taken some effort, in this scattered rural area in a Canadian February, to persuade women to attend the meeting at such short notice. As an extra attraction Adelaide brought a guest with her, a Mrs Rorer, author of a popular cookery book and principal of a Toronto cooking school; perhaps this attracted a few extra women to come. Whatever their reason for coming, there were 101 women, as well as Erland Lee, who took the chair, at the meeting.

Adelaide's son Bernard recalled later:

> It was my privilege as a boy to hitch up her favourite horse, Scotty, and drive her down to Stoney Creek on that stormy night of February 19th, 1897. I can still remember that meeting in the old hall, up a rickety flight of outside stairs, and sliding into a seat at the back and wondering what it was all about. [8]

Adelaide presented the same arguments that Erland Lee had heard at Ontario Agricultural College. She pointed out that if the men felt the need for an organisation, and if it enabled them to grow better crops of hay, grain and fruit and to produce better livestock, then an institute for the women would be equally helpful in their work. The women were convinced and they agreed to form a 'Department of Domestic Economy' in affiliation with the Farmer's Institute, to be called the 'Women's Department of the Farmer's Institute of South Wentworth'.

The following week, at the first formal meeting of the organisation, they replaced this somewhat cumbersome name with the 'Women's Institute of Saltfleet Township' and a little later Saltfleet Township was changed to Stoney Creek. [9] Janet Lee was one of the first committee members and Adelaide Hoodless was invited to be honorary President, which she accepted. She "attended its meetings from time to time entering into the discussions and giving members timely and acceptable advice." For example it is recorded that the WI motto – 'For Home and Country' – was chosen in 1902 by the Stoney Creek committee on the advice of Mrs Hoodless. [10]

As Cheryl MacDonald, her biographer, writes:

> While Adelaide Hoodless has long been credited with founding the Women's Institute, and the membership of that organisation has done more than any other to keep her memory alive, she was only peripherally involved in Institute work. From time to time she attended meetings, such as one on 26th January 1899, when she urged the Institute to affiliate with the National Council of Women. For the most part, however, Adelaide left the Women's Institute in the capable hands of rural women, while she continued her campaign for domestic science in towns and cities. [11]

This campaign was finally successful; domestic science and sewing were added to the Hamilton school curriculum and Adelaide organised the training of domestic science teachers. She wrote a textbook, *The Public School Domestic Science* (nicknamed 'the little red book'), and she became increasingly respected as an expert. In 1899 she travelled to England to take part in the Quinquennial Congress of the International Council of Women. At this conference she gave a paper on 'Technical Education in Canada', in which she stressed the importance of domestic science training in schools and described what had been done recently to carry similar instruction to rural areas – the new WIs – at the same time pointing out that this new venture had already received the moral and financial support of government, but the UK was not ready for the WI … yet.

Later in her life Adelaide Hoodless was to claim, "The education of women and girls has been my life's work," and so it continued to be right up until the end – she died in February 1910 of heart failure just after she had got up to speak at a meeting at St Margaret's College in Toronto, where she was appealing for a school of Household Science to be set up at university level.

There is one quotation above all others that seems to be the message from the founder of the WI to all those women who have belonged to WIs ever since:

> What must be done is to develop to the fullest extent the two great social forces, education and organisation, so as to secure for each individual the highest degree of advancement. [12]

The development of the WIs in Canada

The successful growth of the newly formed WI really depended on Erland Lee and his wife. Erland and two of his friends who were members of the Federal parliament helped the newly formed WI committee to draft a constitution and bylaws. The first constitution, adopted at the initial meeting read, in part:

> The object of this Institute shall be to promote knowledge of household science which shall lead to the improvement in household architecture with special attention to sanitation, to a better understanding of economics and hygiene value of foods and fuels, and to a more scientific care of children with a view to raising the general standards of our people. [13]

Erland Lee also wrote, on behalf of the new organisation, to the superintendent of the Farmer's Institute to ask for affiliation, and to the Minister of Agriculture to request government co-operation and support. It is worth noting here the important rôle that these men played in getting a women's organisation off the ground – this was be repeated, as we shall show later, when the WIs came to England and Wales.

Other WIs were soon started. Several of the pioneer leaders (including Janet Lee) visited other Farmer's Institute meetings at which women were present to encourage the formation of more WIs. The second WI, Whitby in South Ontario, was formed in 1899. By 1919 there were 900 branch Institutes in the Federated Women's Institutes of Ontario.

The education programme of the newly formed WIs

The real purpose of the first Institute, as we have seen, was to educate the members in order to raise the standard of running a home and family. A few quotations from the early minutes of Stoney Creek WI illustrate how the first WI members went about doing this:

A nation cannot rise above the level of its homes, therefore we women must work and study together to raise our homes to the highest possible level.

In order that we may carry out to better advantage the objects for which the Institute was organised, we shall divide them into six divisions or classes as follows:

1. Domestic economy
2. Architecture, with special reference to heat, light, sanitation and ventilation
3. Health, embracing physiology, hygiene, calisthenics and medicine
4. Floriculture and horticulture
5. Music and art
6. Literature, education, sociology and legislation. [14]

At the second regular meeting there was "a paper on 'The proper feeding of children'". At the next meeting a Dr Mabel Henderson spoke on 'The child in health and disease', after which there was a discussion and question-and-answer period. At the following meeting there was a demonstration on 'First aid to the injured' and at successive meetings there were papers, addresses, discussions and demonstrations on such subjects as 'Sunshine in the Home', 'Home Sanitation' and 'Home Making versus Housekeeping'.

By the end of its first year Stoney Creek WI had 75 members with an average attendance of 60. As the WI developed, some of the women met together in a study circle:

The progressiveness and earnestness of these pioneer members is also shown by their purchase, early in 1898, of the Chautauqua Books on Domestic Science, and their meeting regularly once a month to read and discuss them. [15]

The emerging WIs were supported by the Farmer's Institutes, and in 1901 they started to include at their annual conferences sessions of interest to WI members. The Ontario Department of Agriculture also provided a speakers' service for WIs. One WI leader wrote subsequently of these:

by the guidance of the speakers, correct procedure along business lines and methods of work became part of each institute thereby developing leadership... [16]

The speakers are reported to be of

an unusually high standard of merit in the type of material selected and in their standing in their respective lines. Highly qualified medical doctors, registered nurses, opticians, dietitians, teachers, recreational leaders, horticultural, poultry and dairy experts, musicians, writers and educationalist of broad scope were enlisted, all intent on giving service to the women and homes of rural Ontario. [17]

The reports from the WIs in these early years show appreciation of the speakers. The report from North Grey reads:

There are eight branch Institutes in North Grey, all of which are in good running order... The library is not very extensive. A few books have been purchased ... such as 'Dust and its Dangers', 'Emergencies', 'The Chemistry of Cooking and Cleaning'... The grant of $20 which we received last year was spent in securing the services of Miss Agnes Smith of Hamilton, a very capable instructor in Domestic Science.

One of the many benefits derived from our Institute is the bringing together of intelligent women, and also of timid and retiring ones who live secluded lives. The Institute is removing the idea that one's education ceases with school days. Women in rural districts are beginning to realise that more is expected of them than simply to prepare three meals a day and do what little sewing they can do for their families. Many have prepared excellent papers, which have been a happy surprise both to themselves and their listeners. [18]

In 1902, when there were 36 WIs with a membership of 3,000, the Government arranged the first convention of Institute delegates, giving them the opportunity to learn new things that they could share with others. The theme of the 1908 convention was 'Woman's part in the pure milk problem', with speakers on 'Dangers in milk', 'The care of milk', 'Bacterial contamination of milk', 'Food value of milk', 'Milk and children', and 'Infant mortality'.

One district reported afterwards:

Our Institute has educational value. How many of us knew much about bacteria until we heard Miss Maddock at our meetings? We have learned so much now that if we have typhoid fever or scarlet fever, we do not say, "This is the Lord's will", but examine drains, sinks, cellars, walls and backyards where we know there may be conditions favourable to the development of these germs. We have learned that the best way to get rid of them is to let the sunshine stream in. We know that sunshine means health. [19]

In 1910 Miss Watson, Principal of Macdonald Institute (the training college for teachers of domestic science), gave an address on 'Education and the Rural Home-maker'. She acknowledged the rôle played by the one-off lectures but went on to say:

Now the question coming up in many Institutes is, "How shall we move forward for the study of these home problems?" Some are only wishing for better opportunities, but some members are saying boldly, "We ought to have trained teachers who are specialists in their line, going from place to place, giving a whole series of lectures on one subject in each place." And really why not?

As a result of this a programme of short courses in such subjects as food values and cookery, home nursing and sewing was provided. These and other short courses became the main feature of the educational programme of the WIs.

The WIs provided the opportunity for women who had previously lived very isolated lives to meet together on a regular basis At first they concentrated on their own educational needs, but the more they learned the more they started to recognise the deficiencies in their communities compared with urban areas. With the new self-confidence they had gained, these women began to work together to bring about social change. They worked to get libraries, recreational centres, schools, hospitals and health centres provided for their communities. In order to do this the women had to become more informed on matters of legislation and administration of both the country and the province, so that they could begin to influence the decision makers. Their education was continuing.

CHAPTER TWO

THE WI COMES TO WALES AND ENGLAND

The rural areas of England and Wales were an educational backwater at the end of the Nineteenth and the beginning of the Twentieth Centuries. In the urban areas there were many new initiatives in adult education, such as the Workingmen's Institutes, the People's Colleges, the Workers' Educational Association, the University Settlements, University Extension classes, Mechanics Institutes, the YMCA and the Co-operative movement. These developments hardly touched the rural areas.

This was a period of agricultural decline. Between 1871 and 1900 over two million acres of arable land had gone out of production and unemployment was very high among agricultural workers as many farmers went bankrupt. [1] The government tried to encourage the flagging industry; the Board of Agriculture was set up in 1889. In 1901 an Agricultural Organisation Society (AOS) was formed, aiming to start local societies of farmers, smallholders and growers so that they could work co-operatively to improve their output. In 1904 Edwin Pratt published *The organisation of agriculture in England and other lands,* in which he described the Canadian Farmers' Institutes and their associated Women's Institutes. He suggested that WIs might educate British countrywomen, but no interest was raised – could an idea from the Empire be relevant in Britain?

In rural areas there was little time for education. The Vicar of Broughton Blean in Kent described the aims of Sunday Schools as being:

> to furnish opportunities of instruction to the children of the poorer part of the parish, without interfering with any industry of the weekdays... The children are to be taught to read and to be instructed in the plain duties of the Christian religion, with a particular view to their good and industrious behaviour in their future character as labourers and servants. [2]

A 'country gentleman' asked:

> Suppose that some friend of humanity were to attempt to improve the condition of the beasts of the field – to teach the horse his power, and the cow her value – would he be that tractable and useful animal he is, would she be so profuse of her treasures to a hapless infant? Could anything be more impolitic? [3]

In spite of such views, there were some people who could imagine a better way of treating those who lived in rural areas – even the women! Robert Greig, a staff inspector of the Board of Education who had carried out an investigation into agricultural instruction in other countries, wrote in his 1912 report of the Women's Institutes he found in Canada. He explained that a WI is:

an association of farmers' wives, daughters and sisters who meet periodically to hear lectures, read papers, and study books of dairying, poultry keeping, gardening, and all the minor rural industries; on cooking, laundry work, and dressmaking; on household sanitation, home hygiene and ambulance methods; and the choice and care of furniture and pictures; and the rearing and education of children and on any other means for the improvement of country life. The institutes also have a recreative side, and attention is given to music and literary subjects. [4]

He concluded that:

perhaps the most profitable outlet for the expenditure of energy and public money in the improvement of agriculture will be found in widening the mental horizon of the farmer's wife and especially the wife of the labourer, small holder, and working farmer ... the farmer's wife is a partner in his business; on her management of the dairy, poultry yard and piggery much of his profit depends.

Still nothing happened, which is hardly surprising if the attitudes of the vicar and the 'country gentleman' were very widely held. It took more than books or pamphlets to get the WIs started – it took a determined woman from Canada, and a world war.

The determined Canadian woman was Madge Watt. She had been a founder member of the first WI to be formed in British Columbia and she then became involved with forming other WIs. In 1911, when the Department of Agriculture for British Columbia gave official recognition to the WI, they appointed her to the advisory committee to assist in forming and guiding institutes. She was a well-educated woman, having read Honours Moderns at Toronto University, and she had later done postgraduate work in history and pedagogics. Not only had she worked for WIs in British Columbia, but she was also involved with University Women's Clubs and the National Council of Women. In 1913 she was elected to the senate of the University of British Columbia.

However in that same year her husband, Dr Alfred Tennyson Watt, who had worked for the Dominion Civil Service in British Columbia, died. Madge decided to bring her two sons to England to complete their schooling. Once here she wanted to start WIs in this country. She pressed her case hard:

It is difficult to decide how far, if at all, Mrs Watt was influenced in coming to this country by a wish to help in starting an Institute movement here. Certainly this seems to have become a fixed purpose soon after her arrival. In 1913 and again in 1914, both before and after the outbreak of war, we find her addressing public meetings, speaking at gatherings and in private houses, always and everywhere urging that Institutes should be started. She was a Canadian. She had no special knowledge of English village life and a complete ignorance of many of its problems. She was upheld only by a strange, steadfast faith that would turn, when she was thwarted and disappointed, to a kind of sulky obstinacy. She never wavered. She knew ... she knew that she knew what English village women wanted. And she was perfectly right. [5]

Just as the start of the WI in Ontario had required the catalyst of a man – Erland Lee – so the beginnings of the WI in this country had its male catalyst – Nugent Harris, secretary of the Agricultural Organisation Society (AOS). He heard Mrs Watt speaking at a conference and became convinced that WIs were just what was necessary; he wrote:

> For many years as the secretary to the AOS I tried to get the farmer members of the co-operative agricultural societies that I was organising to allow women to become members and failed. Then I got two or three to yield. Several women joined, but we could never get them to say a word at the meeting.

> After the meetings were over the women would come to me and criticise the decisions or some items on the agenda in which they were interested. I asked them why they did not say their say at the meeting. They replied, "We dare not because our husbands and sons would make fun of us."

> I would not rest until I could establish some movement that would give the women-folk a chance to express themselves free from fear of being ridiculed by the men. By the merest chance I met Mrs Watt. I felt I had come in touch with the very movement I wanted. [6]

The social climate in Britain at that time was very different to the pioneer communities of Canada where life was harder, but was also more equal. Rural Britain was a very narrow society, hidebound and with groups who were suspicious of each other:

> When they were old enough they joined the Conservative Association if their parents were Conservative, the Liberal Association if they were Liberal, and the Other Party if their parents were Otherwise.

> Very much in the same way they went to Church or to Chapel or Nowhere. They even bought their tea and sugar, their boots and shoes, their drapery and their ironmongery at Conservative-Church shops or at Liberal-Chapel shops or at the 'Co-op'…

> And during the rest of their lives these party denominationalists seemed to make a habit, if not a virtue, of keeping as much out of one another's way as they could…

> Our population had too narrow an education. It had not been trained to work together, there were barriers of Heaven knows how many classes and sections which would be broken down one day. [7]

Even with Nugent Harris's support it still took considerable time — and one or two more enthusiastic men — to get the new organisation started. Colonel the Hon. Stapleton Cotton was one of the governors of the AOS, and Chairman of the North Wales branch; he suggested that a Welsh village would be a good place to "try out" the idea of a WI. The reason he gave was that in every Welsh village there were several places of worship, each with its own social organisation, where countrywomen met, but they never met together as a whole community. Colonel Cotton's view was that if a non-party and non-denominational organisation for countrywomen could be established in Wales, then its success in other places was assured!

The outbreak of the First World War was also a factor in making the idea of WIs acceptable in Britain. The challenge to help with the war effort by doing all they could to produce food proved an ideal way of getting women involved and organised. The government could recognise the value of an organisation that would harness the energies of the women. On the 4th July 1915, The Board of Agriculture's Conference on Agricultural Education issued a 'blue book' on Agricultural Education for women which included a reference to seeing "an opening in the creation of women's institutes":

> … the reverberations from Flanders … the daily toll of the dead, (in this context) party politics, sects, distinctions of class seemed smaller things… Women, whose enfranchisement had justly come, but before the nation was wholly in favour of it, had their great chance of showing their quality and proving their right. [8]

At the following annual meeting of the AOS a resolution was carried – mostly with the support of men – to adapt the Canadian idea of WIs to suit English rural conditions and that the AOS should become responsible for the work. On the 14th July 1915 the governors of AOS acted on the resolution passed at the AGM and set up a Women's Institute Committee. Nugent Harris was authorised to engage Madge Watt as an organiser.

But Madge had jumped the gun. On Tuesday 15th June she had spoken to a meeting of the North Wales branch of the Agricultural Organisation Society in Bangor, on the subject on 'Women's Work in Agriculture'. This meeting was convened by Stapleton Cotton as Chairman of the North Wales branch. It seems as though it was in some way an exploratory meeting – "the response she elicited could either give confidence to the supporters of the forthcoming resolution or demonstrate to them its inexpediency." [9] Also present at this meeting was Sir Harry Reichel, Principal of the University College at Bangor, who had a real interest in rural education and "had a keen perception of the good that would accrue from extending the benefits of education and social development to countrywomen." [10]

Formation of the first WI at Llanfairpwll

Stapleton Cotton and his wife were impressed by what they had heard at the meeting in Bangor and the very next day called a meeting of women in their Anglesey village, Llanfairpwll. The full name of the village is usually given as 'Llanfairpwllgwyngyll-gogerychwyrndrobwllllantsiliogogogoch'. This is actually the invention of a Nineteenth-Century stationmaster, seeking fame and tourists. Until 1850, the village was just Llanfair (Davies N, *Europe, a History*, OUP, 1996, p310). The report in the *North Wales Chronicle* for 18th June 1915 reads:

> A well attended meeting, presided over by Col. Stapleton Cotton, was held at Graig, by permission of Mrs W E Jones, on Wednesday. The lecturer was Mrs Watt, a lady from British Columbia, who gave an interesting account of the work done in that portion of the Empire, by means of the Women's Institute. It was proposed by Mrs Wilson, seconded by Miss Watts, Aber Braint, that a society of this description be established in the village. The motion was passed unanimously. [11]

Mrs Stapleton Cotton became the first President, a committee was formed, and they agreed to have monthly meetings of "an educational and social character" on the first

Tuesday in each month "at 2pm in the room kindly lent by Mrs W E Jones, until such time as the Women's Institute has its own building." [12]

Stapleton Cotton gave help and support to the new WI. About six months after the opening he wrote to Madge Watt that he had himself been "one of the many who doubted the capacity of women to conduct even their ordinary business with success but," he added, "I have learned more about women than I have learned in forty years… I see and believe that women can and will bring all classes, all denominations, all interests, all schools of the best thought together in that common brotherhood of love … which every man and every women longs for in his or her innermost heart." [13]

Llanfairpwll was a good place to start the first WI. The University College at Bangor, only just over the Menai Straits, had Agricultural Studies on its curriculum. There was a supportive Principal and so there was an opportunity to invite as speakers some of the staff there who knew about the latest developments in agriculture. But all was not easy. As the minutes of the first annual meeting of the new WI show, some of Mrs Watt's ideas needed interpretation:

> Mrs Watt, who was connected with the movement in Canada, attended our first meeting and explained the objects and working, as well as the rules, which we have followed as far as is consistent with the different circumstances of life in Anglesey. [14]

In this country the social fabric was unlike that of Canada. The newly formed WI found supporters in the Marquis and Marchioness of Anglesey, who lived at Plas Newydd, the 'big house'. Lady Anglesey became Patron, and they gave permission for the new WI to use Toll Gate House free of rent, until they could build their own Hall on the adjacent land, which they also donated. Thus they set a pattern of support from the 'big house' which was followed for many of the WIs formed in villages throughout the country in the coming years. Indeed in the early days if the 'big house' did not support the formation of a WI (and often the Lady of the Manor became the President) then the WI was either not formed or did not flourish.

The subjects for the meetings during the first year of Llanfairpwll WI reflect how the programme was adapted to local needs. At the first committee meeting it was agreed "that the food supply of the country be the special subject for discussion", and the programme planned for the first year clearly reflected this decision.

At the meetings "papers were read and demonstrations given":

> Professor Robinson read a most instructive and learned paper on 'Food Values and Diet.'

> Professor Philips, of the University, gave a short talk on the 'Gathering of Wild Herbs'; those required for medicinal purposes. It had been the hope of some members that this might be the objective of the Institute for the summer, but, as the lecturer pointed out very forcibly, each individual effort should be turned towards producing food; any object taking time from this latter should not be started. We shall take the Professor's advice and leave it for the present.

Mrs Hunter Smith of the University, Bangor, demonstrated on the easiest and most humane way of killing a fowl; also the proper manner in which to dress and prepare it, so as to increase it's marketable value.

Other speakers came from outside agencies, for example:

Explanation of The Board of Agriculture's poultry scheme.

… lecturer provided by the Agricultural Organisation Society on the conservation and bottling of fruit.

But local people also spoke. The egregious Stapleton Cotton gave numerous talks and "demonstrated in a masterly fashion on salads and dressings". We also read that:

Dr Williams spoke at length on a nursing and maternity scheme.

Dr Price of Bangor spoke forcibly and to the point on the dangers of flies and rubbish heaps.

Most other talks reflected the primary interest in food production, including 'Fruit and vegetable preserving', 'Autumn gardening and a demonstration of the fireless cooker', 'Food, its value as an asset in the future, with regard to the welfare of the individual and the community', and 'The profitable keeping of goats and poultry'. [15]

The minutes also show that from time to time the members took action following a talk or demonstration. After a talk on 'The Buying of Good Seed', by Colonel Cotton once again, they agreed to buy co-operatively. They heard a talk on 'The women's labour on the land question' and decided that "a canvas of the village be taken as to potential help".

The Canadian WIs, as they became established, had moved towards taking social action. The same thing happened to this new WI. The members began to recognise ways in which their community could be improved. In April 1918 Colonel Cotton was asked to draw up a resolution emanating from the Institute, to be submitted to the Llangefni County Council, as to "whether it would be possible to have some water scheme for Llanfairpwll" and this was followed later by a "deputation to the Parish Council with regard to the Water Question". [16]

The WI took a close interest in anything which could help the war effort; for example they passed a resolution that "a war loan association be formed in connection with the Institute". They were also looking forward to life after the war; they heard a talk on the 'Power women may have in the reconstruction scheme'. [17] When peace came the Parish Council asked the WI "to organise the refreshment part of the Peace Day celebrations. This was done most satisfactorily, with the help of outsiders; the members of the Parish Council afterwards paying a tribute to the organising powers of the Institute." [18] This was probably not what WI members had in mind when they were discussing the power women may have in the reconstruction, and many WI members today will sympathise with the type-casting reflected here. WIs throughout the country will no doubt be asked by their Parish Councils to organise the teas to celebrate the Millennium.

The obvious success of Llanfairpwll WI led to other WIs being opened in places nearby. They responded in different ways to the challenge of increasing food production:

> In response to the urgent need for increased food production and distribution the Criccieth WI (then only six months old) opened a small market stall early in the Summer of 1916. [19]

From this first enterprise sprung what is now WI Country Markets Ltd with over 500 markets throughout England and Wales and a turnover in 1993 (the year in which it became independent of NFWI) of £10.4 million, most of which is returned to the shareholders.

Spread of WIs

In 1915 the AOS set up a Women's Institute Subcommittee to encourage the formation of new institutes. The first members were Samuel Bostock, the Chairman of the AOS and Mrs Roland Wilkins who was a "leading figure" in the small-holdings movement. The new subcommittee held its first quarterly meeting on 2nd December 1915 where Madge Watt was able to report that she had formed the first WIs in England in Singleton in Sussex, Wallisdown in Dorset and Sevenoaks Weald and Kemsing in Kent. The subcommittee supplied model rules which were based on those of the WIs in Canada; these rules defined the non-sectarian and non-political character, which was so important in the early days.

At the Annual General Meeting in 1971 it was resolved to change the non-party political and non-sectarian rules. These now read:

> "The character of the movement is non-sectarian and non-party political, but in order to achieve the objects ... this shall not be so interpreted as to prevent Women's Institutes from concerning themselves with matters of political and religious significance, provided the views of minorities are respected and provided that the movement is never used for party political or sectarian purposes." (NFWI Handbook, May 1972)

In March 1916 Mrs Nugent Harris joined the subcommittee as the honorary WI secretary and, by the Autumn meeting, when there were 24 WIs, two AOS governors had joined and Mrs Stapleton Cotton and Mrs Drage from Criccieth had been appointed to represent North Wales. The committee decided that it was time to appoint a permanent chairman:

> Several names were discussed, and at last it was decided to send an invitation to Lady Salisbury. If she should refuse, then Lady Denman was to be invited to become chairman. Lady Denman was already known to Mrs Roland Wilkins through her interest in smallholdings...

Lady Salisbury declined the invitation and so:

> by this chance and as second choice the Institute movement had acquired the Chairman whose ability and personality were to colour, enliven, and hall-mark the growing organisation. [20]

The organisation was growing fast, and also developing its own distinct character:

In the early days of the Canadian movement the emphasis was upon the home and the work for the betterment of the home. In the early days of the English and Welsh Institutes the emphasis was upon the village community and work for the benefit of the community. [21]

CHAPTER THREE

SOME REMARKABLE WOMEN

When Lady Denman was appointed to be Chairman of the WI Committee of the AOS she was only 32 years old, but she had already made her mark. There is a report [1] that, on hearing that Lady Denman had accepted the post, someone wrote anonymously, "I can see that if rightly worked, we are going to get the pick of county ladies in support of our movement…"

Gertrude Mary Pearson, called Trudie by her family, was the daughter of a wealthy industrialist, who had interests in oil, and was also a newspaper owner. He was a staunch Liberal and in 1910 became Baron Cowdray. In November 1903, the year she 'came out' aged 18, Trudie married a young liberal peer, Thomas, the third Baron Denman. "It was a suitable match in that it added title to money, but one which Trudie herself was less sure about than her Mother." [2] They had two children, Thomas born in 1905, and Judith born in 1907.

In 1908, through the influence of her mother, Trudie was elected to the Executive Committee of the Women's Liberal Federation. This was an organisation of 100,000 women and the main business at this time was women's suffrage – "[the Federation] supported the extension of the franchise in order that the inclusion of women might give the vote to the working man's wife and the mill girl as well as to the property owning woman." [3] In 1909 Trudie was elected Chairman of the Women's Liberal Metropolitan Union.

In 1911 Lord Denman was appointed Governor General of Australia and Trudie, at the age of 27, became First Lady of that Commonwealth. They returned to the UK in 1914 and, after the outbreak of the First World War, she became the moving spirit behind a charity called 'Smokes for wounded Soldiers and Sailors Society' (SSS) – she was a heavy smoker herself. From this point on, she and Lord Denman, although not formally separated, lived very separate lives. Her father had bought her Balcombe Place, in Sussex, as a country house in 1905. She spent much of her time there and it was at Balcombe Place in 1915 that

> Trudie … conceived the idea that a useful and practical way of making use of waste scraps and saving food imports would be for every household to keep poultry. She and Nellie (Grant) accordingly started a scheme to encourage back-yard hen keeping for everyone. They took an office in Pimlico and commissioned a friend to design a model backyard hen-house which they then advertised… She started a poultry farm of her own at Balcombe and began to form plans for a co-operative poultry colony of smallholders at Balcombe. [4]

It was through this activity that she met Mrs Roland Wilkins (p 29), who had been impressed by Trudie's practical and unsentimental outlook, and had also found in her someone whose belief in the right and ability of women to conduct their own affairs was as sound as her own; someone moreover who had been trained in the methods of procedure and administration in the hard school of Women's Liberal Federation, and who, in Australia, had not only become familiar with public life but who had also there shown her special interest in countrywomen. [5]

The WI was not Trudie's only interest, she was also involved with the beginnings of the Family Planning Association. "This is not ... an easy subject. It needs great human under-standing, and ethical insight, as well as statesmanship," which was how Bishop Bell referred to it in his address at her memorial service. [6] Lady Denman was also the moving spirit and Director-in-Chief of the Women's Land Army. She served on various Government subcommittees – as Chairman in 1926 of the Denman Committee on the 'Practical Education of Women for Rural Life'; in 1940, as a member of the Rushcliffe Committee on 'Voluntary service', and in 1941, on the Scott Committee on 'Land utilisation in rural areas'. These brought a whole network of contacts to help the newly emerging WI.

*****

In the Summer of 1916, as more and more WIs started, and women were mobilised to help with food production, Government departments began to show an interest – here was something that could help the war effort. Informal meetings were held between the Board of Trade, the Board of Agriculture and the AOS with a view to linking with other organisations for women who were doing war work in country districts – particularly with the newly formed Women's Land Army .

At the beginning of 1917 the WI Subcommittee of AOS began to get anxious about how they were to support this new area of work, which was developing so rapidly that it needed more paid organisers. When the AOS submitted its usual application to the Treasury for its annual grant it included support for four more salaried WI organisers. The newly appointed Chairman of the AOS thought that the WI work was being expanded to the detriment of the other work of the Society. In September the Treasury decided that the WIs could not be recognised as a branch of agricultural co-operation, and thus no more AOS funds should be spent on them. The administration of the WIs was to be taken over by the recently formed Women's branch of the Board of Agriculture's Food Production Department (which also organised the Women's Land Army).

There was no choice in the matter, and the AOS empowered Lady Denman, and two others, to negotiate the terms of the take over.

> Lady Denman's main concern was to safeguard the democratic and independent character of the Institute movement ... she convinced ... the President of the Board of Agriculture, that the Institutes, once formed, must be self governing. [7]

A Women's Institute section of the department was set up. Trudie Denman was appoint-ed (honorary) Assistant Director and Madge Watt was made the chief of three full-time organisers, whose salaries were paid by the Ministry.

On 16th October 1917 representatives of 60 of the 137 WIs so far formed attended a meeting in Central Hall, Westminster, to approve the severance of the WIs from the AOS and the transfer to the Board. At this meeting the National Federation of Women's Institutes was formed. Lady Denman was elected chairman for the day and led the delegates through the agenda which adopted the draft constitution and rules and elected the 'central committee' of ten members. When it met the next day this first National Executive Committee elected Lady Denman as Chairman.

Voluntary County Organisers

The formation of new WIs was the responsibility of the Department of Agriculture who employed the WI organisers under Madge Watt. By August 1918, 20 new WIs a week were being formed and the team of organisers had expanded to eight. Even so it was obvious that they could not do all that was required, so Mrs Watt suggested that one or two volunteers should be trained and appointed in each County to work under her. The first training school for Voluntary County Organisers (VCOs) was arranged at Burgess Hill in Sussex, and its 23 students were the first of a long and continuing line of willing volunteers who, it could be argued, have done more to sustain and mould the WI than anybody or anything else.

This first residential programme of training given within the WI was reported in a small book from which this account is drawn. [8] It lasted for three weeks and was planned and directed by Mrs Watt, who explained the need for the training as follows:

> When the Board of Agriculture decided that it was impossible to carry on Women's Institute Propaganda without more assistance, and proposed inviting ladies in different counties to act as Voluntary Organisers, I was asked as Chief Organiser to submit the names of the ladies considered suitable to do the work... I felt that the new organisers would require not only training and information but being put absolutely on the right lines. I felt that they must learn from others as well as from me, that they must have practical demonstrations as well as lectures, that there must be ample time for discussions and questions and help, and that all of this should be given in an atmosphere impregnated with institute work and ideals.

This training course was held in a member's (rather grand) house, Wyberlye, Burgess Hill, and the trainee VCOs stayed with local WI members, several of whom also offered to lend cars, not very common in 1918, for transport during the course.

The students had lectures in the morning and 'object lessons' in the afternoon:

> I hoped to have social functions intermingled to have it altogether a very human affair with linked work and play ... but yet there had to be both instruction and examination; I had to be both instructing and examining. I had to judge the capacity and goodwill of those who came to be trained, as well as find out what they had learnt and how they would impress audiences... I always tried when getting organisers tested to have their speeches and contributions serve a double purpose. It was natural to ask them to give an account of some Women's Institute activity, or to make a little speech so that the elocution teacher might criticise, in order to get an opportunity of appraising the speakers myself.

Madge Watt seems to have been an able trainer, and the programme she planned included a range of methods that would stand up well today. The topics included office organisation, starting a WI, planning a programme, the history of the movement, visits to local WIs , visits to local WI industries (toys, smocking, glove making), food production, food preservation and food economy, psychology of audiences, hints on public speaking, and how to present the objects and ideals of WIs to village audiences.

The students visited a farm, a Red Cross bandaging class, a soup kitchen for children, a nursery, a dairy and a bee farm. During the course of the School they visited, in small groups, a number of local WIs (as well as being present at the formation of three!).

The visit to Scaynes Hill WI is reported in detail. The programme for the afternoon seems very full and it included a lecture/demonstration on 'The Bottling and Drying of Fruit and Vegetables' with a lecturer from the Food Production Department. This was followed by a 'Roll Call' – an idea which had been imported from the Canadian WIs in which each member in turn, as her name was called out, had to make a contribution on the chosen subject – at this meeting the subject was 'Cleaning and polishing hints'. Also on the programme for that afternoon was an exchange of seedlings and an exhibition of soft toys made by members. The meeting ended with a co-operative tea, everyone in the WI bringing a contribution. This was an important part of the meeting when members were able to mix together and talk.

At Burgess Hill WI the School students found an even fuller programme than at Scaynes Hill. It included an 'Address' – 'Agricultural Cooperation' by Mr Nugent Harris, and this was followed by a 'Talk' on 'Goat Keeping' by Rev A C Atkins. There was also a 'Paper' written and read by a member and followed by a discussion – 'Rainy day amusements for children' – and an exhibition of basket work. This was followed by tea and entertainment.

This pattern of meetings was largely based on what happened in the Canadian WIs, which is hardly surprising as Madge Watt had been responsible for forming both.

The aims of the WI, the students were taught, were:

1. to stimulate interest in the agriculture industry,
2. to develop co-operative enterprises,
3. to encourage home and local industry,
4. to study home economics,
5. to provide a centre for educational and social intercourse and for all local activities …

but above all:

In our work we aim at helping everything to do with agriculture, and especially just now with agricultural production. We aim at bringing technical knowledge into the farmhouse. If you come to think of it, the farmer's wife has more time for reading than the farmer; she is therefore more open minded. She could attend the technical meeting at the institute and bring back the knowledge into the home. We want this; we want her to be able to get at books on rural economics and demonstrations of labour saving machinery both farm and home. Then she takes back the knowledge she has gained into the farm home, and talks it over with her husband or sons. The farmer will say that science of farming is not a women's job, but it is exactly what she ought to know about. So we want the farmer's wife to attend the Women's Institute; we want her to get into the habit of seeing books and papers on the science of farming, and to link up her own home interests with her husband's business interests.

The students learned how to present these aims to 'the village audience':

... I tell them that their lives may have been dull, and how hard they must have worked, and they perhaps have not had all the advantages that they should have had... I tell them of how other WIs have learned haircutting, to buy a ladder to be able to pick the fruit off the tops of their trees... I tell them that we can teach them where to apply for cheap pig food, where to apply for club rules to run a poultry or rabbit club, where to apply for garden lecturers, where to buy their seed potatoes...

I tell them of starch made with diseased potatoes; how they can dry their own currants at home; how they can learn much by seeing what others can do in the arrangements of the house; how women have learned to paper and paint their own houses; how they have learned tinkering and cobbling and done so many things the country thought a women never could do.

I always tell them, in getting out a programme, to remember three points:
something to hear
something to see
something to do
This provides interest for everyone.

They were advised:

Do not make your programme too long. The matter in one good lecture or two short talks (not more than 20–25 mins each) is quite as much as any one can take in at once. Have tea! it is the cement of WIs over which they will talk and compare notes and generally enjoy themselves. One woman said, "We do so like a meal which we have not had to get ready ourselves; it is such a treat to be waited on."

The students talked to individual WI members. One Wivelsfield WI member said:

I am only a girl in service, but I cannot tell you what help Wivelsfield WI is to me. I learn so much there, and when I am married and have a house of my own I can put it all into practice.

At the end of the training the VCOs sat an examination paper. Those who had learned their lessons well were appointed as VCOs by the Board of Agriculture. In her final report Madge Watt wrote:

I should consider that they might all be authorised.
There are one or two of whom I am doubtful, but I understand from the officers that in these

cases there are reasons for office expediency for their authorization. And it is indeed within my own wish that no one who took a full course at the school should be debarred… Some of them should have further instruction now, and some later. They are all, I feel, confident, and indeed eager to go on to further knowledge, and I hope that this is but a beginning.

The newly trained VCOs began their work, but it did lead to some problems.

> Their function then was to assist the Board in its work of propaganda and formation. Small wonder that they considered themselves to have a more intimate and specialised knowledge of the Women's Institutes than the Central Committee to which indeed they felt no special allegiance. [9]

There did persist something of a conflict of loyalties, and the VCOs formed a private association which convened its own conferences. Even to this day there can be tensions between the VCOs, who are now trained by National Federation of Women's Institutes, and the elected Executive Committees in their respective Federations.

In July 1919 Madge Watt returned to Canada, but not before she had "the satisfaction of starting a WI at Sandringham of which H M The Queen is President." [10] The WI has never had a Royal Patron, only members of whom two happen to be the Queen Mother and the Queen.

The directing of the VCO schools was handed on to Mrs Nugent Harris and by the end of 1919 there were 89 trained VCOs working in 26 County Federations among a total of 1,405 WIs. VCOs today still go on residential training courses. The examination paper, though, is a thing of the past.

The National Federation of Women's Institutes as an independent body

After the war the Board of Agriculture lost interest in the 'propaganda work and the formation of Institutes' and the organisation had to decide how it should be run. The National Executive Committee took over all the running of the Federation, though they did receive a grant of £10,000 from the Government to see them on their way. They also had to decide what kind of an organisation the National Federation would be in peace-time. During the war much of the emphasis had been on producing food; now was the time when strong leadership would plan the direction in which the WIs should develop.

When the NFWI Executive Committee elected its officers, the leadership of the organisation was settled, and for a number of these formative years two women above all others influenced the development – Trudie Denman, as Chairman, and Grace Hadow, as Vice-chairman.

Grace Hadow

Within a few months of its first meeting, the Executive Committee decided that it should also have a vice-chairman. Grace Hadow was elected to the post and thus began a long and distinguished partnership that led the organisation into its peacetime form:

Recalling in after years the beginnings of a close, happy and lasting partnership that was to give the Women's Institute movement so much of its future aims and purposes, Trudie, always conscious of her own academic shortcomings, wrote characteristically that she "could not believe that anyone of Miss Hadow's knowledge could give such serious consideration to the views of anyone as ignorant as myself." [11]

Grace was born on 9th December 1875, the youngest child of the Revd William Hadow and his wife Mary, of South Cerney near Cirencester. She went up to Somerville College, Oxford, in 1900, at a time when a first class education was rare for a girl. The few women who were at Oxford were allowed to study, and could take examinations but were not allowed to receive degrees. In 1903 Grace was awarded a First Class in the Honours School of English Language and Literature and in 1904, following a teaching engagement in America, she took up the post of English tutor at Somerville. A year later she become resident English tutor at Lady Margaret Hall.

When her father died she returned home to look after her mother. During this period, which included the First World War, she was involved in a variety of initiatives to improve the status of women. When Cirencester WI formed in 1916 she became its President. In mid 1917 she was appointed Director of the Welfare Department of the Ministry of Munitions, where the health and well-being of women munitions workers was a priority. In the same year she was elected to the NFWI Executive Committee, and became its Vice Chairman, a post she was to hold until her death.

She was a well-trained, well-read, alert, kindly woman, with a gift of clear exposition which was to make her invaluable to the movement, and she had a deep sense of public service. She not only had intelligence and friendliness but fibre – I have heard that all her aeroplaning has been done in the open air alongside the pilot. It is told of Miss Hadow that when her services were later on accepted at the Ministry of Munitions, her chief said to somebody, 'well, she won't cry!' [12]

Grace's eldest brother, Henry (Plate 4, pp 128–129), was 16 years older than her and was also her godfather. When she was at Lady Margaret Hall he was a tutor at Worcester College and, in spite of the difference in their ages,

the bond between them was very strong and they spent as much time together as they could snatch from their multifarious duties. It was a common sight to see them walking and talking round the Parks at amazing speed. We used to say that they walked so fast that they went in front of themselves, and talked before their mouths had time to open. [13]

In 1909 Henry went on to be head of Armstrong College in Newcastle (later to be Newcastle University). From 1916 to 1918 he was Vice-Chancellor of Durham University, and was knighted in 1918. In 1919 he became Vice-Chancellor of Sheffield University. He chaired the committee which produced the Hadow report of 1926 on 'The education of the adolescent', which set the foundations for the modern structure of secondary education.

Henry influenced his sister, and through him she had contacts with the wider education world. Soon after being elected to the National Executive Committee of NFWI, Grace briefly shared a house with Henry, who was at that time working on a project to provide an 'educational bridge' to help soldiers returning from the First World War. Grace at the same time was considering ways of using adult education to help women to deal with the changing social climate, through her work in the WI.

Grace's professional life continued alongside her work as Vice-Chairman of NFWI. She was Secretary to Barnett House from 1920 to 1929 and Principal of the Society of Oxford Home Students from 1929 to 1940. This Society grew out of the Association for Education of Women which was the origin of women members of the University. Women were first admitted to degrees in 1920 and the Delegacy for Oxford Home Students was constituted in 1921. During her ten years as Principal Grace was able to move the OHS towards its later status as St Anne's College through the acquisition of land and the building of the library, which was opened in 1938.

Always concerned about life in rural areas, she assembled a group of people in Oxfordshire with similar concerns which grew into the first Rural Community Council in the country. She also fought for the provision of public libraries for rural areas, travelling the countryside at the wheel of a snub-nosed Morris car named 'Andrew' after Andrew Carnegie, whose trustees had supplied a grant for rural development. [14] She was a member of the Executive Committee of the National Council for Social Services, a member of the BBC Advisory Council, and a member of the Adult Education Committee of the Board of Education, as well as being Vice-Chairman of NFWI. Her wide range of contacts was important in the developing educational work of the WI.

She died of pneumonia at the age of 64, not long after returning from a holiday in Norway where she had enjoyed, as she always did, strenuous walks and climbs. There is a memorial tablet to her in the University church of St Mary in Oxford, which bears the following quotation from the Wisdom of Solomon (7.22–23):

> Wisdom which is the worker of all things taught me, for in her is an understanding spirit. Holy, Subtil. Clear in utterance, loving the thing that is good. Quick. Steadfast, ready to do good.

A remarkable partnership

We have given a brief biography of Trudie Denman at the beginning of this chapter. She was an astute business woman, too. As a director of S Pearson and Son, the Cowdray Trust, and the Westminster Press, she had very wide experience and skills which she brought to the newly formed independent WI organisation. The partnership of Trudie Denman and Grace Hadow, which lasted until Grace's death in January 1940, provided for the WI exactly the balance that Adelaide Hoodless had spoken of when she said:

> What must be done is to develop to the fullest extent the two great social forces, education and organisation, so as to secure for each individual the highest degree of advancement. [15]

Trudie Denman brought the "great social force of organisation" and Grace Hadow brought the "great social force of education", and together they worked "so as to secure for each individual" WI member "the highest degree of advancement".

And in doing this they fulfilled the objects of the WI which had been laid down in the Constitution of 1919:

The main purpose of the Women's Institute movement is to improve and develop conditions of rural life. It seeks to give all countrywomen the opportunity of working together through the Women's Institute organisation, and of putting into practice those ideals for which it stands. For the purpose of securing and furthering the said objectives the Women's Institutes shall have power to:

1. provide for the fuller education of countrywomen in citizenship, in public questions both national and international, in music, drama and other cultural subjects, also to secure instruction and training in all branches of handcrafts, domestic science, health and social welfare. [16]

The talents of Trudie and Grace were complementary:

... Chairman and Vice Chairman each contributed qualities that were just right for this work as well as for their specific functions. They were at one in their wholehearted devotion to public service, in their belief in a women's movement for women and in democracy as its form of government, in their keen interest in the administration of rural affairs and their bent towards social reform. Both were ready to welcome new ideas and glad to encourage new workers and leaders. [17]

Nancy Tennant, who became Vice Chairman in 1940, after the death of Grace Hadow, knew them both and later recalled them:

Lady Denman had clear judgement and great precision ... she was immensely respected, but she was not loved in the way that Elizabeth Brunner was loved, as a person, as a warm person. She was looked up to enormously and was very valuable... Miss Hadow was an academic. She looked like a bean pole, very tall and angular with pince-nez, but attractive and funny, and gay and sweet. I would love to have known her better... Lady Denman and Mrs Watt worked in totally different ways, but they were both absolutely necessary, and I think that Miss Hadow was a sort of king pin in between, because she was more approachable than Lady Denman, by a long chalk, but had all the precision of an academic. [18]

They were also supported by an executive committee of able women. Lady Brunner, reflecting on those who started the WI, said:

The women who started the WI had enthusiasm, originality and organising ability, and they were slightly idealistic ... there was a feeling that if you had the privilege of education, and the privilege of position, you wanted to give it back, you wanted to give other people the opportunities you had. [19]

The polices agreed by the Executive Committee were implemented by committed and competent staff. In the very early days the secretariat was that of the AOS, and then later the Board of Agriculture's women's department, Miss Talbot and Mrs Nugent Harris. The first General Secretary was Mrs Kilroy Kenyon who fell ill and had to resign after only a few months. Her successor, Inez Jenkins (1919–1929), was assisted by Mrs Nugent Harris as chief organiser, and editor of *Home and Country*. Inez Jenkins had "distinguished herself at St Hilda's Hall", and came to the Federation after some years with the National Union of Societies for Equal Citizenship. [20] The Hon. Frances Farrer (later Dame Frances) followed Inez Jenkins as General Secretary and was still in that post when Lady Denman died. She had a particular interest in, and knowledge of, public affairs and had a "fine power of written expression, and an exact and retentive memory." [21]

These were indeed remarkable women who moulded and guided the newly independent organisation as it emerged from the war years and had to find a new identity and rôle.

CHAPTER FOUR

EDUCATION IN THE WI : 1919–1939

Towards the end of the First World War, a WI president said regretfully, "When the war is over I suppose the Women's Institutes will come to an end." [1] The WIs did not come to an end, indeed they grew rapidly in number, but the emphasis of their activities changed somewhat to adapt to post war life. This was reflected in the Constitution, (p 39) which was concerned less with the production of food and much more with rural development and education. The Adult Education Committee of the Ministry of Reconstruction, in their Final Report of 1919, described the main purpose of education as "to fit a man for life, and therefore in a civilised community to fit him for his place in that community... The whole process must be the development of the individual in his relation to the community." [2] As befitted the conventions of the day, this referred to women too, and the WI embraced this purpose.

A woman's life in the rural areas

A typical village and its inhabitants in the time between the wars was described by Grace Hadow:

> An average village of some four hundred to a thousand inhabitants contains a considerable variety of interests... There are the squire and his family, who may be in residence for most of the year, or may only come for the hunting. There is a little group of farmers, the elder, as a rule, men of a certain shrewdness and narrowness, with little imagination, kind hearts, and an impatience of book learning bred partly of well-meant endeavours on the part of theorists to find them short cuts to prosperity. There is possibly a hard worked village doctor, the only man in the place with some knowledge of science. There is the schoolmaster, and in these days possibly one or two weekenders or artists, beings of another world who may or may not become part of village life, and there are agricultural labourers and their families. [3]

One of the great strengths of the WI was the way in which it crossed social boundaries, and allowed women who had never previously met on equal terms to do so. There was a considerable difference between the lives of the ladies in the 'big house' and the women who served them. The following article condensed from an early number of *Home and Country*, the WI magazine, was written to assure the WI member who was a 'domestic servant' that she was also a valued member of the organisation. It may seem rather patronising today, but it was making a very radical statement at the time:

Domestic service and the WIs

We are told the title domestic servant is not popular nowadays, but no sensible worker ever objects to a title that is a fair description of an honest occupation. Domestic comes from the Latin domus – a house – and simply means belonging to the house; whilst servant comes from servire – to serve. Hence, one of the house who serves the house is the right description of anyone who belongs to the honourable profession of Domestic Service. The most important thing in life is to find out what work we can do best, fit ourselves for it, and then do it to the best of our ability, with the happy assurance that the honour of work and its reward lie in how it is done, not in how a misguided little world regards a special piece of work from a worse than stupid standpoint… Domestic service is as much a skilled profession as any other, and is certainly not among the worst paid. The more its members prize training, and the more they appreciate the advantages of the calling without dwelling on its disadvantages – every occupation has some disadvantages – so much more quickly will the status of domestic service be recognised as second to that of no other profession in the kingdom…

Domestic servants are amongst the most useful WI workers, and we want them to realise that there is a special welcome for them in every Institute. We want to bring to their notice the Guild of Domestic Employment, Roland House, London SW, which, among many other benefits, has promised to find out for any member if a WI exists in a village to which the member is arranging to go. The subscription is one shilling. Two remarks heard lately from Institute members need no explanation. "My cook just got married. She was a splendid WI worker. The new cook is doing well. I have had no servant problem since the Institute was started". " I didn't believe I could stay in my place at first, the village is so lonely; but since I joined the Institute I am happier that I have ever been in my life." [4]

Another article showed concern for a particular group of women who were to be found after the war which had resulted in the deaths of so many young men. Headed 'Surplus Women', it showed an awareness of, and a sympathy for their special needs:

Those who point out that the census shows a surplus of women should follow up their argument by advocating at the same time better training, better openings and equal pay for equal work for women, since by their own showing a large number of women must support themselves all their lives or become dependent on their men relations. [5]

The leaders of the WI had to plan an educational programme that would begin to address the needs of this wide range of women. One of the ways in which they did this was to concentrate on the newly acquired vote and to encourage all women to become active citizens. They also explained the educational rôle of the WI to the members in no uncertain manner, as witness this article published in *Home and Country* in 1920:

The WI as an educational factor

Q	What is education?
A	The gaining of knowledge whereby the development of the mind and the formation of character are helped
Q	What is a factor?
A	One of the means whereby a result is obtained.
Q	In what ways can the Institute be an educational factor?
A	1. by bringing all the women of the village together and teaching them to respect each others opinions
	2. by teaching democratic principles through the equality of members, one women one vote, government by a representative committee elected by a ballot of members

3. by teaching that the will of the majority of the members must be carried out loyally by all
4. by proving the value of co-operation i.e. working together
5. by teaching that organisation and business like methods are necessary if the institute is to remain a permanent part of country life
6. by developing the social spirit and proving that a happy community life depends on the desire and action of all the people in the community
7. by providing lectures, classes, study circles, demonstrations, social gatherings as desired by members
8. by teaching the responsibility of citizenship
9. by developing the sense of comradeship
10. by expecting members to share any expert knowledge they possess with fellow members
11. by giving the opportunity to each member to develop her best powers of head, heart and hand
12. by creating that atmosphere of kindliness, goodwill and good humour that is characteristic of the Institutes. [6]

At the 6th meeting of the Consultative Council, held in Exeter in November 1921 (by which time there were 2,174 WIs), delegates endorsed the following recommendations:

That there is a need in the counties for teaching and instructing speakers on such subjects as Local Government and that the County Federations should act as the channel for any scheme of instruction, Headquarters being prepared to help them wherever possible.

That a subcommittee of members of the Executive, county representatives and educational experts be formed to discuss technical and higher education and to draw up an agenda on these subjects for the next meeting of the consultative council. [7]

There was, alongside this education for citizenship, a very practical concern to try to improve the lives of members, especially those who had heavy domestic duties. Other articles from *Home and Country* give some idea of the everyday lives of many WI members. Some of the subjects covered include:

Helpful hints for the busy housewife, on clearing the ashes, the use of blacklead box, broom, and dustpan; and how to make soap. (1922)

How to manage on a housekeeping allowance of £2 5s. 0d. a week for a working man and wife. (1922)

Rats and how to destroy them. (1925)

WI members encouraged to keep goats to provide more milk for the villages. (1930)

How to manage the earth closet. (1944)

There were letters from members which gave an insight into their lives. In 1936 a WI member in Staffordshire wrote:

> I have lived in this cottage for over six years. During the first four and a half years we had no water supply and had to fetch if from a draw well 40 ft deep 70 yards away. We had to make three journeys a day which would take about half an hour.

– and Adelaide Hoodless was concerned in 1896 that women were still having to carry water to the house.

Developing the educational programme

Lady Denman and Grace Hadow were remarkable women who influenced the way the educational purposes of the organisation developed. As we have seen, both came from privileged backgrounds – one in society, with money, influence and all the right contacts, the other in academia, but also with wide-ranging interests and contacts. They were both comparatively young when they started their WI careers: Lady Denman was 32 and Grace Hadow was 41. They both used their knowledge, influence and contacts in the interests of the new organisation. For Trudie Denman the main thrust was citizenship and agriculture; for Grace Hadow it was liberal education and widening the horizons of village women.

Under their guidance the National Executive Committee agreed the educational policy of the new organisation and set up programmes for its implementation. There were five main strands to the educational programme of the 1920s and 1930s: teaching members to run the new organisation; education in citizenship; practical instruction in domestic matters; revival of crafts; and liberal education.

Running the organisation

The women who were joining the newly formed WIs needed help and advice on how to run an organisation on democratic lines, help and advice that the VCOs provided. In the March 1920 edition of *Home and Country* the training of the VCOs themselves is described. This is one of the earliest examples of the WI using short stay residential courses:

> The women's branch of the Board of Agriculture and fisheries is retaining as part of its future work the training of organisers for WIs. It proposes to hold two schools during the current year at University centres, one in England and one in Wales. Each school will last a fortnight and 25 organisers will be trained at each. [8]

Lady Albermarle, who succeeded Lady Denman as National Chairman, remembered that:

> Lady Denman had always been very keen on the organisational side of things, that the business should be clearly and well run. The WI offered a very good training on how to run things, and I think she saw the WI as a training ground for women so that when they went into public life they were aware and knew what they were doing and how to handle things. There was a lot of training in those days. At the time people rather enjoyed that kind of thing because it gave them confidence. I dare say people would find it dull now, but at that time we were really hungry for it. You see countrywomen had not done an awful lot of public work.

But when WI members went onto Rural District Councils, to a great extent they met the same procedures that they had already met in the WI, so they didn't feel out of their depth. [9]

Lady Denman herself wrote pamphlets on how to carry out various rôles, for example 'The Duties of WI Secretaries', and 'Planning Work and Programmes'.

By 1921 every English county had its Federation though some of the Welsh and Island Federations were formed later. In order to ensure that all these Federations were being run in a similar way, and that similar standards were being maintained, the National Executive Committee ran regional officers' schools and conferences to cover particular aspects of the work. In the four years 1922–25 there were four training conferences held in different parts of the country, taken by Lady Denman herself, assisted by one or two senior staff members from London.

Education in citizenship

In its final report (1919), the Adult Education Committee of the Ministry of Reconstruction wrote that they believed the "economic recovery of the nation" and the "proper use of their responsibilities by millions of new voters" (including women for the first time) depended on a more intelligent public opinion; therefore it concluded that "adult education is a permanent national necessity, an inseparable aspect of citizenship" and that the opportunity for adult education should be spread uniformly and systematically over the whole community. [10]

The National Federation took this matter very seriously and felt that it was important that they should inform members and encourage them to make use of their new power. Some extracts from *Home and Country* illustrate how they did this while remaining within their non-party-political boundaries:

Many more women have the right to vote now than three years ago – the wives of men who are local government electors, as long as they are over 30 years of age, as well as those women over 21 years of age who are qualified in their own right as occupier, whether as owner or tenant... [11]

Proportional representation is in the air, and its adoption for practically all public elections in this country cannot be long delayed, for it is by its use public bodies can be made really representative of those who elect them... [12]

This was followed by a long article explaining how proportional representation would work. How dismayed the writer would have been to find that it had still not been adopted over 70 years later.

Revival of handicrafts

Home and Country reported, after the first Consultative Council, that there was

a demand from the Institutes for teachers and for a standard of work. There is a necessity of getting rid of our false standards and getting back to the old right standards. WIs could help by learning suitable handicrafts, and could also help to revive old crafts such as rush weaving, which had become almost forgotten. [13]

At a conference of Educational Associations at University College, London, held as early as January 1920 reference was made to the revival of practical rural skills by WIs:

> It is said in connection with 'Homemaking as the basis of citizenship' that a great loss had come to the home through the habit of supplying needs with the ready-made ... in order to regain the true homemaking spirit it is necessary to recover those lost arts within the home ... on the practice of these arts rests the basis of good citizenship. Reference to this side of rural domestic life by the WIs ... is worthy of all encouragement... [14]

In January 1920 the 'Guild of Learners' was set up with the following aims:

1. To regain the practice of home handicrafts with a view to restore the best traditions of English workmanship.
2. To assist in bringing the best instruction in handicrafts within the reach of villages.

Membership was in two categories:

1. Associates – WI members who will undertake to become proficient in some handicraft connected with the home.
2. Members
   a) WI members who are already proficient in some handicraft;
   b) WI members who are proficient in some handicraft and are willing to use their knowledge for the furtherance of such craft in their neighbourhood.

There was a separate subscription for Associates and Members. [15]

In order to set up such a Guild of Learners there had to be suitably qualified and trained teachers, demonstrators and instructors. NFWI developed a series of 'proficiency tests' which a member had to complete to prove that she was competent at the appropriate craft before she could train as instructor, demonstrator or judge. Judges were required to judge WI competitions and County shows. One of the indirect educational methods that has always been used in WIs is to hold a competition, perhaps for a particular craft item, e.g. a soft toy. The competition is judged and comments given by the qualified judge; these comments help the individual to raise her standards.

Competitions, judging and proficiency tests were not for everyone, as the following extract from *Home and Country* shows:

> The Lace Test – Do members of the Guild of Learners lack courage, or is it a fact that minorities are clamorous in indirect ratio to their size? Urgent appeals for this particular Test were made, but when it came to the point, like the guests at a certain wedding feast, hindrances were pleaded and the results so far as numbers are concerned are disappointing.

Three members are then congratulated on passing their test (in Carrickmacross lace, Buckinghamshire lace and Russian lace) and the report goes on:

Lacemaking is not a very largely practised craft at present but many classes have been held in Institutes scattered up and down the country, and while beginners might not expect to gain their certificates at once, fear of failure should not deter anyone from trying. Much besides a certificate may be gained in the attempt to complete, as perfectly as possible, a set piece of work within a given time; great improvement in the capabilities of the worker will be one reward of such concentrated effort, while the criticism received from the judge should be very helpful and stimulate the student to further efforts. [16]

WI members were able to develop skills either through classes and tuition in the WI or by classes provided by the Local Education Authority. East Sussex County Federation engaged a professional teacher in the craft of toy making. She visited many WIs, cycling on a bicycle bought by the Federation for £5. [17]

Even in the days when the WIs were organised by the Board of Agriculture, it was recognised that there were commercial possibilities. A draft memorandum setting out NFWI's reasons for claiming financial help from the government reads, in part:

… the exodus from the country will not be checked until village industries are sufficiently well established to give employment to those women who are not able actively to devote themselves to agriculture proper but whose home duties do not take their whole time. [18]

In 1918 a standing Industries Subcommittee was set up, and a 'lecturer on industries' was appointed to advise counties. The committee also administered the £1,000 grant which had been received from the Carnegie Trust for craft work. From this grant loans were made to counties who wished to establish industries. *Home and Country* reported that Lindfield WI, in Sussex "has produced 1,900 toys during the year and one member has made £20 pocket money as the result of her share in the industry." Another Sussex WI, Ticehurst, set up a WI industry in smocked dresses and jumpers for children, which were advertised in *The Lady* and traded well during the 1920s and 1930s. In *Home and Country* there are numerous accounts of other enterprises; in Warwickshire for example there was skin curing, fur craft, and glove making; in Devon, dyeing, weaving and making socks.

There were problems however in ensuring that the crafts, toys in particular, met the standards required by the trade, and it was difficult for a small local industry to hold its place in a competitive market. Gradually the initiatives to set up industries died out and after 1920 loans and grants from the Carnegie Trust were made solely for educational purposes. The 'lecturer on industries' gave up her post in 1919 and a 'technical adviser on handicraft' was appointed in her place. She was one of the instigators of the Guild of Learners.

Practical instruction in domestic matters

The most popular subjects for most WI members were the practical ones which helped them to do their job better, whatever it might be – housewife, mother, small holder, farmer…

There were speakers at the monthly meetings and instructors and tutors who went to the villages to run practical classes. In the early days many of these classes were to help to 'make do and mend'. Photographs of the Scaynes Hill WI in Sussex (one of the ones visited by Mrs Watt's trainee VCOs at the first VCO school, p 34; Plate 12, pp 160–161) show members learning tinkering in order to be able to mend their pots and pans, and being instructed in cobbling to enable them to mend their families' shoes. These were skills that most women had not had before; the instructors were men and they were teaching women things previously considered as 'men's work'.

Lady Denman particularly supported instruction on how to make the garden, the small-holding, or the farm more productive. This part of the programme primarily provided the technical information required to grow produce, milk cows, keep poultry, etc, but skills related to the preparation of food in the kitchen and management of the house were also included.

The County Federations of WIs built up links with their local county councils. For example:

Lectures, demonstrations and classes in agriculture and horticulture have been held in Shropshire under the auspices of the county council and since the inauguration of the WI Movement ... the work of agricultural education among women has considerably developed, the county agricultural committee working in co-operation with the WIs. [19]

The 1922 AGM resolved

that this meeting recommends the NFWI Executive Committee to represent to the Government the great need for the continuance and development of adult education in rural districts and the possibilities of economy by using the assistance of voluntary societies in this work. [20]

Some county councils responded well. In 1924 the AGM expressed

... its cordial appreciation of the valuable assistance given to the Institute movement by those county councils which have aided the Women's Institutes in their areas by providing lectures, demonstrations and educational facilities generally and it further urged all county councils to make full use of the opportunities for the development of adult education in rural areas afforded by the Women's Institute movement. [21]

Because of her particular interest in this field, Lady Denman was asked by the Government in December 1925 to chair a committee set up jointly under the Ministry of Agriculture and the Board of Education to "consider the general question of the practical education of women for rural life". The result was the Denman Report of 1928:

Fundamental to the whole report was the concept that village women make a unique and twofold contribution to agriculture; the 'independent' contribution of women farmers and paid workers (of whom there were over 100,000 in 1926); and the 'co-operative' contribution made by a very much larger number of women and girls by virtue of their position as wives or daughters in village homes and where they have a far greater influence on the work of their menfolk than is the case in other industries. Practical education for women in rural life must therefore embrace not only the growing of produce in the field and garden, but also its subsequent utilisation in the kitchen, and instruction in home management and crafts. [22]

Following this report the Ministry of Agriculture provided special grants to train teachers in farm household management as well as appointing women inspectors to advise the County authorities on the education of women in agricultural subjects. By the end of 1930 the first Rural Home Economists were trained.

As part of this whole thrust of improving the quantity and quality of home produce the various publications by the Ministry of Agriculture were promoted to WI members – allotment cropping, pig-feeding, bees and rabbits, fruit growing, etc. – in order to help members increase the productivity of their gardens and small holdings.

In 1931, as a consequence of the economic crisis, WI members were encouraged by NFWI to "produce, conserve and market good food." [23] NFWI organised two regional courses in cooking and food values, taught by experts, and only open to WI members with previous experience who were willing to teach. Five places were also kept for WI members on the Board of Education's course for uncertificated teachers. Within a year all the students who had attended these courses were employed by their Local Education Authorities. This provides an early example of WI members being trained to train others, a 'cascade method' used on many occasions since.

The increased interest in this area of work led, in 1939, to the formation of the NFWI Produce Guild which brought together the schools and classes and the training of teachers and judges. A grant of £500 from the Development Commission helped towards the running costs of the Produce Guild. Individual WIs could set up a branch of the Guild and members paid a small sum to join and have access to its activities.

The marketing of surplus food also gained in importance at this time of economic depression. In 1932 NFWI called a conference of all the Women's Institute Markets which until that time had existed in isolation. There were about 20 of them and at that point they became registered as Provident Societies. The Carnegie Trust made a grant that enabled NFWI to employ a marketing organiser who was able to support the existing markets and promote the development of new ones. This was the beginning of the WI County Markets, now established as an independent unit.

Liberal education

While reporting all this practical activity, *Home and Country* also warned:

> Whilst busy over classes for the provision of food and clothing and for the artistic decoration of the home, members of WIs will not forget there are other ways by which they may become good home makers besides purely practical means. The village has need of its Marys as well as its Marthas. [24]

Grace Hadow felt this strongly and worked actively in Oxfordshire to promote lectures on a wide range of cultural subjects. She herself gave talks on miracle plays, folk lore, poetry, and village history, and shared her own experiences of travel abroad for holidays and work. [25] She was also able to persuade some of her fellow Oxford dons to talk to WIs on such subjects as 'Medieval England', 'Women in Local Government', Classical Novels', 'Ancient Greece and her Love of Beauty', 'Medieval Guilds', and 'Wild Life in the Country'. These subjects were listed in the Report of HM Inspectors on the 'Educational Work of Women's Rural Institutes', 1926.

Music and drama became an important part of WI life. There were schools to train conductors of 'Village Singing'. 'Folk Dance' classes, plays and pageants were organised, and Federations gave advice and ran schools on how to produce plays.

In the 1930s the Carnegie Trust gave a regular grant to help with the training of village producers and conductors. These grants were administered by the joint Music and Drama Committee of NFWI and the National Council for Social Service (do we see the hand of Grace Hadow here?) and contributions were made to Counties for their festivals. It was a way of maintaining an equal standard throughout the Counties, but it also allowed access to specialist training which WI members living in rural areas would not be likely to get in any other way.

In East Sussex, for example, Gertrude Lampson started a County Choral Festival. At the first one, held in Lewes Town Hall in 1923, 11 WI choirs competed, but during the next 18 years the Festival grew into an event, the Lewes Music Festival, which covered six days, with over 2,000 competitors, and included classes for mixed choirs and children's choirs as well as soloists. To support this huge undertaking the County Federation also ran annual conductor's courses. At the fifth one, in 1928, 200 students were supervised by Dr (later Sir) Malcolm Sargent. [26]

Report of HM Inspectors

In 1925 The Board of Education carried out an inspection of the 'Women's Rural Institutes and … the Educational Work carried on under the various County Education Authorities in connection with them'. They published their report in the form of a white paper. [27]

The report starts by noting the rapid growth of the WI. There were 3,328 WIs all "set up within the last 10 years". It continues:

> The extension of educational activities amongst country women has steadily increased with the growth of the institute movement… Not all country women are ready to receive the more formal type of instruction usually given in towns. Home occupations often prevent their following a course of lessons; as do also inclement weather and seasonal events such as haymaking and fruit gathering. It is therefore often found more convenient to arrange short intensive courses in crafts and to rely for other educational expansion in single lectures, demonstrations and discussions; much of this work is aided by local education authorities… One of the important aspects of this work is that as a result of single demonstrations and

lectures followed by discussions, regular though short courses have frequently been asked for. Women have not known before of all the interests of which by reason of the remoteness of the village they have been deprived. These needed to be brought to their doors to arouse attention, to cultivate the keen intelligence and interest which hitherto had lacked opportunity, and to give outlet to latent natural ability.

Country women do not naturally think quickly, they need time for reflection and for the application of the knowledge gained, but they know what they want and what is worth having. For example, Northumberland provided between 20 and 30 courses of instruction as the outcome of single lectures given in the previous year. In Staffordshire, 100 short courses were held in one year, largely as a result of the policy in the previous year of holding single demonstrations.

The report goes on to review the subjects being taught and the training of instructors and the facilities required. It concludes:

Up to the present time practical subjects have made the strongest appeal because their immediate value is evident. The time is yet to come when the same effort will be made for courses in more academic subjects. That this may be confidently looked for is shown by the growing number of lectures in music and health subjects, and by growing interest in subjects bearing on the historical, sociological and literary questions.

National training programme

The National Federation ran a centralised programme of training. Most of this training was for the leaders who were involved in running the organisation. The residential training schools for VCOs have already been mentioned (p 33). In January 1922 the first recorded correspondence course was set up for VCOs:

Correspondence course in Economics
In concurrence with the wishes of many WI organisers, and in view of the importance of economic questions in the national life, rural as well as urban, it is proposed to arrange a three months' course in General Economics to begin January 1922, for NFWI organisers, and if vacancies occur for WI members.

The course will be in the charge of Dr E W Shanahan, D.Sc.(Econ), M.A, of the London School of Economics, who will address a meeting of Institute organisers in London … on the subject of Economic Studies. Dr Shanahan prescribes a simple course of reading, so that students may prepare in advance for the correspondence course. The syllabus … under the heading of general economics deals with Wealth, Agents of Production, Markets, Values and Prices, Rent, Interest, Profits, Wages, Incomes, Money and Functions of Government.

Papers containing questions for written work and directions as to study, will be sent every three weeks by Dr Shananhan…

If this first course proves successful a second will be arranged, dealing more particularly with Agricultural Economics. [28]

The text book set cost 4/6, and the fee for the course was 10/6.

This was indeed a rather formidable programme and it is not clear how many actually followed it.

In order to develop a programme of training for those in the Federation who would lead in other areas of work NFWI appointed a number of 'Organisers'. The Handicraft Organiser has already been mentioned; there were also a Marketing Organiser and a General Organiser (who dealt with forming WIs). At the end of the 1930s a further post was created, that of Education Organiser. Cicely McCall was appointed to this post:

> I was asked to lunch by Lady Denman ... and half a dozen other executive members – a rather formidable form of interview. In spite of my being appointed at a higher rate of salary than the other organisers I found my fellow organisers wonderfully supportive and keenly interested in this new endeavour. [29]

The work of the various national Organisers was mostly out in the Federations, they worked to one of the national subcommittees and usually had a close working partnership with the relevant subcommittee chairman. Cicely McCall relates:

> In Adeline Vernon, I had an enthusiastic chairman of my education sub-committee, and she and I went on many county tours together. The usual routine was to spend a week per month in the Eccleston Street Headquarters to attend committees and write reports, and three weeks touring the counties. In my eight years with the WIs I visited every county in England and all but one of the Welsh counties. The WIs provided a car, and each organiser averaged 15,000 to 20,000 miles per year. [30]

Residential conferences

In the period between the wars the National Federation organised residential conferences. Some of these were for training purposes; for example in 1937 and 1938 the Board of Education held refresher courses, each of a week's duration, for WI teachers of cookery, and local authorities and Federations jointly selected 41 students to attend. [31]

With the appointment of an Education Organiser, the training given for many years on committee procedure was added to by Speakers Schools:

> If WI members of the future were to play their part in local government they must not only know accepted procedure but they must also be articulate enough to negotiate it effectively. [32]

After such courses and conferences the participants returned to their WIs and passed on what they had learned to their fellow members, providing a valuable source of education to women who lived in villages where, until that time, little had been available to them. The rate at which the WIs were formed and the membership increase show clearly how the new organisation was welcomed.

WI members, when they were delegates to conferences, or when they came to the AGM, often had to travel considerable distances and would also have to stay away from home overnight. For many of the women then, as is still true today, this was a difficult thing to organise. But most women found that the value of coming together from all over the country compensated for all the difficulties.

Belonging to the WI increased the confidence of many women in their ability to run their own affairs. In 20 years they had developed, sometimes in co-operation with other agencies, a well-run educational service to women in the countryside. In 1939, with the outbreak of a second World War, their efforts, yet again, had to be deflected from education for their own personal and community development towards helping once more with a war effort.

CHAPTER FIVE

INTERLUDE : A LOOK AT
ADULT EDUCATION IN BRITAIN

The WIs throughout the 1920s and 1930s had become an established feature of the educational scene in rural areas, but the WI did not exist in isolation. In this chapter we will review some of the other educational developments that were happening in Britain, albeit largely in the urban areas, and largely aimed at men. Some of these were to influence the WI when it founded Denman College.

The Nineteenth-Century legacy

Adult education in Britain has its roots in the activities of Nineteenth Century voluntary bodies, especially the Mechanics Institutes, the Co-operative movement and University extra-mural work. The desire to bring about social change was the underlying motive of many of those organisations, and most of them were aimed at the urban male.

The first Mechanics Institute was founded by George Birkbeck in Glasgow in 1823, and by 1851 there were 700 in the UK, mostly in urban areas. They offered an opportunity for men who were 'skilled mechanics' to improve their education. This was usually done through single lectures, and most Mechanics Institutes banned politics and religion as being too controversial. As we have seen there was a similar ruling in the early WIs. The rule that banned these topics was not changed in the WI until 1971.

The name 'Institute' is defined in the Shorter Oxford Dictionary as "a society or organisation instituted to promote literature, science, art, education or the like". The name was adopted quite widely, and was used to refer to the building in which this type of education occurred as well as to the organisation that provided it. 'Institute' suggested liberal education, provided in an accessible way and shared with like-minded people and with associated social activities. As well as the Mechanics Institutes, a number of other organisations chose this name: the City and Guilds of London Institute, the City Literary Institute, the British Institute of Adult Education, the National Institute of Adult Education, etc. It was a name which was already recognised when the Women's Institutes were started in this country and happily adopted by them. When a similar organisation to the WI was formed in the USA, the name chosen was 'The Farm and Home Bureau' and in Ireland 'The Countrywomen's Association'.

The Co-operative movement began in the Lancashire cotton town of Rochdale. The Rochdale Pioneers, as they were first called, decided on their formation in 1844 to devote a percentage of their profits to educational purposes. With this money they established schools, libraries, reading and lecture rooms, and debating clubs. Notably for our theme, they set up in 1883 the Co-operative Women's Educational Guild to train women to take a full part in the movement. This training included public speaking, committee work and policy formation.

University extension work, or extra-mural education, was started by Cambridge University in 1873; Oxford University followed in 1878. The primary aim was to provide further education for working men, but also to bring further and higher education to women, who at that time were otherwise denied it. University lecturers travelled around the country, usually to the large urban centres – Leeds, Liverpool, Sheffield and Manchester – to deliver short lecture courses. These were particularly popular with middle-class women. In addition, residential Summer Schools were run in both Oxford and Cambridge.

The first summer school was held in Oxford in 1888. Oxford was chosen because the university could provide teachers, and there was an opportunity to visit museums, libraries, and galleries. Summer schools lasted for about ten days and used university buildings. "There were lectures during the morning and in the evenings eminent men spoke on literary or scientific subjects," [1] – a pattern that others were to follow in the future, and which was used in the early days of Denman College. For many of those who experienced it, the opportunity to study intensively in the atmosphere of an ancient university, with some of the country's leading academics, affected them for the rest of their lives.

One such person was Albert Mansbridge, who attended the Oxford summer school of 1899. He was an employee of the Co-operative Wholesale Society and he envisaged how a closer alliance between the University extension movement and the worker's associations, such as the co-operatives and the trade unions, could make the benefits of a university education more readily available to the working class. In 1903, with a small group of other like-minded people, he founded the Association to Promote Higher Education of Working Men, which was renamed the Workers Educational Association two years later.

From the 1830s onward many elementary day schools opened in the evening for adult students. Initially these were private enterprises or attached to a church, but in 1851 government funding for these evening schools increased, so that by 1858 there were over 2,000 in England and Wales. Two thirds of the 81,000 students who attended them were male, however, and the majority were adolescents. [2] At first the curriculum provided basic education, but by the 1870s many evening schools prepared students for vocational qualifications offered by the City and Guilds of London Institute, or the Royal Society of Arts Examination Boards. Meanwhile, in 1885, the Recreational Evening Schools Association had been set up to encourage the use of school buildings for recreational purposes. Practically all these activities were in urban areas, and the rural provision, especially for women, was negligible.

1900 to 1939

The new century started with two educational developments, one statutory and one voluntary. The 1902 Education Act set up Local Education Authorities and gave them the responsibility for adult education. In 1903, as mentioned above, the Workers

Educational Association was founded. The first branch of the WEA was started in Reading in October 1904; Mansbridge believed that at least three quarters of the members should be "actual labouring men and women." He also "emphasised objectivity and study for its own sake, uncontaminated by the pursuit of material goals". [3] The WEA grew rapidly and by 1939 there were 28,652 members. In 1924 the WEA received 'responsible body' status, receiving grant aid directly from the government. The WEA developed its own network of tutorial classes, but in the early years few of these were available to women who lived in rural areas.

During the First World War the Ministry of Reconstruction established an Adult Education Committee. It's final report in 1919 presented a blueprint for adult education as part of mainstream provision. The report "depicted adult education not as a side issue to be resigned to the fanatic or the crank but as an activity indispensable to the health of democratic societies and to be regarded therefore as a necessary and normal part of the country's educational system." The rationale of adult education was to be "the creation of a well ordered welfare state or Great Society ... a free and fully partici-patory democracy." [4] As a result of this report the President of the Board of Education set up an Adult Education Committee to promote and develop liberal adult education, to bring together national organisations concerned with the provision of adult education, to secure mutual help and avoid waste of effort, and to further the establishment of voluntary organisations and their co-operation with the LEAs.

The WIs grew and developed in this supportive atmosphere, where the Government was actively encouraging voluntary organisations, and WI County Federations worked collaboratively with their LEAs to organise classes in villages. The first leaders of the WI had themselves, for the most part, been well educated. They were aware of the opportu-nities available, of other adult education providers, and of the whole network of people who could help them.

The 1927 AGM of NFWI carried the Executive Committee proposal:

> That as there is an ever increasing demand in the Institutes for demonstrations and classes in dressmaking, cooking and housewifery, the NFWI should consider the possibility of arranging for short courses in domestic science, to include food values and household budgeting for WI members and should urge the county and other authorities to have special consideration for the needs of the rural areas both in the provision of teachers and in the conditions regulating classes. [5]

The records show that many local authorities did work with the WIs to this end.

A new means of communication came with the invention of radio. From the beginning broadcasting had a strong commitment to adult education. This was a means of delivering such education into homes in the most remote rural areas, so the WI was quick to see its value. In 1928 Grace Hadow's brother, Sir Henry Hadow, who was then the Vice-Chancellor of Sheffield University, chaired a Committee of Inquiry set up jointly by the BBC and the British Institute of Adult Education. This committee included a represen-tative of the NFWI among its members along with representatives of the National

Council of Social Service, London County Council, the Carnegie UK Trust, the WEA, and the Board of Education. Subsequently Grace Hadow served on the BBC's Advisory Council. Following the recommendations in the report of this committee (*New Ventures in Broadcasting: a study in Adult Education*), the BBC introduced listeners' discussion groups, and printed study guides supported by a handbook, *Discussion Groups and How to Run Them*.

NFWI has continued to be represented on BBC Advisory Councils and was also represented on the Adult Education Advisory Council of the Independent Broadcasting Authority (IBA) until it was replaced by the Independent Television Commission (ITC). Some joint initiatives with broadcasters are referred to in Chapter 13.

Development of residential colleges for adult education

The early history of residential colleges for adults was greatly influenced by developments in Scandinavia. The 'father figure' was N F S Grundtvig (1783–1872) who was a pioneer of adult education in Denmark. In the Nineteenth Century, 80% of the population in Denmark were dependent on the land, and led restricted lives. Grundtvig planned to offer the mass of the population a way to enjoy a better life through his idea of a 'School for Life'. This was to be a place where people after they were past school age, preferably over 18, could go to stay for five months and learn "knowledge for citizens and peasants for both practical use and for pleasure, not with the emphasis on livelihood or business but to teach people to become sons of their country and citizens of the state." [7] He also advocated interaction between the student and the teacher and much opportunity for discussion, both between teacher and student and between students, something which was possible in the residential setting. At least some of his inspiration for this came from his visits to Oxford and Cambridge, where he had experienced and admired the system.

Under the influence of Grundtvig, the first Folk High School was set up in 1844 for men and boys; the second was started by Christian Kold (1816–1870), who also pioneered a three months' summer course for girls. The Folk High School movement was founded on a belief that life is a development and continuing education allows people to live that life more fully. It was also intended as a vehicle of community development, for what people learned they would take back and share with their families and communities. This certainly seemed to happen, for when they returned home some of the students built halls and invited their Folk High School teachers to come and give talks. They also formed clubs and societies and played a much more active part in their community.

The first equivalent venture in Britain was Toynbee Hall, in the east end of London (1884). In this University Settlement the residents were tutors and undergraduates who provided educational opportunities to the local people, mostly men. Other new ventures were long term residential adult colleges. Ruskin College (1899) provided one year courses for working men, and was supported by trade unions. Other colleges followed. Fircroft (1909), in Birmingham, only provided courses for men in its first year, but in the following year one-week summer schools were provided for women, who, it was assumed, would not be able to get away from home for more than a week. "Although primarily intended to give the women a break from their hard existence, [the courses] also had a cultural and educational element." [8]

Other long stay residential colleges were founded in the years between the wars. Coleg Harlech, opened in 1927, offered one year courses for workers from Wales, and also provided some summer courses. Wincham Hall, near Northwich, in Cheshire, was opened in 1933 to run short courses for unemployed men from Merseyside. They were asked to stay six weeks with the option to stay on for a further three months, which most took. The Wincham Hall Annual report for 1935-6 asserted the value of the residential experience:

> It enables a man to escape for a time from the limiting conditions. He can sit back and, looking at the limitations objectively, reshape his values, rediscover himself. As some men have put it, they did not realise there were so many things a man could do with his life. [9]

Apart for the University extension summer schools in Oxford and Cambridge, the first permanent centre for short-stay residential education was the Quaker 'Guest House' opened in 1905. Joseph Rowntree offered his villa, Friendensthal, in Scalby, in Yorkshire, as an adult school guest house. It was run by a committee and the guests came for the weekend; they had to make their own beds and clean boots as part of the routine. The programme was educational, although the details of what was offered are not recorded. The evenings were an opportunity for social gatherings and there were singsongs. The Guest House finally closed in 1919, although numbers attending had been much reduced during the war.

In the inter-war years the ideas and experiments of two men, Ross Waller and Richard Livingstone, were of paramount importance.

Ross Waller 1899–1988

Ross Waller was appointed as Director of Extramural Studies at Manchester University in 1936, and from the beginning he wanted to set up a residential centre for his students. In that year he founded The Lamb Guildhouse, which might be said to be the prototype for all the short-stay colleges that were to follow. Before being appointed Director, he had been a lecturer in the English Department for twelve years, and during that time had worked for the WEA, taking regular tutorial classes and residential summer schools. As a result of this experience he felt that a permanent residential base would be good for his adult students:

> I thought an element of cheerful activity might be useful in adult education, even of the academic kind, and that the pursuit of the true and the good ought to be accompanied by a greater regard for the beautiful. [10]

Ross Waller found the right house for his residential college close to his own house in Bowdon, ten miles southwest of Manchester. There was a large ornate Victorian house called Denzell, with ten acres of garden, which had been owned by Samuel Lamb, a prominent business man and Liberal. After he died Lamb's sister gave the house to the local council, but when they could not find any use for it they were considering demolishing it. It was at this point that Ross Waller's wife heard about the place.

> Next door to us lived a solicitor who was a member of Bowdon Council; his gardener was not only a member of the Council, but at that time also Chairman of it ... my wife used to talk to him through the garden hedge about garden operations and sometimes about the affairs of the world in general. And that is how the idea of a residential college suddenly attached itself to a home. The gardener-chairman at once thought the idea wonderful; in fact he said it was 'a star in the sky,' so much better did it seem than demolishing Denzell altogether... [11]

In due course the council rented the house to a limited liability company set up by Ross Waller and his colleagues for use as a residential college. They renamed it the Lamb Guildhouse, after Samuel Lamb.

Because of Ross's close association with the WEA, there were plenty of people prepared to come and teach at the weekends, and in planning the programme Ross was able to call on fellow university lecturers who gave their services free of charge. Only the caretakers were paid, everyone else was a volunteer.

In its first brochure of 1938, the Guildhouse described itself as:

> ... a place where friendly people from far and near may meet on the common ground of respect and admiration for true, good and beautiful things, where they might find interest, good fellowship and peace. A place of refreshment light and peace. [12]

The College could accommodate 30 people. At first there were no single rooms; people who did not like sharing rooms with strangers were encouraged to come with friends. A weekend from Saturday afternoon to Sunday evening cost 7/6 (a tradesman's weekly wage was about £4). There was an extra charge for a bath: 3d cold and 6d hot.

The courses that were offered had a distinctly academic bias, as can be seen from the listings of the weekend courses from September to Christmas 1938:

Sept 10	Mr WM Speight M.A., on a Biological subject. Field expedition on Sunday if weather permits.
Sept 17	Mr W Mansfield Cooper, LL.B 'The Partition of Palestine'.
Sept 24	Long weekend for Accrington Branch WEA ... Mr and Mrs Waller will give a joint lantern lecture, two sittings on Dante's 'Divine Comedy'.
Oct 8	Professor H B Charlton: 'Profitable Theatre-Going'.
Oct 22	'Comus' Weekend. Directed by Mr and Mrs R D Waller The purpose is to read and act and sing Milton's 'Comus' ...
Oct 29	Professor T H Pear. 'The Psychology of Social Stratification'.
Nov 5	Mr C Day Lewis, the Poet and Novelist, will stay in the house and will give readings from his poems.
Nov 12	Dr L R Palmer. 'Language, Race and Nationality'. (Lantern illustrations.)

Nov 19	Professor E F Jacob. 'Our Spiritual Debt to the Middle Ages'.
Nov 26	All-French Week-end. Professor E Vinaver will preside ... A play will be read and there will be some French music ...
Dec 3	Professor W J Pugh. 'Glaciers', with special reference to glaciation in the Cheshire area (Lantern Illustrations).
Dec 17	Professor J Jewkes. State Intervention in Industry. [13]

The Lamb Guildhouse was built on a democratic foundation, and it involved the local community, inviting them to come to lectures. It depended on voluntary help and on financial contributions. When war broke out, the college was requisitioned 'for more important work'. The company had to be wound up because the income tax commissioners refused to recognise it as an educational charity and demanded property tax. This was a warning to the short-stay colleges of the future. There would continue to be misunderstandings about the nature of short-stay colleges and adult education. Even today the National Institute of Adult Continuing Education is arguing vigorously with the VAT inspectors on behalf of the short-stay colleges.

In 1945 Manchester University set up a Department of Adult Education and Ross Waller became the first Professor. He was involved in the setting up of Holly Royde, another short-stay college in a house offered to the University of Manchester by a benefactor, and was briefly its first Warden.

In his 1946 book, *Learning to Live - a short and long view of adult education*, he appealed to other universities and LEAs to set up such colleges:

> Residential colleges of adult education are not, as some seem to think, a luxury to be postponed till all other important kinds of provision have been made. They are essential in the same way that retreats are necessary for the religious. They are Interpreter's Houses, wells of inspiration, places of refreshment and light. One week in them should give point and meaning to a whole year's work in a local centre. [14]

Sir Richard Livingstone 1880–1960

While Ross Waller was setting up his prototype college in the north, Richard Livingstone was promoting similar ideas in a more theoretical way from Oxford. After gaining a double first in classics from New College, Richard Livingstone was elected a Fellow of Corpus Christi College, Oxford, in 1904. He remained there as Fellow and tutor in Classics until 1924 when he became Vice-Chancellor of Queen's University, Belfast. He was knighted in 1931 in recognition for his work in Northern Ireland, in particular in promoting better health in the province. In 1933 he returned to Oxford to become President of Corpus Christi.

His interest in adult education had been kindled during his period in Belfast and he developed this interest in parallel with his classical studies. He believed that education should continue throughout life, referring frequently in his writing and lecturing to the Danish Folk High School model and also to the work being done by the WI.

In 1936, in his Presidential Address to the Education Science section of the British Association, Sir Richard said:

No doubt the lamp of wisdom can burn in solitary shrines and even in dismal lecture halls. But for the many its right place is in the simple but pleasant buildings of a Danish High School with its gardens, its pictures, its music, its corporate life. Few women's institutes are so well housed, but there is in them that social and corporate element, which exists in a residential university and which both educates and makes education attractive. Here also this country has the germ of the future in summer schools, and in such institutions as Fircroft, Coleg Harlech … these are the pointers to the adult education of tomorrow. [15]

He expanded his thoughts on the importance of adult education, and residential education in particular, in two books, *The Future in Education* (1941) and *Education for a World Adrift* (1943). [16]

Adult education, instead of being created from above, may grow up from below, as Women's Institutes [which were] started with quite different objects, have developed into an agency of informal education, and may further develop residential colleges of the Danish type. [17]

While our future educational developments … bring adult education into the foreground, economic conditions give an exceptional chance for its development on residential lines. There will be no need to build colleges. All over the country great houses will be vacant, calling for occupation and purchasable for a song. Why should not each Local Education Authority start its own House of Education? It need not follow the exact lines of the People's High Schools, if that is found impracticable. It might be used for weekends, or for weeks, of study, for educational and other conferences. Out of small beginnings great developments might grow. [18]

Sir Richard realised that 'Education' can be intimidating and needs to be attractive:

It is as important, for practical purposes, that education should be attractive as that it should be good. For, unless it is compulsory, one of the great difficulties is to induce people to take it… A minority will follow knowledge for its own sake; but most people need their pudding sweetened. It is not only the studies and the degree which attract people to Oxford and Cambridge, to Reading and Exeter; (I mention only these among the newer universities because, like the PHS [People's High School, Danish Folk High School], they are largely residential) it is their amenities and their common life… Hence the importance of the residential element; I doubt whether any voluntary nation-wide system of adult education is possible without it. To attend lectures after a day's work, and regularly, week after week, to leave one's fireside for a room in one of our dismal provincial towns, which is generally much less attractive and comfortable than the local cinema, requires an effort that is only overcome by a real desire for education: and most human beings have a capacity for education, rather than a desire for it.

… I do not think that we shall succeed in developing adult education unless we make it more social. [19]

Sir Richard was convinced that the education to be offered to adults was to be 'liberal', and in his definition of 'liberal' he drew on his classical background:

To understand it, we must imagine ourselves in the Greek world where the great distinction was between free men and slaves, and a liberal education was the education fitted to a free citizen … the free man, the real man, the complete man, must be something more than the breadwinner, he must have something besides the knowledge necessary to earn his living. He must have also the education which will give him the chance of developing gifts and faculties of human nature and becoming a full human being. [20]

He argues for education for citizenship; education which continues through life – "one of the greatest problems of the age, the problem of how to keep the middle aged young". [21] He considered the Folk High School system the ideal way of providing education for adults, and it was mainly through his influence that the system became so well known to educationalists in England. There does not seem to be any evidence that Sir Richard went to Denmark himself. [22]

His influence on educators of his time is inestimable, and he played some part in the development of almost all the short-stay residential colleges that are in operation today.

Laying plans for future adult education

The years of the Second World War were fruitful times for debate over adult education. In planning for the post war period and the prospect of reconstruction there were many opportunities to build on the ideas and developments of the immediate pre-war period.

In 1943 the Board of Education published a White Paper, 'Educational Reconstruction', which was followed by the 1944 Education Act. The White Paper opened with the words, "Upon the education of the people of this country the fate of the country depends." Of particular relevance to our theme was the paragraph:

> While more serious and solid studies that have formed the backbone of adult education at its best in the past must be maintained, there will be room for new methods and new approaches to meet new demands. In particular, there will need to be developed appropriate centres, including a number of residential colleges, which will not only provide the educational courses which the adult population may need, but will add to them the values associated with the life of a corporate institution. [23]

The Education Act failed to realise the promise of this section of the White Paper however and only gave a brief mention to non-vocational post-school education – it did not even use the words 'adult education', but it did make it the duty of a local authority to:

> secure the adequate facilities for … leisure time education, in such organised cultural training and creative activities as are suited to their requirements, for any persons over compulsory school age who are able and willing to profit by the facilities provided for that purpose. [24]

Development of short-stay residential colleges

Denman College is only one of a number of short-stay residential colleges which partly grew out of these social and political developments. The first such college was the

Wedgwood Memorial College at Barlaston Hall in North Staffordshire. This was a joint venture between the Local Education Authority, the WEA and Oxford University Delegacy for Extramural Studies. The first courses were held in February 1945, although the 'official' opening, by Sir Richard Livingstone, was not until 22nd July 1947.

Other colleges followed. Pendley Manor, near Tring, in Hertfordshire, was opened in 1945 by Sir Richard. Westham House formed by the Warwickshire Rural Community Council, Urchfont Manor in Wiltshire, and Missenden Abbey in Buckinghamshire all opened in 1947 (see **Table 5.1**):

Table 5.1 – British Short-Stay Residential Colleges

College	Sponsor	Opened	Closed
Ashridge College, Herts (1959 changed to Management Centre)	None	1939	1959
Holly Royde, Manchester	Manchester University	1944	
Wedgewood Memorial College, Staffs	LEA	1945	
Pendley Manor, Herts	None, aided by LEA	1946	1983
Kingsgate College, Kent	None, aided by LEA, YMCA	1946	1974
Urchfont, Wilts	LEA	1947	
Missenden Abbey, Herts	LEA	1947	
Westham House, Warwick	Trust	1947	1994
Burton Manor, Cheshire	LEA	1948	
Denman College, Oxon	NFWI	1948	
Debden House, Essex	LEA	1948	
Attingham Park, Shropshire	LEA	1948	1975
Battle of Britain House, later Ruislip College, Middlesex	LEA, then commercial	1948	1984
Belstead House, Suffolk	LEA	1949	
Grantley Hall, Yorks	LEA	1949	
Wansfell, Essex	LEA	1949	
Dillington House, Somerset	LEA	1950	
Moor Park, Surrey	Trust, then LEA	1950	1980
Knuston Hall, Northants	LEA	1951	
Lambton Castle, moved and became Beamish Hall, Durham	LEA	1952	1994
Alston Hall, Lancs	LEA	1956	

The information in this table is based on a list drawn up for the Adult Residential Colleges Association (ARCA) conference held at Denman College in 1959, and updated with with information from Walter Drew's thesis (see Bibliography).

The Wardens of these first short-stay colleges met informally from time to time. As more colleges were opened these meetings formed the nucleus of the Association of Wardens of Short-Term Colleges (1950) set up in close association with the National Institute of Adult Education (now NIACE). Subsequently it changed name to the Adult Residential Colleges Association (ARCA) membership of which is restricted to those adult short-stay colleges which have a Warden (or Principal) involved in developing the programme of courses; those residential centres which just host conferences are not included.

In 1959 when the Wardens' conference was held at Denman College there were 29 colleges with a total of 50,066 students attending during the year. [25] In 1969 the number of colleges had reached 32 (the greatest number) and it was estimated that at least 100,000 people a year attended.

> This increase is one of the outstanding developments in education and in the social behaviour of the last 20 years. [26]

The decision makers at NFWI were aware of these other adult education developments, and especially of the beginnings of the short-stay residential college movement, and gradually the way forward for the next big educational development by the WI became clear.

Chapter Six

Planning for a Brave New World

At the outbreak of the Second World War the WIs were filled with uncertainty. During the Munich crisis in 1938, the Home Office had asked the WVS and the WI to co-operate and deal with the probable evacuation of all children under the age of five from London. In fact this was never necessary. When war was declared in 1939 one Federation Secretary wrote:

> The WI had apparently no definite place; some members left us, feeling hurt and frustrated. Perhaps mercifully our vision was limited and we could not see the great part we should be called upon to play, as WI members, in the coming six years. [1]

Grace Hadow reassured members that the WI did have a rôle to play when she wrote:

> It is for every individual to decide for herself how best she can serve her country in peace or war, but the fact that the Institutes were called into existence in 1915 because an organisation was needed, and that it was a Government department which fostered their growth at such a time, should make all of us consider whether possibly this work in our own village and our own county, work for which we have been specially trained, may not be that for which we are best fitted and in which we can be of most use. [2]

The WI membership did decrease during the war, reaching a low of 288,000 in 1943. Many members were called into active service. Those who remained did become involved in helping to house evacuees. An article in *Home and Country* reported that:

> When members of a WI were asked what they found most disagreeable in present war conditions someone called out 'mending evacuee schoolboys' trousers!' [3]

The WIs' part, however, was wider than this, as the East Sussex Federation secretary wrote:

> ... and how grand a part it was: to keep the countryside sane and to give mental, moral, and spiritual courage to the women of England's villages... The County Federation office dealt with nearly half a million articles of fruit preservation equipment ... two and a half tons of vegetable seeds ... a ton of wool... [4]

In spite of all this 'war work' NFWI reminded the Institutes that it was

> important to maintain the educational and social character of the monthly meeting, which should provide 'a centre of tranquillity and cheerfulness in a sadly troubled world': [5]

Equally some of the staff wondered if they were in the right place. Cicely McCall, Education Organiser at NFWI, recalls:

> Some time after war had been declared I felt that perhaps I should be doing more for the war effort. I telephoned Lady Denman and said I was considering joining the services. I have never heard her more vehement. Didn't I realise I was helping to prepare women for after the war? Wasn't that more important than joining up and being relegated to some clerical job in a barracks? Very subdued, I agreed, and stayed on. [6]

One of the many other things that Cicely did subsequently was to write one of the Collins series 'Britain in Pictures', in which she told of the ways in which WI members coped with wartime. The illustrations show WI members making fur coats for Russia, running market stalls, using a mobile canning van given by the USA, fruit bottling, jam making, looking after evacuees and spinning wool gathered from the hedges. The book concludes by looking to the future:

> Institutes have taught countrywomen to be articulate, they have taught citizenship and they have revived forgotten crafts… The test time for the institutes is going to come after the war. Tired elderly members will have to make room for demobilised younger members, not to be replaced but to work alongside them. [7]

Even in the darkest days of the war the country was looking ahead and planning for the post-war world. In 1941 the Luxmore Committee was set up to consider and advise the Ministries of Education and Agriculture on post-war agricultural education, and the Scott Committee was set up to advise on building and the location of industry in rural areas. Lady Denman served on the latter, and WI members expressed their views through her, many of which became incorporated into the final report. [8]

NFWI urged its members to become involved with national planning:

> The war must be won, but so must the peace. The Government has recognised the need to think ahead and plan now. Women's Institutes have their contribution to give to the official planners… [9]

With a coalition government it was much easier for the WI, with its non-party political rule, to discuss political issues, because "the whole side of party politics was so much more civilised." [10] In January 1943 *Home and Country* carried a leading article on 'Shaping the Future' which outlined the government proposals for two new ministries, the Ministry of Town and Country Planning and the Ministry of Social Security. A subsequent issue of the magazine carried an article, 'Benefits for All', which outlined the contents of the Beveridge Report.

WI members also considered what they wanted of the education system. In 1943 the government published its White Paper on 'Educational Reconstruction' which stressed the need to provide a proper training in democratic citizenship through adult education. The NFWI Education Subcommittee decided to find out members views:

What kind of education do we want? The Board of Education want to know. So NFWI is drawing up a questionnaire which will be sent to counties shortly. [11]

The questionnaire was circulated to Federations, and members were told that the "evidence from these questionnaires will be forwarded to the government departments now considering education after the war"; 4,000 questionnaires were returned. At the same time conferences were held in 33 counties, with members of the Education Subcommittee, and Cecily McCall, helping to stimulate the discussions:

It was my job to break down the intricacies of these plans into a form which our WI members would find easier to digest. [12]

In May an international conference on education in London was chaired by Ester Neville-Smith, a member of the National Executive Committee and an Oxford graduate, who was herself deeply committed to adult education. The main speaker was Chuter Ede, Parliamentary Secretary to the Board of Education, who referred in his talk to the People's Colleges of Denmark. Cicely remembers:

We spoke of the new idea of village colleges and discussed the adult education schemes of other countries, such as Denmark. My Chairman, Adeline Vernon, and I talked of the possibility of some such college one day in the far future for the WI members. [13]

In the January 1943 edition of *Home and Country*, Nugent Harris, that long-standing male champion of the WI, wrote an article that described his visit to the Folk High Schools in Denmark, so from various quarters WI members were being made aware of the People's Colleges and their value.

Conference at Radbrook College

In September 1943 NFWI held an experimental Residential School at Radbrook College in Shrewsbury, attended by 50 students from 26 counties. (These are the figures quoted in the 1944 NFWI Annual Report. *Home and Country* reported 34 counties and nearly 100 WIs!) Called 'Questions of the Day', it "proved a most successful experiment which it is hoped to repeat." [14] The hope was fulfilled by residential schools in the following two years: in 1944 on 'Home and School', and in 1945, when over 100 students attended a week's residential school at Oxford to consider 'The Future of the Village'.

The first four-day conference in 1943 was chaired by Adeline Vernon, an Oxford graduate and "an enthusiast dedicated to education." [15] The main speaker was Sir Richard Livingstone, who spoke on 'Education in a World Adrift', similar to the title of the book he had published in 1943 – *Education for a World Adrift*. Cicely McCall remembers how:

during the lunch break Adeline Vernon suggested I should ask him to put forward our ideas of a college in his afternoon speech. He willingly agreed and the audience was surprised but wholly welcoming to the idea that one day WIs might have a college of their own. [16]

It was Cicely who subsequently wrote a report of the conference for *Home and Country*:

> The next day our speaker was Sir Richard Livingstone. He spoke of the "vision of greatness" without which moral education is impossible. He said that most electors of the next thirty years would have left school at 14. Yet the new Government proposals made no provision for adult education. Why shouldn't WIs, who had shown such remarkable common sense in their education questionnaires, fill that gap and provide a People's College?... Later in the evening a recommendation was put to the meeting by a Herefordshire member that a WI People's College should be founded. This was carried unanimously.

> ... They were indeed two full days. Full of thought and action ... but the high spot of the conference was the idea Sir Richard Livingstone left with us. A Conference house where we could meet together for a day or longer, a hostel, holiday home (with nursery attached), and perhaps somewhere in the grounds a WI cottage built on the Institute housewife's design for convenience and beauty! Just an outsize dream? Not if we really want it enough. Then it might become a thrilling possibility. [17]

This shows how enthusiastic Cicely was for the idea. Her enthusiasm was shared by another NFWI staff member, Betty Christmas, who was General Organiser. Together they drew up the first 'blueprint' that was presented to executive by Adeline Vernon:

> Its success, we knew, depended on the reactions of Lady Denman. Lady Denman listened gravely and then said, "Do you think anyone would come?" Mrs Vernon and others soon persuaded her that WI members *would* come, and that this really was an extension of the day schools and conferences that we had already been holding... [18]

Thus the idea of setting up a WI college began to take root. In order that the idea might be shared with all WI members, Sir Richard was invited to write an article for the December 1943 edition of *Home and Country*. He wrote:

> ... Two things about our present [educational] system are absurd. First 80% of our population have no education after 14. Mr Butler proposes to sweep away this scandal ... but it is nearly as disastrous to stop education at 18 or 21. We might almost as well expect to go through life on the food we have eaten by 18 or 21. New problems continually appear, new interests develop. We ought to have a chance to think about them and pursue them ... the remedy is a nation-wide system of adult education, so that everyone has a chance to learn and think in later life.

> Adult Education already exists in this country. The Workers Educational Association is one form of it. Another (though it may not so think of itself) is the Women's Institute Movement. But across the seas are four countries where it is far better developed...

and he went on to describe Denmark, Sweden and Norway and their People's Colleges. He suggested that the WI could found such a college and that he hoped that "Mr Butler's forthcoming Education Bill will contain provisions by which [the] running expenses can be met." He continued by stressing the advantages of residential education in fine buildings in pleasant country surroundings. People get away from work and domestic worries, and can give their whole time and mind to study. They meet others from different jobs and different parts of the country, with different views, live with them and have endless chances of discussion: one learns as much from a good discussion as from a book... Out of this common life come community feeling, understanding of others and sympathy with them...

Such colleges would give education, but education in the right sense of the word. Dismiss from your minds schools or examinations. Think instead of a chance to find new interests or pursue old ones, to study religion, politics, conduct, to learn something of the meaning and power of science, to understand life and its activities better, and so to make more of them, to escape from the daily routine and have leisure to think and learn. This has been hitherto the privilege of the few; adult education, properly organised, would make it possible for all... Then we might attack with high hopes the task of making the Britain of our desires.

In the same issue there was a letter from Margaret Turner of Limpsfield in Surrey:

Our College

Dear Editor,
I think the idea of "going to school", even if we go to school at our own WI College, will at first sound too dream like altogether to many members with heavy household responsibilities. On second thoughts however perhaps we can take heart. Through the years our families have got used to Monthly Meeting Day when Mother has her fling, and more and more families are pleased and proud when she pops off for the whole day, to the Albert Hall perhaps, to set the world to rights. It is only one step farther if, just for once in a life time, she goes off for two days or even, giddy thought, for a week to mix with WI members who she has never seen, and listen and discuss and talk her head off with them about bottling or schooling or housing or hospitals from morning till night.

Believe me, the WI "Questions of the Day" school held recently was as cosy as the very nicest monthly meeting! The generosity of the most gifted members to the shy and inexperienced, so that you found yourself earnestly holding forth to a member of the national executive, as one learner to another, these things we've known before. "Going to school" for WI members will be something familiar and dear. If the dream of our college ever comes true, it will be a homely place. We could all help to make it, even if it is only a few stitches, or a pot of jam, and afterwards, we and our sons and daughters would have it to share and enjoy.

Margaret Turner
Limpsfield, Surrey [19]

Enter Lady Brunner

The idea of the WI college was kept alive by two groups, not all of whom had been at the Radbrook conference. There was a nucleus on the National Executive Committee, and a small group of the Oxfordshire Federation. This latter group included Helena Deneke, Grace Hadow's friend and biographer, an historian and Fellow of Lady Margaret Hall. She had been at the Radbrook conference and also knew Sir Richard Livingstone well. Another member of the Oxfordshire Federation Executive Committee, and a keen advocate for the idea of a WI college although she had not been at the Radbrook Conference, was Elizabeth Brunner. She had just been elected to the National Executive Committee and was to become the key player in the move to form a college.

Elizabeth Brunner comes from a famous theatrical family. She is the daughter of Dorothea Baird and H B Irving and granddaughter of Henry Irving. She had herself been an actress (by the time she was 16 she was playing Titania in 'A Midsummer Night's Dream' in the West End) but gave up her career on the stage when she married Felix (later Sir Felix) Brunner. In 1937 when they moved to live at Greys Court near Henley, where she still lives, she joined the WI. Lady Brunner became central to the development of the WI college and we are remarkably lucky that she is still alive today and able to talk about the foundation of the college, and to reflect on life then and now:

> When I first got to know the WI during the war most of our members had left school at 12, 13 or at the latest 14. In preparing for the Butler Act we were all absorbed in how to provide fuller, longer education … education for jobs of necessity to provide skills for industry; training for the professions but alongside a strong skein of history, literature, music, art and crafts to widen horizons and develop gifts to achieve a complete individual … [20]

If the WI was to have its own college, the idea had to be put to the members at an Annual General Meeting. Unfortunately the next AGM, in 1944, was cancelled because of events in the war, so in the meantime an *ad hoc* committee was set up to "work out a scheme and find a house for the WI college." [21] This committee, to which Elizabeth Brunner belonged, did some exploratory work, collecting information about existing colleges and conference houses, for example Foxlease owned by the Guides Association.

In 1945 the AGM could be held and on the agenda was a resolution submitted by the Oxfordshire Federation. The resolution was proposed by Elizabeth Brunner.

The defining moment

The AGM was held on 5th June 1945. Lady Denman, in her Chairman's address, paved the way for the Oxfordshire proposal:

> The [Education] Act also provides for greatly increased facilities for adult education and lays down the principle that there should be consultation … a voluntary society such as ours, doing educational work, should be consulted and encouraged to play its part in the general system of adult education, and may be given financial help to do so.

The proposal was:

> that this meeting welcomes the suggestion of a Women's Institute College and notes with satisfaction the power to provide grants for such a purpose in Clause 100(1) (b) of the Education Act.

In her eight minute speech (the full text of which is given in **Appendix 1**) Elizabeth Brunner started by assuming that her audience already had a knowledge of the People's

Colleges – which was reasonable considering the articles already published in *Home and Country*. She then tackled the fear of the word 'education':

I am afraid that quite a number of us here today may have been put off by the phrase "adult education", and even by the somewhat formal and severe word "college". Let us be frank. There is something a bit intimidating about the former – and grim about the latter. Together they neither of them describe what we are after. They sound bleak, institutional, portentous. But when we are using these words – especially when we are thinking about our own WI college – I want you to imagine a place that will be homely and welcoming, where in the pleasantest possible surroundings, away from responsibilities and distractions of our usual lives, we can learn about useful practical crafts, and in addition where we can become better informed about the things going on in the world today, where we can learn more of our   heritage, and consider and discuss our future.

She shared a vision of a place which would "continue the work we have begun in our Institutes" and where "we should be free to experiment along our own lines in the kind of courses we think would best suit our members needs". She saw the value of meeting other WI members – "women of all kinds and ages from the whole of England and Wales, we should have a richer and more diverse common background than would students at a local or regional college."

This was to be a college with a wide curriculum:

Subjects we would wish to include would be ones of general interest and which would create an active interest in citizenship – the future of the village and rural life – local government and education and housing – life in other countries as Lady Denman suggests – history and literature – as well as the more specialist ones of music, drama, handicrafts, agriculture, horticulture and the domestic arts. Besides these we should want to have occasional schools and conferences for the study of our own institute affairs.

She paints a picture of a "traditional country house, with small holding and garden attached, and from which the college could be supplied with farm, garden and dairy produce" and a homely place where you would "see in all bedrooms and living rooms examples of our handicrafts – cotton printing, patchwork, quilting, weaving, rug making." She envisages the students themselves helping so that "the costs for the students could be kept down. No institute member would feel it unreasonable to carry out a rota of household jobs for an hour in the morning, with occasional turn at washing up and laying meals. But comfortable beds, well cooked plain food, plenty of hot water and central heating, combined with the goodwill engendered by the Institute spirit, will make short work of a lot of odd jobs."

She is honest about finance, explaining that:

we do not know what grants the Ministry of Education envisages in the clause we are welcoming. If the idea of a college gains support today, it will then be possible to approach the Ministry in order to find out to what extent they are prepared to help us. But WIs in supporting the idea of a college of their own, must expect to have some financial responsibility in the raising of funds, whether for purchase of premises or endowment. By careful planning it should be possible to keep student fees reasonably low, and in some cases local education authorities and county federations might give bursaries.

She summed up by saying:

A college centrally situated could become a much needed home and focus for our movement. It would provide a means of attracting and interesting the incoming younger members, and it would open new vistas to our older ones. It must be able to welcome our most reluctant and diffident members; it must provide them with the sympathy and encouragement that their first approaches will undoubtedly need. It must provide fun and relaxation as well as instruction. It must not be a place where only our most forceful intellectuals vie with each other in solving the world's problems. What we teach must be related to the everyday practical things that make up our members lives. In addition, there must be inspiration and a vision of wider horizons, so that life and the living of it becomes more important and worth while. [22]

This proposal was seconded by Mrs Hopkinson of the Cambridgeshire Federation who suggested "a model nursery school in the grounds, where young mothers could ... leave their children for the time they wanted to be at courses" and also "a pooling of fares and pooling of fees?" [23]

Not everyone was in favour of the idea, a Warwickshire member spoke against:

... wherever a permanent college is built, it will be inaccessible for some people... WIs should cooperate with their own local educational establishments ... the estimate of £30,000 for building is too low and £3,000 for annual upkeep too low ... will not get huge grants ... those of us who would wish to attend these courses would have very great difficulty in leaving our homes and children. [24]

The Shropshire Executive Committee said:

It is not fair to ask the ordinary member to raise money for something for which she will on the whole receive no direct benefit. It will be for the few, whereas the money will be raised by the many. [25]

East Kent WIs advocated local provision, and said that:

only 3,000 would be able to come in a year and 300,000 women are being asked to contribute. [26]

However the majority of delegates were being swung in favour of the idea and South Stoke WI, Oxfordshire, proposed an amendment that would add the phrase "and instructs the Executive Committee to make necessary arrangements." They argued that in the post-war planning period they should move as quickly as possible:

Who knows, the right house in the right place may be discovered at any moment ... how grievous it would be if the executive were not in a position to be able to clinch a deal ... we must work quickly if we are to bring our plans of a brave new world into being ... please get going with it at once. [27]

The Gloucestershire Federation Executive Committee agreed:

> We want to do more than welcome the suggestion; we want to get started. We do not want this college when we are all so old we have to be taken in bath chairs to it; we want it now. [28]

The amendment was carried.

Mrs Neville Smith, a member of the NFWI Executive Committee, spoke:

> One reason why I support this resolution is because of a group of countrywomen to whom the WI college will be of particular value. This is the Institute member whose schooling stopped at twelve or thirteen. She has been educated by the rich experience of country living, but now she is demanding more. She does not want specialist instruction or long university courses, but she will go with a WI friend to their own institute college to study and discuss the questions of the day outlined by Lady Brunner, or to receive instruction and practice in the skills of the home. That is going to equip her with confidence and knowledge to take a responsible position in the community as well as to hold high office in this movement. [29]

The resolution was carried by a large majority; Lady Denman announced, "That is carried, so now we are pledged to a very important piece of work." [30]

The Denman College story had finally begun.

CHAPTER SEVEN

VISION INTO REALITY

The WI in Britain grew out of the First World War and it can be said that Denman College grew out of the Second. It was a difficult time to be setting out on such a large venture, but the WI had a great commitment to education and the 'brave new world'.

The day after the 1945 AGM an NFWI Conference in London on education was attended by representatives of 48 Counties. Members had already spent much time thinking about the sort of education system they wanted after the war, and now that the war had ended they were keen to express their views. They also wanted to press ahead with plans for the college that they had agreed at the previous day's meeting. At the Conference the delegates agreed a memorandum to be sent to the Central Advisory Committee of the Ministry of Education about adult education in rural areas and urged NFWI to ask the Minister for Education for support for the WI college.

In July 1945 NFWI ran another residential school, this time for seven days, at Somerville College, Oxford. The theme was 'The Future of the Village', and it was attended by over 100 students. [1] The success of this residential school supported the view that the WI was indeed ready for its own college. To start the process the National Executive Committee appointed a College *Ad Hoc* Committee to "deal with this proposal [to make necessary arrangements for a WI college]" and they were given "power to call witnesses." [2] Elizabeth Brunner became its chairman and Sir Richard Livingstone was one of the 'witnesses', continuing to give help and advice. Lady Brunner remembers him as "inspirational, ... he was a sort of prophet, and he loved the WI;" [3] "... he so fully understood the good in the 'Marthas' as well as the 'Marys' – valued their potential, recognising how much the two strands were woven in the WI movement." [4]

The shared vision of the place

Both N F S Grundvig and Sir Richard Livingstone considered that residential adult education worked best in the atmosphere of a big house or country mansion, to which you came as guest; having a host or hostess was all part of providing that atmosphere.

Lady Brunner envisioned "a place of your own where you will meet WI members from all over the country." [5] She also wanted those members who had themselves been 'in service' in big houses to have a 'big house' of their own. [6] She wanted 'the best' for WI members: a well-equipped college, without being ostentatious or over luxurious. She was insistent that the college should be warm, and should have comfortable beds. "Those academic beds were so uncomfortable!" [7] she recalled from the NFWI residential schools held in colleges. She also imagined a place with a smallholding attached which would produce its own farm, garden and dairy produce.

The shared vision of the learning

Sir Richard Livingstone had written, in *The Future in Education*:

> The vegetation of a district reveals the capacities of its soil, and we can find our answer [How can people be trained to understand and enjoy the best] by noting some new plants that have recently grown in English earth. Men's and Women's Institutes, Townswomen's Guilds, Community Centres... These developments both show the demand for adult education and suggest how it may be met. Their weakness is that, for the most part, the education which they give is casual and episodic, stray lectures or course of lectures, stimulus rather than education, a cocktail rather than solid food. We need something more systematic and methodical. [8]

The college would become a place which could provide a focus for, and give a framework to, the educational work of the organisation. Somewhere that could provide that 'something more systematic and methodical'. It would have the best lecturers and teachers who would offer women a chance of learning, "to discover new interests and needs in later life and help to pursue them." [9] It would be a place that offered liberal cultural education – history, the arts, science, handcrafts, and much more.

It was also to be a place where a "member whose schooling stopped at 12 or 13 ... will gain confidence and knowledge," [10] and a "place where one can get away from household duties and worries and give one's whole time to the business in hand." [11]

Here a member might widen her horizons, and be led on to something she might not even have considered doing or learning. Lady Brunner saw it as a place where

> we should be free to experiment along our own lines in the kind of courses we think would best suit our members' needs. [12]

The shared vision of a focus for the organisation

The college would provide a place to meet and talk with others, to learn more about the WI, a place "to continue the work which we have begun in our own institutes." [13] Lady Brunner hoped the college would become a "much needed home and focus for our movement." [14] There would be a welcoming family atmosphere, where a member would feel at home; a place that would provide gentle, friendly support for learning. The new college would give NFWI a great tradition to maintain and be inspired by – a college of continuing excellence.

Sir Richard could imagine how the college would feed outwards: "[Members] will take home to their institutes what they have got here and their homes and institutes and villages will gain." [15]

THE VISION OF THE FOUNDERS

- That WI members would have as their college a comfortable and well equipped 'big house' of their own in beautiful surroundings.

- That the college would be a friendly and welcoming place where WI members would be able to meet others from all over the country, learn more about the WI and feel part of a national organisation.

- That it would be a place that offered the best in liberal adult education.

- That here a member might widen her horizons, and be led on to something she might not even have considered doing or learning.

- That the college would provide a focus for, and give a framework to, the educational work of the organisation.

- That the college would provide a place to continue the learning begun in the local WI, and from which to take back fresh inspiration to share with others.

Finding the house

The committee started by deciding what sort of a house they were looking for and what accommodation was required. Besides Lady Brunner the members of the *Ad Hoc* Committee were Nancy Tennant (Vice-Chairman, with a special interest in music), Ester Neville Smith and Dora Tomkinson. Lady Brunner remembers the last as "a great bane to people – a very strong character. Her coming onto the committee was due to the kitchen garden and it made life difficult," [16] which probably explains why the discussions of the committee about the use of the college are recorded in the following order.

USES OF THE COLLEGE

Agriculture
Miss Tomkinson felt that it would not be practicable to combine a farm with the college. It was thought best to find a house, possibly near a farm institute, with a large vegetable garden, and to concentrate on the study of horticulture, poultry, bee-keeping, small livestock for the present
Handicrafts
to have a permanent well fitted room for demonstrations etc
Music and drama
large hall with dressing rooms
Education
hall, with smaller classrooms
Cookery
two kitchens – one for demonstration purposes, instruction in fruit preservation, etc.; the other to be ordinary staff kitchen. [17]

The committee considered using the college for exhibitions. "There might be a standing exhibition of latest household devices." They certainly intended to have National Federation literature available and hoped that "a cinema projector should be installed;" a "central library might be combined with a museum in a common room."

They wanted a house that would provide sleeping accommodation for a minimum of 25 students plus nine or ten staff, and teaching space for classes of up to 60. "If a house capable of accommodating these numbers could be obtained, sleeping accommodation might be added later, possibly in a separate building…"

Sir Richard suggested that some of those who were planning for the college should visit the Danish Folk High Schools, so in 1947 Lady Brunner and Joan Yeo travelled to Denmark "at their own expense." [18] Joan Yeo, a member of the NFWI Executive Committee, who subsequently became Chairman of the NFWI Education Committee and a member of the first College Committee, was a friend of Lady Brunner. In Denmark they visited about ten Folk High Schools. Lady Brunner reports that they found them "very bleak, but it gave Joan and I an experience that influenced our view of life at that time." [19] They brought back some ideas that were incorporated into the structure of courses in the early programmes:

They [the courses at the Folk High Schools] were good courses for practical farming and domestic economy and that kind of thing, but into every course they introduced something about the history of Denmark and the culture, so that they kept it alive… I think, possibly, at the back of our minds, was the thought that the essence of a rural community, would, after the war, need fostering, although it was being given every possible service, electricity, housing and so on, we could nevertheless less, lose touch with our roots.

The courses that the college was to run were enormously varied, but into each of them we cunningly inserted, rather like the Danes with their own history during the German occupation, cultural subjects – literature, art, drama and so on, and then we sort of canalised people who enjoyed a touch of literature or what ever it might be to take a literary course and this was very good; it was purposeful, done by people who valued education. [20]

Lady Brunner also recalls visiting Foxlease, owned by the Girl Guides. There were other short term adult education residential colleges developing at the same time and the *Ad Hoc* Committee made contact with some of them. Lady Brunner remembers that George Trevelyan, Warden at Attingham Park, in Shropshire, gave them some helpful advice. [21]

Sir Richard Livingstone wrote in *The Future of Education*:

There will be no need to build colleges. All over the country great houses will be vacant, calling for occupation, purchasable for a song. [22]

The WI wanted such a 'great house' somewhere in central England, so that WI members from all over the country could reach it. They wanted it sited near a university and possibly an agricultural college so that they could be near a supply of potential lecturers. Very soon they were concentrating their search in the Oxford area. [23]

Buying the house

The house hunting group continued to visit houses and start negotiations, but it was not until November 1945 that they found Marcham Park in the village of Marcham near Abingdon – in those days in Berkshire, though now in Oxfordshire. It had come on the market de-requisitioned from the Air Ministry, and was a late Georgian mansion in a hundred acres of parkland. There were a small lake and two cottages and a large walled kitchen garden and it seemed to meet all the requirements. It was sited in the village, next to the parish church, and there was plenty of space for expansion in due course, and even a kitchen garden to keep Dora Tomkinson happy (see sketch map, p 10). In December they signed a contract to purchase it for £16,000.

There was essential work to be done before the college could open for the first students, all of whom would be sleeping in rooms in the house. There were very few single rooms and some of the large rooms were more like dormitories. Future plans included building additional accommodation for students; initially the college could house no more than 30.

Naming the college

In 1945, soon after the AGM which had agreed to set up a college, and long before a house was found, it was reported that some members were alarmed by the implications of the title 'College'. [24] The uncertainty about a name found a happy solution at the 1946 AGM.

This first AGM after the end of the war was a memorable one. The Queen, who was President of Sandringham WI, came on the first day to pay special tribute to Lady Denman, congratulating her on all that the WIs had accomplished under her leadership both in peace and war. On the second day, after speeches from two women MPs, Ellen Wilkinson, Minister of Education, and Megan Lloyd George, Nancy Tennant, as Vice-Chairman, announced to the members that Lady Denman had decided not to stand again for the Chairmanship.

Trudie Denman had served as the National Chairman for thirty years. Towards the end of the meeting Lady Albermarle (who was to succeed her) said:

> … suggestions have been coming in of ways in which we can keep Lady Denman's name in perpetual association with the work of the Women's Institutes… The most popular one is that the Women's Institute College should be known as Denman College. We want this to be a memorial of the sort that would appeal to her. [25]

Lady Denman replied, "Thank you. I think that is a lovely idea."

It solved the problem, because within the WI the college is rarely referred to by its full name, but is just called 'Denman'.

Getting the money

To purchase a suitable building, and to equip and endow it satisfactorily, was estimated to cost about £60,000.

The first possible source of money was the Government. When the delegation from NFWI met with Ellen Wilkinson the Minister of Education, they were disappointed to find out that clause 100(1)(b) of the Education Act did not provide for the direct recognition by the Ministry of Education of the NFWI, as they had hoped, nor would there be any money available for the purchase of a WI college. [26]

The next option was to seek grant aid from a charitable trust. The obvious one was the Carnegie United Kingdom Trust, especially as Lady Denman was a trustee and the link continued through Lady Albermarle. The Carnegie Trust had already given money to NFWI in 1918 for rural industries, in the 1930s for training drama producers and choir conductors, and for a national organiser for WI Markets. The request for a grant to purchase the college was sympathetically received, and the Trust agreed to give a grant of up to £20,000, provided the WIs gave a similar amount, and to provide an additional loan to help with any cash flow problems.

The WIs themselves were to be the main source of money. In July 1946 Lady Albermarle wrote to every WI reminding them that in 1945 they had passed a resolution to start a WI college "with money raised by the members themselves" and inviting every WI to raise £10 over three years. Her appeal letter also explained that the college would be a

> centre for cultural and practical education, i.e. for conferences, schools and courses in all branches of Women's Institute work ... open to all WI members in England and Wales. [27]

By the end of 1946, £4,000 had been received in cash, and promises of a further £27,000 had been given. This was still a long way from the £60,000 target and so a further appeal was made once the purchase of Marcham Park was completed. In this immediate post-war period, new WIs were being formed, and women who had been in the forces or doing war work were returning to the WIs, so it was felt that there could be a fresh surge of support. Lady Albermarle wrote to all WI secretaries:

> You will have seen on the cover of the February *Home and Country* a picture of Marcham Park – the house which the NFWI has bought for the Denman College. You will be wanting to know more about this new venture...

> ... As soon as the house is released from requisition the federation will:

> Furnish the dining rooms, sitting room, library and lecture room.
> Adapt and furnish the bedrooms, to accommodate about 30 members.
> Equip the kitchen.
> Adapt and equip outhouses for work rooms and extra sleeping accommodation. [28]

The letter went on to explain more about what members would experience when they went to the college and concluded by explaining that:

> in order to make the College available for all members, charges will be kept as low as possible and to do this a College Endowment Fund will be built up. So I ask all the Institutes which have not so far replied to my letter to do so now... [29]

By the beginning of 1947, in less than two years, 4,000 Institutes had contributed £41,000. When the appeal finally closed in 1953, £66,000 had been raised, which meant that there was £37,000 in the endowment fund.

An additional minor source of income came from renting part of the property that the college was not using. The shooting was let to Mr Duffield, the previous owner, for 1/- an acre.

Furnishing and equipping the college

The restrictions of the immediate post-war years meant that it was a very difficult time to be setting up a college:

> ... very depressing interview with Mr Davies of the Ministry of Education, regarding help with furnishings. The quota of raw materials for educational purposes is so low that we must do all we can to obtain our requirements on the normal market. [30]

So the organisation appealed to its members.

Very early in the planning the Isle of Ely Federation had written asking if they might be solely responsible for the furnishing of one room. The committee accepted the offer and suggested that they send their proposal to *Home and Country* to encourage other counties to follow suit. Further encouragement came in a letter to WIs from Lady Albermarle:

> Before long there will be another way of helping. County Federations will be asked to assist with the furnishing of the college rooms. This will provide a special opportunity for those of our members who are skilled in handicrafts. [31]

The County Federations rallied to this call. The challenge of producing something 'special' for their bedroom that reflected a local theme appealed to members. The Worcestershire bedroom (shared with Warwickshire), for example, had

> curtains of neutral-coloured linen, printed in pink with a design in squares, featuring the pear tree of Worcester alternatively with the bear and ragged staff of Warwickshire, hand-blocked by a Worcester Centre member. [32]

The members collected clothing coupons. There was a working party at the college in August 1948 to make loose covers for some of the chairs in the public rooms. Friends from near and far sent contributions, the Institutes in Ontario sent sheets and pillow cases. Lady Brunner remembers that they tried not to accept a gift unless the committee agreed that it would be appropriate. "That very awkward thing – taste – can be divisive," she added somewhat wryly. [33]

In spite of the fact that one of the criteria for the choice of the site was originally that it should be near a convenient railway station, this was not the case. The nearest station in 1948 was Abingdon, closed in the Beeching cuts.

Because of the distance from a railway station, it was decided to obtain some college transport and "as no utility car was large enough to carry 12-14 people, [it was] decided to buy a 25 cwt Commer van with a utility body." [34]

The redoubtable Dora Tompkinson was given permission to order 25 head of poultry and the necessary houses. The greenhouses were found to be in poor condition and they were repaired (at a cost of £941). This expense was justified as it was estimated that by 1950 the outlay on the gardens should have been repaid and the profits would start. Even before the college opened there was a produce stall supported by those WI members who came to view the new college, which took £105 in April and May 1948.

As an 'accredited training college', Denman College was eligible to have pictures from the Victoria and Albert Museum on loan for up to six months. In addition Lady Listowel (a member of the National Executive Committee and also a Governor of the V & A) was able to arrange for a loan from the Collection of Embroideries to be on display at the opening. Perhaps the first example of 'cunningly inserting' some culture? [35]

The same minutes noted that the Arts Council had offered an exhibition of litho-reproductions, *What is modern painting?*, for 3/- a day. This was declined for the opening but would be offered for a course.

As the opening day approached, teams of volunteers helped in very practical ways. As they have continued to do ever since, they helped with gardening, decorating, cleaning, sewing…

The management and the staffing of the college

Once the college had been purchased the *Ad Hoc* Committee had fulfilled its purpose and was dissolved. A decision then had to be made about how the college would be managed. Lady Albermarle suggested that a Board of Governors should be appointed, to include "well known educationalists", and alongside this a house committee. The National Executive decided instead to appoint a Denman College Subcommittee which met for the first time on 26th March 1947 with Elizabeth Brunner as its Chairman. The terms of reference were:

> to advise the Executive Committee on all matters concerning the Denman College and to be responsible for such matters of detailed administration as the Executive shall decide. [36]

The minutes of the first two meetings of the Denman College Subcommittee show that the main matters of concern were the buildings and the market garden. However they did agree to "begin considering the plan of teaching at the next meeting." [37] Who was to be responsible for planning the courses was still uncertain. NFWI already had a General Education Subcommittee and its members obviously felt that they should be involved in the planning of any 'teaching'; a way to share out of this responsibility had to be devised. These tensions between NFWI subcommittees and staff and the Denman College committees and staff have produced 'stresses and strains' at intervals through the past 50 years as different structures of management have been tried (see Chapter 13).

The staffing of the college had been considered early in the planning stage:

> The residential staff might consist of a permanent warden (£200.00), secretary to the warden, capable of helping with the catering, accounts, reception etc (£150), cook (£100), a resident working gardener who would give instruction and take students to whom she would give six months preliminary garden training (£150). The salary bill would probably be less than £1,000 per annum.

> ... students might be asked to help with washing up, making beds and dusting their own rooms; daily cleaners to be engaged for other household duties. [36]

These were very low salaries in comparison with those on offer in other short stay colleges. They perhaps "reflect the enthusiasms and voluntary spirit of the WI movement of the time. Wardens appointed by Trusts and local government enjoyed salaries of between £800 and £1,000 ... the Warden's salary here amounted to well below half of that of a schoolteacher." [39]

The NFWI Executive Committee decided that the responsibility for the appointment of the first Warden "should rest with the General Education Subcommittee in conjunction with the Denman College Subcommittee." [40] The first Warden, Elizabeth (Betty) Christmas, was an internal appointment. She was only 37 years old but had been the General Organiser with NFWI for eight years, during which time she had travelled widely; before that she had been secretary of the Buckinghamshire Federation. In the Spring of 1945, she went to visit Canada "to convey personally to the WIs of Canada the gratitude of Britain for all that had been done to help and encourage them during their years of horror and suffering." [41] This visit was paid for jointly by the British Ministry of Information and the Canadian War Information Board. During the war years the Canadian WIs had sent NFWI donations of $15,000 for the War Distress Fund, 11 hand sealing machines to use in the fruit preservation scheme, wool and sewing supplies and over $10,000 worth of garden seeds to be distributed to every county and to thousands of villages in England and Wales. During her visit Betty Christmas was photographed beside the portrait of Adelaide Hoodless (Plate 1, pp 128–129), a pleasing link between the foundation of the WI in Canada and Denman College.

In her farewell message to the Canadian WIs Betty wrote:

Keeping ourselves alive to the needs of others will still be our aim in this post-war period, but perhaps the most important work which Institutes can do is to train the members to be the sort of citizens who will think for themselves and not be blindly led; who learn to do a first class job of homemaking, but whose vision is not bounded by the kitchen sink; who will work intelligently for the welfare of the community and who understand the world where we all depend so much on each other, the community is not limited to our township, but comprises the world and every other human being. [42]

This shows the sort of person Betty Christmas was; although she had no formal academic background she was familiar with the WI and WI members. Many of the executive members who were on the General Education Subcommittee did have academic qualifications and they all worked together in planning the programme for the early days at the college. Very soon after her appointment, Betty Christmas went to a conference of the Educational Centres Association [43] and the letters she wrote and the internal memoranda that are in the archives show that she learned rapidly.

Planning the programme

In March 1947 all the NFWI specialist subcommittees were invited to "put forward courses, conferences, and other educational activities that they would like to hold at the college." [44] Subsequently they were asked to provide "syllabuses for courses of one week or longer, giving the number of students in each case." [45]

The first draft programme, referred to as a 'syllabus', was based on these suggestions. It covered a year and included a holiday period in July/August when local County Federations could use the grounds for 'rallies'. Only one course at a time was planned, leaving room for others to be added later; the courses themselves are described more fully in Chapter 10.

The draft programme was circulated to all subcommittees, who considered it and then met with the National Executive members to agree the final form. Sir Richard Livingstone attended this meeting and played an influential part in developing the educational framework for the college.

Telling the WI members about the college

Since the AGM which agreed to set up a college, the WIs had known about the college and had been raising money for it, but members were interested to know more about what the college would provide. NFWI provided speakers who visited County Federations to explain more. [46] It was reported that speakers had found great interest in the Countrywomen's Courses – these are described on p 118.

Parties of WIs were invited to visit the college in the spring of 1948, prior to the opening, and local guides were organised from nearby WIs to show members round. One particular open day was reported with enthusiasm:

A Day at Denman College

"A great day – the fulfilment of so many hopes" – thus one WI member spoke to another in the crowd gathered at Denman College on April 29, when 640 of the AGM delegates, mostly from long-distant counties, were taken in 20 motor coaches to have a first glimpse of the countrywomen's college they had asked for in 1945. Crowd – yet it scarcely seemed so. House and grounds expanded in welcome to their owners, offering hospitality, it seemed, not only to these but to all WI members represented by the day's visitors. They emerged ... asking about courses – how soon? how many? how long? [47]

By the end of June 3,000 members had already been on visits and a further 117 parties were expected.

The opening

By September 1948 the college was ready to be opened. Unlike so many other similar occasions the 'official' opening did actually coincide with the real opening. On Friday 24th September Sir Richard Livingstone performed the opening ceremony, [48] and the first course started that evening with Federation representatives attending an education conference. On Monday 27th September the first 'ordinary members' arrived, those who Ester Neville Smith thought would get "particular value" from the countrywomen's college. (see p 73).

PART 2

DENMAN COLLEGE
REVIEW OF 50 YEARS

PART 2

INTRODUCTION

The second part of this book describes how Denman College has developed over 50 years.

The following chapters take up in turn each of the 'vision statements' of the founders (p 76) and attempt to show to what extent developments in that area of the college's life have fulfilled the founders' vision.

Each chapter ends with a selection of comments to show how today's students view that particular aspect of the college.

The chapters cover:

Chapter 8   the house and grounds and how they have been developed to provide more acceptable accommodation and better teaching facilities.

Chapter 9   the way that the college provides a friendly and supportive environment in which women can learn.

Chapter 10   the changing programmes offered over the years.

Chapter 11   the tutors, who they are, where they come from, what they think of the college and the students and what the students think of them.

Chapter 12   the students, who they are, why they come, and what they get out of the college.

Chapter 13   the management and finance of the college.

Chapter 14   the way in which the work of the college is integrated with the work of the WI as whole.

Most of these chapters include information which was obtained from questionnaires. These were circulated at the end of 1996 to WI members who had been Denman students, and also to a control group who had never been on a Denman course. About 500 of the former and 200 of the latter were returned. A comparison of the results of this exercise with a survey of Cheshire WI members   suggests that the sample is representative of the WI as a whole. Some details of these questionnaires can be found in **Appendix 2**.

A simpler questionnaire was distributed to tutors in February 1997 and 46 were returned. Some details can be found in **Appendix 3**.

CHAPTER EIGHT

"... A Big House of their Own ..."

> **VISION OF THE FOUNDERS**
> That WI members would have as their college a comfortable and
> well-equipped 'big house' of their own in beautiful surroundings.

The buildings

When the college opened in 1948 there were 31 beds available in the house, five single rooms, seven double rooms and four treble rooms. There were also a 'common room' that seated about 50, a lecture room, a rather cramped dining room, the Grace Hadow library, and a large entrance Hall. The huts left in the grounds by the RAF remained, and in due course were converted into teaching rooms, and the old stable buildings also remained, ready to be converted when permission was granted and money was available. There was not a great deal of space available for larger meetings or conferences. The Warden, writing to the NFWI General Secretary, suggested:

> For a large meeting the garage could be used and will accommodate 150 or so. There is lighting in the garage but no heating. [1]

There was even a suggestion in 1949 that the garage might be adapted as a theatre [2] – there is no record that the garage was ever so used, but several members remember courses held there. Pottery was one of them:

> The workshop was the garage – we were not allowed in the college for mid-morning coffee or afternoon tea, it was brought out to us. Dirty! we were filthy – water everywhere plugging the clay. We were taken to see a potter at work – hardly a dribble of water! [3]

Those who remember the early days recall a somewhat Spartan "dormitory life". [4] It soon became clear that when the college was full the lavatory and washing facilities were inadequate. [5] At the first Consultative Council after the College opened, there were questions about what was being done for those who did not like sharing rooms. [6]

These issues were not as important as the provision of more accommodation and specialist teaching facilities. The way in which this has been done is outlined in **Table 8.1.** Other improvements were gradually achieved. All the residential building in the table contained single and double rooms only, with the emphasis on single, and the number of multiple bedded rooms in the house was gradually decreased. Bedrooms in the most recent buildings have had *en suite* facilities from the outset, although, as Lady Brunner

Table 8.1 – The College Building Programme 1949–97

Year	Building	Opened by
1949	CROFT Stables converted to make 7 double rooms and 2 single bedrooms. *Converted into storage, staff flat and games room in 1953; demolished in 1961*	Mr Salter Davies Chairman of CUKT
1953	HOMEACRES Renovated RAF huts, shared with Berkshire CC Rural Home Economy Centre. *Demolished in 1970*	Florence Horsburgh MP Minister of Education
1953	NEW CROFT Specially built block of 18 single rooms, reduced to 16 in 1985 with extra staircase to meet fire regulations. *Demolished 1997; rubble used for carpark*	no official opening
1957	DINING ROOM built onto the College and paid for by the Lady Denman Memorial Fund	Lady Burrell (Lady Denman's daughter)
1961	TWO ESTATE COTTAGES Jasmine and Clematis. Used to house staff. *In 1996 Jasmine was converted to the NFWI Training Unit*	no formal opening
1970	TEACHING CENTRE AND BRUNNER RESIDENCES Provided studio, lecture room, craft room and workshop in teaching centre, with 10 single and 2 double rooms and 3 staff flats	Queen Mother
1979	HOLLY AND JUNIPER bungalows for staff; then Holly converted for tutors and Juniper for offices. *Juniper demolished in 1996 to make way for new building*	no formal opening
1979	HOME ECONOMICS CENTRE Demonstration and practice kitchen with preparation rooms, storage and offices	H M Queen
1991	TEACHING CENTRE FOYER Extension of the foyer to provide space for displays and group discussions	no formal opening
1993	BEECH AND WILLOW New houses with 12 single *en suite* bedrooms and two twin-bedded rooms suitable for disabled members and helpers	Lady Brunner and Lady Anglesey
1997	MAPLE AND OAK New houses with same accommodation as Beech and Willow	Lyndsay Hacket Pain, World President ACWW, and Anne Stamper, Education Adviser

has said, "in a way it was more cosy before it was quite so grand." [7] Nowadays, when even the road-side signs for bed and breakfast advertise *en suite* facilities, these are what members expect, and they are appreciated:

> The accommodation continues to improve; the new blocks are first class, and my personal preference is for single rooms. [8]

The buildings also reflect the changing requirements for teaching, and the continued improvement of facilities. In the early days, huts left by the RAF were converted into teaching rooms. Gradually, as money became available, more permanent provision was made. Any short-stay college must provide accommodation which is flexible to meet the needs of a wide range of courses, and yet able to satisfy some quite specialist needs. The well-established traditions of the WI demanded that Denman College should have specialist provision for crafts and home economics, and how this has been met over the years is described on pp 214–216. Provision for other subjects is less specialist. Art, drama, country dancing, public speaking and tutor training courses all have to use the studio, for example.

There is a greater demand today for courses with physical activity, such as short-mat bowls, which require more space than the college can provide. The largest space is still the garage, currently used for a couple of cars and storage. In 1994 planning permission was given to build an Activity Hall on the site; and at the time of writing negotiations are underway to seek funds for this work. (See p 10 for map of college, showing building programme.)

The big house feel

Members continue to be surprised on their first visit to the college to find it so elegantly furnished and comfortable; comments such as "I thought it would be like a boarding school" are common. It is elegant because the founders wanted members to have "a big house of their own," and that meant furnishing it as such. To a large extent this has been done through the generosity of members, as the following description from 1973 illustrates:

The Drawing Room

The *Steinway piano* was a gift from a Cambridgeshire member.

The *vases on the mantlepiece* are French. They were a gift from an 84-year-old member from Surrey.

The *chandelier* was here when the house was bought.

The *portrait of Lady Brunner* was painted by R G Eves.

The *carpet* was presented by Sir Felix and Lady Brunner.

The *convex mirror over the fireplace*, the *grandfather clock*, the large *couch in the window*, and *golden velvet sociable*, and the *rose wood firescreens*, and the two *standard lamps*, were all given by Lady Brunner. The *drawings* were done by Leonard Rosoman.

The *bookcase* was bought by the College.

The small *folding table in the window* belonged to Lloyd George, and was given by his family.

The *green velvet Victorian chair* was given in memory of Mrs G Melbourne, Downham Market and Saltford WIs.

The *smaller green velvet Victorian chair* was given by Mrs Edward Bawden (Essex).

The *double chest (18th Century)* was given by Miss Pleydell-Bouverie (W Suffolk).

The *hearthrug* was presented by Cornwall.

The *brass cooking pan* on the windowsill was given by an East Kent member.

Rush log basket given by Norfolk, made by Mrs Florance. [9]

Some of these items of furniture already had a 'family history'; on one occasion Robert Schumann's daughter, Eugenie, had given the donor a lesson on the piano. [10] In other rooms of the house there are 'family portraits', one of Lady Denman in the entrance hall, and one of Grace Hadow in the room which was originally the Grace Hadow Library, but is now the bar! Other pieces have their own more recent story to tell:

> [In 1967 the college had] a marvellous tabby cat called Tiger ... known by numerous students for sitting in the most comfortable chair in the front hall and if anybody tried to stroke him, as everyone did, he either bit them or scratched them. He finally demised but is commemorated by a carved wood doorstop, carved by Donald Potter, a wood sculpture tutor. [11]

The author recalls, when at the college recently, watching, at the end of the evening, as two members walked down the beautiful main staircase. One of them escorted her companion to the front door and bade her good night as she went off to her room in one of the new buildings, then turning to me she said, "I was just pretending it was my house" ... but of course it *is* her house.

The park and gardens

In 1948 the 'beautiful surroundings' were in a poor state and much in need of work. A letter to The Carnegie United Kingdom Trust explained:

> The grounds and gardens have been sadly neglected during the Air Ministry's occupation, and some expense on labour and tools is necessary before use can be made of them... It is difficult to estimate the cost, but we fear it may mean quite a substantial sum in the neighbourhood of £1,000. [12]

The Trust made a grant of £1,000 for this work and useless shrubs and trees were cleared, the fish pond was restored, walls and fences repaired and 32 acres of woods replanted and wired against rabbits. The wiring was not very effective for by June 1949 a neighbour had written to ask that NFWI take steps to exterminate the rabbits which were overrunning his land. It was agreed that, with the shortage of meat, the rabbits should not be gassed out, but that Colonel Sinclair, to whom the shooting had been let, should be informed. At the same time, inside the house, "the activities of the cats on the ground floor have driven the mice into the bedrooms." [13]

More to be welcomed was the news that His Majesty's Swan Keeper was sending two pairs of swans, though the committee would have to pay for catching them and transport. They arrived in March 1949 and the cost was £5.3.11. [14] Swans on the lake have continued to contribute to the elegance of the grounds. In 1978 the Principal, speaking at the AGM in the Albert Hall, was able to announce the first birth at the college – three cygnets, who were immediately named A G and M. [15] In the last year or two the swans have deserted the lake, but Charlie, a peacock has arrived unbidden to replace them. He seems to enjoy displaying his beautiful tail to students as they go to their classes, and is much admired and photographed, but also cursed when his squawks keep members awake.

From the beginning there was new planting; in the spring of 1949 an avenue of 300 lime trees was planted in memory of Madge Watt (p 24), who had died in Canada the previous autumn. WIs were invited to contribute £1 each for a tree – but it was recorded that "some small institutes combined for a joint gift." [16] In 1988 members of WI Markets planted a shrubbery garden in memory of Agnes Salter, the National Chairman who died in office, and who had been a keen marketeer.

The intention has always been to keep the lay-out of the garden appropriate to the period of the house, and over the years there have been a number of advisers who have helped with planting schemes. There have also been parties of volunteer gardeners who have been prepared to come to the college from time to time to give extra help to the garden staff. In 1948 a herb garden was planted on the site where some of the RAF huts had been. In 1970 a woodland path was opened up round the perimeter of the estate and laid out as a nature trail. (See map on p 10.)

These quotations from the questionnaire replies show how members enjoy the gardens and park:

I have extended my knowledge with an excellent tutor in a beautiful house with excellent company and a peacock.

A wonderful setting for courses; takes you away from the kitchen sink; shame about the peacock!

Interesting … wildlife around the college including the heron that ate the gold fish, the peacock without a mate that woke members early and the lovely family of hedgehogs in the shrubbery.

I enjoyed living in such beautiful surroundings.

Members can be seen walking in the garden, round the lake and round the nature trail from very early morning, and in all weathers.

The grounds are also used for some of the courses. Hilda Jones, who was Director of Studies, 1961–77, and Principal, 1977–81, introduced archery courses. She claims that the worst bit of planning she ever did was to have an archery course on at the same time as a herb course; the novice archers were in danger of shooting the students in the herb garden. [17]

The art courses often use the grounds. One member recalls a visit in the '80s on

a painting course during brilliant August weather when the gardens were magnificent. Some members were experienced artists, others like me were beginners. After two days of instruction, we were turned loose on the grounds to paint a picture. Most of us drifted to the lakeside. I set up my temperamental easel on one of the grassy footpaths and began. I had filled in the back-ground of bushes, the rushes at my feet and a not-so-glorious version of a glorious tall tree. I don't think I've ever seen a better stick of rhubarb! After lunch it looked no better. My easel, still misbehaving, fell with my 'masterpiece' face down in the newly mown grass. Just as I was about to tear up the painting, the tutor came down the path.

'Rip, what are you doing?' she asked as she put the painting back on the easel. We both looked at it and giggled. The grass had done what I couldn't. It had smudged the stick of rhubarb into quite a presentable tree and the blades of grass all over my lake made it look most realistic, practically a collage. So my effort went up on the wall. [18]

In 1956 the college programme included:

'The Countryside in Summer' – flowers, trees, animals and birds – the woodland, parkland, and the banks of the streams in our 100 acres surrounding Denman College are a happy hunting-ground for naturalists and a good basis for study.

The 100 acres is now reduced because some of the land has been sold, but much of it remains as it was, and students can still use the nature trail, although the college no longer owns the land.

The market garden

The walled garden, which was such an attraction when the house was purchased, had been worked during the war and so was in a much better state than the rest of the grounds. Under the guidance of Mary Clarke who was appointed Head Gardener in April 1947, the garden provided fruit and vegetables for the college's needs, as well as for sale. Mary Clarke was involved in teaching and demonstrating to the students as well as running the commercial side of the market garden. [19] At first all worked well. In 1949 new planting included one eighth of an acre of soft fruit and twelve dozen cordons of apples and pears. Fruit and vegetables were provided for the house, and external sales were over £1,000.

In 1951 it was decided to make the garden, together with the packing shed and the glasshouses, into a commercial operation run by a special committee. However it never proved profitable, partly because there were a number of very dry summers, and in 1953 it was let, with a cottage, to a new tenant. The livestock that were purchased at the beginning did not prove any more successful. First the hens were killed off and used for the table and finally in 1959, Mrs Ferguson, the acting Warden, was instructed by the Denman College Subcommittee to "dispose of the geese." [20] It is not recorded if they also appeared on the college menu.

In 1974, in order to release much needed capital to provide more teaching and residential space, it was decided to sell the now derelict market garden. Having obtained planning permission for low-density housing, three plots within the inner walled garden were sold for £18,000 and the adjacent four acre market garden was sold for twenty four houses for £110,500. At the same time permission was given to convert Market Garden Cottage into additional accommodation for five students and a tutor. This was the end of one of the visions of the founders.

Improving the facilities

In the Autumn of 1949 the old stables were converted into bedrooms, so that the College could now sleep 50. However only 40 people could squash into the dining room; when the college was full some people had to have a buffet meal. When Lady Denman died in 1954, a memorial fund was set up and used, among other things, to provide a new dining room, which was built as an extension to the main house.

> The two new improvements which students appreciate most, however, are the new sound-deadening ceiling and the washing up machine. Normal conversation is now possible at meals, and there are no more washing up rotas for students. [21]

It seems that not everyone shared Lady Brunner's prediction (p 71) that members would not mind doing domestic chores. They did them when required, but were glad to be rid of them!

Gifts to the college have continued over the years and have varied from very practical gifts of equipment to more luxury items that add to the 'gracious living'. Some donors have been individual WI members; Lady Castle Stewart gave an epidiascope, screen and table in 1949. Other gifts been given in memory of WI members – the revolving summerhouse was given in 1949 in memory of Miss Simpson.

We have already described how the Federations adopt bedrooms and furnish them with care and imagination (p 80). Federations have also been generous in gifts for other parts of the college; Staffordshire for example donated Wedgewood china in 1958. There have also been gifts from manufacturers – Courtaulds gave soft furnishing and carpets in 1973 and the Hoover Foundation gave new chairs and sewing machines in 1981.

In 1952 the Government gave a wall hanging, designed by Constance Howard for the Festival of Britain and called "The Country Wife", to NFWI, who decided to house it at the college. It is mounted on the wall at the back of the studio and, as it is now becoming quite delicate, it is protected by curtains, which are regularly, but briefly opened to give new students the opportunity of seeing the work.

In 1962 a bronze bust of Sir Richard Livingstone was presented to the college:

> [The bust] was unveiled in the garden at Denman by [Sir Richard's] old friend Sir John
> Christie, the Principal of Jesus College, Oxford, before a gathering of relatives and old friends.
> Not long before his death at the age of 81, in 1961, Sir Richard sat for the sculptress Kathleen
> Parbury; since then she and his family had felt that they would like the bust to stand in a place
> with which he had special association and their choice had fallen on Denman … .it stands on
> the north side of the house, showing Sir Richard with head thrown back, in the characteristic
> pose he so often adopted when lecturing. [22]

The receipt of so many gifts is an advantage that a college owned by WI members has
over many of the other short-stay colleges:

> By all these gifts the college is made more gracious and beautiful, and they contribute greatly
> to its welcoming atmosphere. [23]

Crisis at Denman 1984/5

As we shall see in Chapter 13, the finances of the college have always been a source of
concern, and there has always been a determination to keep the fees as low as possible.
As is usual in such circumstances regular maintenance was kept to a minimum and very
little provision made for major repairs should they be required. Sooner or later a crisis
was bound to result, and it happened in 1984 when three major unavoidable items of
expenditure coincided: work associated with changes in the fire regulations for public
buildings; the regrettable effects of a design fault in Brunner House and the teaching
centre; and a large backlog of maintenance work on the original house including
electrical rewiring, work on the roofs and chimneys and damp treatment.

The introduction of new fire regulations meant that extensive work had to be done.
Second staircases were needed in New Croft and the top floor of the main house; a fire
break on the main staircase and emergency lighting throughout was also required. The
fire officer said that unless the work was put in hand he would have no choice but to
close the college. Estimates for fire safety work had been obtained in 1978, but at the
time the committee, not feeling it to be a matter of urgency, decided the college could
not afford it. This time they had no choice.

Brunner House and the teaching centre, then only 14 years old, were designed in striking
hexagonal modules (see Plate 9, pp 160–161). Each had its own roof lantern and rainwater
drainage was carried down inside the structure. The effect was much admired but the result
was expensive and provided constant problems with leaks and penetrating damp.

To carry out all the work would cost in the region of £500,000, and the total estate was
only valued at £750,000. [24] The Trustees, faced with this dilemma, had to decide if it was
worth keeping the college. They consulted their financial advisers on whose suggestion
they employed John Spicer, "a professional trouble shooter, having worked in a
merchant bank." [25] He visited the college in January and reported that he felt that

"a move might be necessary, and whatever the outcome the college must spend £60,000 on fire precautions without delay." [26]

John Spicer presented an interim report [27] to an NFWI Policy Day in February. He felt that there had been no consistent maintenance provision in the past and now faced with estimates of £30,000 for repair of the Brunner roof and £60,000 for works in the main house, the cost of three different staircases and the screen at top of stairs required by the fire officer to be completed in in three months, the situation was very serious.

In his subsequent final report [28] he wrote:

> With assets of some £1.25m the Trust cannot advance a claim to be unable to fulfil its central, educational, purpose. The strategic decision is how to do so. There are four possibilities:
>
> 1. Residential at Marcham
> 2. 'Otherwise' at Marcham
> 3. Residential elsewhere
> 4. 'Otherwise' elsewhere.

If the choice was to stay at Marcham then the organisation would need to raise at least half a million pounds. If this amount could be raised it would be reasonable to approach the Charity Commissioners for release of endowment funds to enable them to carry out the required work. This would, however, remove the 'cushion' of income that these funds provided (at that time £28,000 per annum) and this would necessitate an increase in fees. He felt that it would be preferable to make the appeal for a larger amount, so that the Trust would retain a significant financial asset.

From the tone of his report it is obvious that John Spicer thought that the members were unlikely to raise this amount of money and that the college would not be viable, so:

> an alternative method of fulfilling the Trust's purpose would have to be worked out and approved by the Charity Commissioners (whose approval for the sale of the estate would also be required). It might be assumed that the Trust's assets would be reduced by £1M by the costs of repairs and closure. I am no expert on adult education or the wishes of WI members, but I have suggested that a peripatetic college with a small central staff organising courses at a number of different centres throughout the country might have advantages. Bringing the college to a membership which is dispersed and whose roots may be stronger at a local level, might be popular. With Marcham sold and annual expenditure reduced to a fraction of that at Marcham, Trust funds should again stretch to subsidising course fees. [29]

The National Executive Committee called a special meeting of all the Federation Chairmen and Treasurers to explain the gravity of the situation. Members were "forced to face the possibility of losing one of their most precious assets." [30] The options were put to them and it was explained that if Denman College was to be saved then the members would have to raise at least half a million pounds. The Federation Chairmen went home to discuss this with their members to be ready to bring their views to the National Council meeting. At that meeting in September two thirds of the Federations voted to 'save Denman'.

In their rejection of the suggestion that the college should be 'peripatetic' the members showed that they believed the place to be important, just as Ross Waller and Sir Richard Livingstone had considered that a 'beautiful place' is important.

Ross Waller wrote:

> Residential colleges ought to be beautifully situated in rural surroundings … particularly colleges providing short-period courses, the most strenuous and most exacting of all forms of adult education. [31]

Speaking at the celebration of Denman's fifth birthday Sir Richard had said:

> I sometimes think that buildings take on a colour and quality from the purposes for which they are used, and the people who live within them. I think that you may regard Denman College as exemplified in being a concrete image of certain virtues – virtues which are present when you do a fine thing in a fine way. I am certain that anyone who sees this place – its grounds, the house, the furnishings, will know what Aristotle meant when he spoke of "magnificence" – the sense of a magnificent thing done in a magnificent way. [32]

The members recognised that they had a 'magnificent thing' and wanted to keep it.

In the following week the National Executive Committee unanimously voted to launch an appeal for £1 million. The National Council had turned down the suggestion of using professional fund raisers, so Executive member Lyndsay Hacket Pain master-minded the appeal with administrative help from one part-time book-keeper (a member's husband). The Executive Committee knew that if this target was reached all the repairs and alterations could be carried out, and the increased endowment fund would allow for regular repairs, renewals and maintenance to be done properly in the future. A year after the appeal had been launched members had raised almost half the target; it reached £1 million in time to celebrate at the College's 40th birthday As the annual report commented, "The amazing result fully justified the committee's faith in the members and the future of the WI." [33]

The work was able to start in September 1986 when the college was closed for four weeks. This caused loss in income, as indeed had happened over this whole period of uncertainty, when applications fell off, but confidence began to rise again once the builders came in and the repair work started. One of the public rooms in the house, the Livingstone Room, had a suspended ceiling that dated back to when it had been used as an operations room by the RAF. During the rewiring work Jean Varnam, who at that time was a national Vice-Chairman, recalls:

> During August … I, as Vice Chairman, took over responsibility whilst the Chairman and Treasurer were on holiday. One Saturday morning I received an urgent call from David Austin, the Bursar. During Friday, the workmen removed the lights from the suspended ceiling in the Livingstone Room and found, in almost perfect condition, the most beautiful carved ceiling. They wanted permission to remove the suspended ceiling and reveal the original one… I went to the college the next day and climbed the scaffolding, put my head through one of the light sockets and with a torch and a hard hat viewed what had been covered over for 40 years.

I could find no-one to consult … and as the workmen had to proceed on Monday morning, I took the decision to remove the suspended ceiling, bring in an expert from London to assess the damage and estimate the cost of repair… Having thrown all to the wind with the ceiling, I also asked whether they could uncover the fireplace – yet another gem and I persuaded Wedgwood to give us the lovely vases which now grace it. [34]

In the Livingstone room, not only was the original ceiling reinstated, but two of the dummy windows were opened up as well. When all the repairs and renovations were completed the College was perhaps more gracious than before.

The 'crisis' had the effect of raising the profile of the college, and applications increased rapidly once the decision had been made to raise the money:

It is difficult to think now that the future of Denman hung in the balance in the early 80s … that there should have been any question of not pulling out all the stops to save it for future generations… North Yorkshire West members quickly and enthusiastically raised money for the appeal. What I would have missed in the last 10 years if Denman had closed doesn't bear thinking about. I feel Denman has gone from strength to strength in recent years. On every visit there is some improvement and always new courses being tried. [35]

Staff accommodation

When the college opened there was a small staff: Warden, College Secretary, Warden's Secretary, Gardener, Resident Housekeeper, Cook-Caterer, and two Swedish girls, and all but the Warden's Secretary lived on site. The Warden (and later, after the change in title, the Principal) has always lived on site, with one or two very brief exceptions. The first Warden lived in the cottage now called after her – Christmas Cottage. More recently, Principals have lived in one or other of the thatched cottages. One of the characteristic features of all short-stay residential colleges in the past has been that the Warden is resident:

A good residential college is a home, ideally of the Warden and his family and sometimes also, if accommodation is available, that of his deputy or other staff. It then also becomes the home, even if only for a few days, of the students in residence. [36]

Denman College is rather different to other short stay colleges because the family atmosphere is generated by the members themselves, but the Warden/Principal provides a continuity that might not be found otherwise.

In 1948 there were two small residential suites in the main house for the Cook-Caterer and Housekeeper. The thatched cottages were used for gardeners. In the 1950s, two three-bedroomed semi-detached houses were built for staff and in 1979 two staff bungalows were built. Brunner House included a staff flat for the Bursar. In those years the ability to offer accommodation to staff was an aid to recruitment – Hilda Jones recalls that it was the fact that accommodation was offered that influenced her in accepting the job as 'Studies Secretary' in 1961. [37]

As the college has grown, and offered more courses to more students, the number of staff employed has increased. The additional staff have been largely recruited from the locality and the need to provide residential accommodation has decreased. Since the early 1990s only four of the staff have lived on site – the Principal, the Deputy Principal, the Bursar and the Maintenance Officer. There is likely to be an even further reduction of resident staff in the future.

Although the need for accommodation for resident staff has reduced, the amount of space required for offices has increased. The college is now open continuously all year round with two, and in some weeks, three intakes of students, and with five courses running concurrently for much of the time. There are over 6,000 students a year, and this requires a considerable amount of administration to keep it all running smoothly and an increased number of staff to do it. In 1995, in addition, the newly formed NFWI Education and Training Unit was located at Denman; they have offices in one of the houses which was originally built for Denman's residential staff.

Fulfilment of the founder's vision?

The founder's vision does seem to have been met. Today's students have confirmed it in their questionaire responses (**Appendix 2**):

> There has been a gap of about 10 years since my last visit and in that time considerable changes have taken place at Denman – all for the better. It is a lovely place for the WI to own, and it's good that more members are attending.

> Denman offers so much: very good tutors, good varied company who also contribute, peace to study, wonderful surroundings, accommodation and food. What more could one ask?

> How lucky we are to have our own college in such wonderful surroundings. [38]

> Living in a beautiful manor house gave me a taste of the gracious living enjoyed by the gentry of old that I would not have experienced otherwise. 'Denman College' are magic words like 'Open Sesame'; it opens doors to kindness and friendship as well as a wealth of knowledge, to be obtained within its walls. [39]

CHAPTER NINE

"... A FRIENDLY WELCOMING PLACE ..."

VISION OF THE FOUNDERS
That the college would be a friendly and welcoming place where
WI members would be able to meet others from all over the country; learn
more about the WI and feel part of a national organisation.

Before 1948, unless they were chosen as the delegate to the AGM, the majority of WI members never had a chance to meet fellow members from other parts of the country. Only a few had been able to attend national conferences or schools of the sort held at Radbrook College in 1943 (p 67) or Somerville College, Oxford, in 1945. The opening of Denman College gave the 'ordinary' member a chance to meet with others from all over the country, and to feel part of a national organisation.

For many of the WI members who come to the college it is a new experience to be away on their own without their family. For many even the term 'college' can be intimidating, especially if they have not had any experience of formal learning since leaving school. Lady Brunner, in her speech at the AGM that proposed the setting up the college, acknowledged this when she said some members may be put off by the "somewhat formal and severe word 'college'," but she went on to say that the WI college would not be like that. "I want you to imagine a place that will be homely and welcoming." [1]

College Chairman

When a student arrives at Denman she is welcomed at the front door by a fellow WI member, the College Chairman, who is the 'hostess' for that week or weekend. There have been College Chairmen since the college was first opened. In the early years the Chairman was usually a member of the National Executive Committee, but when the college began to be open for more days in the year the team was enlarged to include members of the College Management Committee and past members of the Executive Committee. In recent years Federation Chairmen, and Federation Denman Representatives have also been invited, and now there are two Chairmen on duty at the same time to share the work. The Chairmen are all volunteers and come for expenses only.

It is the rôle of the Chairman not only to welcome the members and act as hostess, but to work closely with the staff to ensure that all the students' needs are met so far as is possible. At night, when the staff are off duty, she is the responsible person in charge.

This can be quite daunting. The telephone by her bed will ring if there is some emergency in the night and she will then decide if she needs to call the doctor or the staff member who is on call. The minutes of the College Committee of 1st March 1968 record that the College Chairman, during the week when a student at the college died, thought that "this crisis had shown clearly the need to know who was in charge when the Warden was absent from the college." As a result of this a deputy warden was appointed. Fortunately such extreme emergencies are rare.

The College Chairman is the first point of call for the members during their stay, from reporting a burst hot water bottle to asking for information about the nature trail. The College Chairmen also help to staff the college shop when it is open, help to pour out coffee, and sometimes get even more involved if there is a crisis:

> My highlight was on the occasion when – mid afternoon – word rustled through the office that the cook had gone home sick and they'd had to send for the 'boss' from the catering company. Well, I wasn't doing anything and as it happened I'm a trained cook. I sent in a message "I'm a cook – can I help?" Back came the single word "Yes!" So off I went to the kitchen expecting to peel potatoes or do some other mundane task. I was handed a white coat and hat and told to "sort out the sweet for tonight – there's cream in the larder, a tin of cherries and chocolate," and I was on my own.
>
> I looked at the 'sweets' and there were ten of the saddest looking chocolate cakes I've ever seen. They'd all sunk in the middle and most had broken as they'd been turned out of their tins and lay in sorry heaps. No wonder the poor girl burst into tears and went home I thought – I nearly joined her!
>
> Well, though no one knew it, years ago I used to teach cake decoration and cookery at Tech: but I had never, ever, done more than one elaborate cake at a time, and I had never had to resurrect one, let alone ten! I set to work.
>
> I lost count of time, but when I finally got a bucket and mop and cleared up the cake crumbs and grated chocolate from the floor, and left my work tops pristine, I heard the ding dong of the dinner gong. Music to my ears. I had done it!
>
> … The 'boss' did say thankyou as they loaded the really quite smart gateaux onto the trolley, but I got the impression that he'd really expected no less from the WI. My accolade came when I saw someone who I knew was a first rate cook take a second helping! [2]

Not many College Chairmen have quite such challenging experiences, but their friendly and helpful attitude is vital in developing the ambience which so many members mention. Just how much effect the College Chairman can have is illustrated by one of the very rare complaints from a member who reported:

> The College Chairman was more interested in scoring Brownie points with members of the national executive who were there for a meeting than providing me with information. I asked to be shown to my room but was refused and sent in pouring rain to the wrong building. My whole visit was soured by this first impression; I have not been since. [3]

Happily this is not the usual experience; much more common are comments like these:

> Thank you for a wonderful experience. I learned in a relaxed and caring atmosphere. The staff were motivated, interested and truly professional in their approach. It did make a world of difference to me. [4]

> I first came to Denman 25 years ago – was delighted this time to find nothing had been compromised during these years. The physical improvements are great and necessary for the 90s and the friendship and fellowship remains. As then we were welcomed at the threshold – so important. The Chairmen were superb – thankyou, please let us fly the flag for this superb college and organisation. [5]

The tutors share this feeling. When asked in the questionnaire if there was any thing which they felt was 'special' about Denman College the responses included:

> Very warm friendly atmosphere.

> I think that the fact that all the students have the WI in common creates a cohesive atmosphere, it is their college.

> Warm welcome.

> The college chairmen have a key role in creating a thriving and successful ambience.

> Everything is special at Denman, the welcome, the atmosphere, the lovely grounds. [6]

And from a tutor who works at other short stay colleges:

> The atmosphere of support, friendship, good fellowship and warmth is more pronounced at Denman than anywhere else. [7]

Course Chairman

As well as a College Chairman to act as hostess, in the early years of the college there was often also a Course Chairman. The need for such a person was recognised after the first ever open course:

> It will be necessary to have someone present at the school who can take the chair and be able to link the whole course together. Mrs Yeo came in for two days and by being there she kept the sessions together, which otherwise would have been disconnected. [8]

Until the new teaching centre was opened it was only possible to accommodate three courses at a time. Two of these were usually practical courses and were limited in number to about 15 people. The third course was a 'lecture' course, often with a series of lecturers coming in over the three-day period. The course chairman was the hostess to these visiting lecturers, and also chaired the course and ensured its continuity. She chaired the discussions and helped the WI members see how what they were learning might be used in the WI.

Lady Denman had been particularly keen that members who came to the college should learn more about the WI. She wrote:

> ... something of the work of the NFWI should always be included... Examples should be given where appropriate; these might have to be given by the chairman, by the mover of a vote of thanks, or brought up in discussion when the outside speaker is an outside expert... I realise that this will need some thought and occasional research, but I am convinced that Institutes do not appreciate that their strength lies in the fact that they work together through NFWI and County Federations and that therefore every conference at Denman College should strive to bring this point home. [9]

She gave a number of examples which were later incorporated into 'Notes for Chairmen of Courses at Denman College'. These 'Notes' formed part of a comprehensive file which was given to every course chairman. Included also were particulars about the college and the course, a copy of the Handbook and the Public Questions Handbook [now the Public Affairs Handbook, 'Speaking Out'. AS] – the list of all the mandates and follow up work done on them. The Chairmen were told that part of their function was to:

> relate the content of the course to the everyday experience of members and particularly with their knowledge of the WI movement, and to link it up with the opportunities in their own Counties. [10]

For example:

> *For a course on the English house or similar architectural subject*
> the work done on rural planning, and to safeguard ancient buildings (PQ Handbook pages 62–64)

> *For a course on books*
> AGM resolution on libraries, with information about County library services (PQ Handbook pages 25–28)

> *For a Handicraft course*
> resolution on plain sewing being taught in schools (PQ Handbook page 25) [11]

Finally:

> The dual purpose of the movement – the improvement of social conditions in rural areas, and the bringing of knowledge, skill, and enjoyment to individual members – should also be mentioned. [12]

In recent years, there have been fewer large lecture courses and the course chairman is no longer required for open courses because they are usually now taught by a single tutor. However, the members still learn about the WI by the informal exchange of ideas:

> Meeting other members has widened my experience of the WI.

> [I now have] broader perspectives of the WI in England and Wales.

I really enjoyed meeting fellow members from other parts of the country, I have kept in touch and corresponded with a member from Berkshire ever since.

[I have] a better understanding of the WI.

[I have] more confidence in my area of WI responsibility; it was a wonderful exchange of ideas with others in the same role. [13]

The members are also reminded of the history of the WI as they walk around the college. The portrait of Lady Denman greets them in the entrance hall and some of the rooms carry names associated with the past: the Nugent Harris room, the Bawdon workshop, the Livingstone room. Members who have not been to the college before are taken on a tour, in which the guide points out these links with the past.

Staff

Friendliness and approachability is as important in the staff as it is in the Chairmen. This starts with the Warden/Principal:

My main memory of early Denman is of watching Betty Christmas, the first Warden, welcoming in women for many of whom, then, this was their first resident visit outside their own villages. Betty set a standard for warmth, hospitality and sympathy which is still evident. Her wide smile, shining eyes and Sam her large black dog really made Denman. [14]

Members obviously did find her sympathetic:

… she wore herself out because all the members wanted to confide in her, and share their problems … [15]

The friendly welcome given by the Principal to the members attending continues with her successors:

My first visit to Denman was when my sons were quite small. I was taken by my husband and the boys were welcomed with delight by Miss Jones the Principal… [16]

At the initial gathering of students for each intake, Graham Jones, the current Principal, says, "Welcome to your college", underlining the importance for all the staff of the fact that the students who come to the college are their employers.

Types of courses

Lady Brunner, in her speech proposing the setting up of the college, suggested two types of courses that the college would offer. The first would be courses of general and specialist interest to WI members, and the second would be "occasional schools and conferences for the study of our own institute affairs" (p 71).

When the college opened the courses were divided in this way and the two categories were designated 'A' and 'B'. The 'A' courses were planned and run by Denman College as open courses for which any WI member could apply; the 'B' courses were planned by NFWI Headquarters staff and were training courses for which the County Federations applied and nominated those who would attend. Those who came on 'B' courses were expected on return home to use what they had learned for the benefit of their Federation and fellow WI members. Many of these 'B' courses trained tutors, demonstrators, judges, officers and other leaders to give them the skills to do their jobs competently and to maintain a national standard.

In 1950 a further category was introduced, the 'AB' course. These were planned by NFWI Headquarters but open to both Federation nominated students and those who applied directly. These courses tended to be of a more academic nature and the intention was that the participants would share their knowledge with others. The first such course was in February 1950, on 'Health and Safety in the Home', and was planned by the NFWI Public Questions Subcommittee.

The terms 'A' and 'B' were dropped in the 1980s but the same general division of courses still holds – open courses, NFWI training courses, and the modern equivalent of the 'AB' course which is the 'cascade conference'.

A 'cascade conference' is usually sponsored by an outside body. Members can apply, but they are expected to 'cascade' the information when they return home. For example, in 1980 Kellogs sponsored the first of a series of nutrition conferences in the newly opened Home Economics centre, and in 1995 the same sort of pattern was followed by 'Genetics Now', a conference jointly funded by The Wellcome Trust, the Medical Research Council and the Biotechnology and Biological Research Council (see p 147).

Lady Brunner had said in her speech at the AGM, "If we succeed in making the college all we wish it to be, perhaps people will even come for holiday courses." (p 247). There are members who come on open courses and consider it to be a holiday. One member related how she had been saving up the money she earned from the goods she sold through her WI Market in order to go on holiday to Greece, but in fact she spent it on a course at Denman instead. She goes on to say:

> I never got to Greece, but I'm on my 14th visit to Denman! [17]

Another member wrote:

> I attended this course for a holiday; the first I have had for 29 years. What an experience! It was like being let out of school; everyone was laughing and chattering, the surroundings were fantastic and the tutors excellent. I came back with batteries recharged and feeling relaxed... [18]

For a woman on her own it can be a holiday:

> Being retired and widowed I find the courses suitable for a single person's holiday as well as being of a high standard intellectually. [19]

There are some courses which are more recreational, and which have been advertised as 'Country House' weekends. Sometimes these are linked with an outside event like the 'Royal Ascot Country House Party', or with Henley or Newbury Races. Denman College is the WI member's own country house and for some members, especially those on their own, it is an ideal holiday venue. In the Golden Jubilee year there is to be a country house party for members and associate members to see in the New Year. The publicity reads:

Don't be alone on New Year's Eve... Ask for details of course 211 and get 1998 off to a brilliant start, pamper yourself with aromatherapy, join in a treasure hunt, enjoy a Viennese concert, work off excess calories with line dancing or just sit by the log fire.

In recent years there have also been some educational tours arranged, with Denman tutors taking parties to other parts of England and abroad, to Cornwall, the Welsh Marches, Turkey or Greece.

Guests on courses

Although at first it was intended that members should apply individually and come on their own, it was soon recognised that there were many women who would prefer to come with a friend. So in the second programme, in 1949, two courses were specially reserved for members who would like to come with a friend, although they were welcome to do so on other courses also. In the early years the 'friend' had to be a WI member, but gradually others were able to come as well. Even today 33% of students on open courses come with a WI colleague and 6% with a guest. [20]

In 1958 it was agreed to accept "a limited number of husbands on certain courses at 25/- a night," [21] and 26 husbands came during the year. [22] Out of a total of 2,032 students attending, they hardly swamped the college. Husbands are still accepted on some courses, although the description is now 'guest', and they must be accompanied by a WI member who is also on a course (though not necessarily the same one). The policy of allowing men to attend a women's college does not meet with universal approval; there are some members who feel that the college should be for women only; there are others who feel that allowing men to attend may prevent a member getting a place at her college. Tutors also have views on the way in which the presence of men may affect the course, and the way that the students participate (see p 234).

There are members who appreciate this opportunity to come with husbands:

My husband wanted to go on 'Looking at Cricket', so I went on this course.

I always wanted to join the flower arrangers at church, so I went on a course combined with other church activities, husband bell ringing and daughter choral singing.

My favourite stay at Denman was when I went with my husband who tutored 'The Drama of Motor Sport'. It was wonderful to share the Denman Experience with him. [23]

Another member tells a story that particularly emphasizes the caring qualities of the college:

My husband and I were booked to go on a microwave course, but two weeks before we were due to go I had a mastectomy after being told that I had breast cancer... The college were very understanding but said not to be too swift in saying we could not go, to leave it till the day to decide ... so I came out of hospital on the Sunday and went to Denman on the Friday. From the minute we went through the door and were greeted by the hostess I was treated like royalty... The whole weekend was so relaxing and everyone was so kind. We both went to almost all the lectures and when I didn't my husband was able to take the notes, he did all the practical cooking and enjoyed himself very much.

I am sure the whole weekend did us both a lot of good and sums up what a stay at Denman is all about – caring, learning, relaxing and enjoyment.

Attached to one of the returned questionnaires, a husband described his own experience. He was a retired physicist, who had been booked on a course by his wife when she was going to be at the college as College Chairman.

Other than our tutor there was only one other man visiting the college. The first instruction at dinner on the first night was that nobody was to sit with their friends and that we must sit with different people for each meal... [This is not always done, and is not enforced but suggested. AS]

The whole atmosphere is of a college and people working to advance their skills. It is nice to study and work without having any domestic chores to intervene. The ladies accepted a man in their midst without any problem and I received very little leg pulling. Quite a number of the ladies thought I was very brave to go to the college as they said their husbands would never dare to go. I would recommend any husband or guest to go to the college as the courses are all excellent and well worth while.

Families

The seconder of the resolution at the 1945 AGM proposing the setting up of the college had suggested that there might be a "nursery school in the grounds where young mothers might leave their children."(p 72) This was not quite achieved, but in 1959 14 courses were available for mothers with babies under the age of three. 31 babies came with their mothers and a day nursery was provided and supervised by an experienced nurse. There were also four courses available for mothers with children between the ages of eight and 15 years. The children camped in the grounds. A member recalls doing this:

My first most momentous visit to Denman was in 1959 when I took my twins Hilary and Felicity to the first camp in the grounds. The twins were very used to camping holidays but never one with other children, so were very excited. My own course was 'country house-wives' and I was subsidised by the two WIs to which I belonged ... after my husband had died. We were driven, with camp beds and sleeping bags to Marcham by a WI member... The children were in tents and were very well looked after and amused – their only disappointment being that there was no specific course for them ... they were taken swimming in Abingdon... (Plate 15, pp 160–161).

Some years later when Felicity was investigating University entrance, she stayed for a weekend in York with … one of the girls who shared the tent they slept in at Denman. [24]

By 1970 there were still family weeks, but they took children from 11 to 15 who slept in dormitories in the house. This seems to have been because so many of the camps had been 'washed out' and the college had problems with all the drying. The 'Mother and Baby' courses however had ceased by this time. The college staff had found coping with these difficult, and the number applying for them had decreased. In 1960 a 'Mother and Baby' course had to be cancelled because of lack of applicants. It would seem that members preferred to leave the children at home and come to have a time completely to themselves.

In 1962 a 'Mothers and Daughters' week was introduced; the daughters had to be 15–20 years old – no babies! 14 daughters came with their mothers and the courses were repeated. This idea was reintroduced in 1994, when there was a 'Mother and Daughter' course held over the Mothering Sunday weekend. This time there was no upper age limit and the college was filled with mothers and daughters spanning the generations. There were two parties involving three generations and one involving four. It would seem that WI members enjoy sharing the experience with their daughters (and mothers- and daughters-in-law). 'Mother and Daughter' weekends are now a regular feature of the programme.

There is a real feel of a shared 'inheritance'. After 50 years there are members who still remember being at the AGM:

I was at the Albert Hall when Denman was suggested and was instructed to vote for it. [25]

A member who came to the college in 1996 for the first time wrote:

I have been a member of the WI for over 50 years and have always wanted to come to Denman. [26]

Another member recalled:

When I first became a WI member in 1948 the WIs were furnishing bedrooms for the new college. [27]

Others remember their mother's stories:

I have photographs of my mother on her first visit to Denman in the early 50s plus a lot of house rules which told where the dusters were and what time to make the early morning tea. [28]

Federation visits

The original intention was that WI members would come from all over the country and so get a 'national' feel. However it was acknowledged that some members would be more attracted to come, at least for a first visit, if they came with their Federation. These

Federation courses were first introduced in the early 1960s, but in the 70s and 80s they were discontinued as at that time the college was fully booked with open courses. It was not until the mid 1980s when the crisis at Denman had caused a fall in the number of applications that the Federation visits were re-introduced.

Federations book the college and work with the staff to plan the programme. Sometimes they bring their own tutors but more often the Federation will decide what subjects they would like to have and Denman staff are able to find tutors for them. The Federation bookings are a valuable way of bringing first-time students to the college, and they are also economically attractive for the more distant Federations, because they can hire a coach and everyone can travel together. There is also a valuable educational spin off as the work begun on a course at Denman can be followed up back in the Federation if the Federation arranges further classes. On the other hand the national dimension is lost when the whole college is taken by one Federation.

Since the reintroduction of Federation visits all but one of the 70 Federations has organised at least one such visit, and many have had several. The Management Committee tries to keep a balance so that the national nature of the college is not lost.

Making friends

The friendly welcoming atmosphere has always made it easy to get to know others; the one thing that all have in common is WI membership, and to ask about someone else's WI is a good way to get talking. A member explained it this way:

> [I had] a feeling of being part of a family of women from all areas and walks of life. [29]

> As a widow living on my own I gained much from the company and very welcoming atmosphere at Denman. [30]

This friendly atmosphere affects the way that students learn and is commented on by tutors:

> The safe feeling of the college fosters an openness and group warmth and trust.

> The students come from a common background – the WI – and so there is a group atmosphere established already at the start of courses. [31]

When the college first opened most of the students had to share rooms and many remember their room mates. One member who went in 1959 wrote:

> I shared the Welsh room in the main building with two very charming and friendly Welsh members, one a farmer's wife and the other a teacher. [32]

On one's first visit it was a good way to get to know someone. This was certainly what happened to the author on her first visit when she was still a little anxious about how her husband and two small children would manage without her. One of her room mates, a cheerful older member who had been through it all before, assured her that they would cope – and they did. The 'dormitory' life was friendly in other ways. Those who slept in the same parts of the house met up when filling hot water bottles in the pantry, and there was a rota to take early morning tea.

One member remembers:

> I first went to Denman in 1968 and really enjoyed it… Early morning tea was arranged – meeting members in dressing gowns over a kettle did make for a really friendly atmosphere. Having tea-making facilities in the bedrooms now is a good idea in some ways but part of the social life has been lost. [33]

The bedrooms are a constant source of delight to members, as they reflect the character of the County that has adopted them, and they all include personal touches, noted by members, that make them feel at home:

> … comfortable and beautifully furnished with its matching curtains and bedspread. I appreciated too the small thoughtful touches, the copy of *Lincolnshire Life* and needles and cottons ready for possible running repairs. [34]

Many of the rooms have visitor's books which provide another view of the college experience. From the visitor's book in the Tyneside bedroom:

> A very comfortable stay and much pleasure from the beautiful patchwork furnishings.

> As a Geordie I am delighted to be in the Tyneside room.

> A bright comfortable room. The patchwork makes the room and has inspired me to have a go myself!

> Two days hard work but this comfortable room gave a welcome refuge.

> Comfortable room, charming decor, excellent course.

Students meet those on other courses over meals, and in the evening. In the early years there was no bar in the college, but an evening cup of tea was provided from a trolley in the Hall, poured out by the College Chairman. There are some students who remember that and regret that it is no longer so. There are others who remember that, before the college had a bar:

> our tutor led those who would go, to the pub; and we invariably had to knock them up to let us in… [35]

In 1966 the first licence was obtained "to allow members to enjoy a drink before dinner." [36] At first the drinks were served from a trolley which was wheeled out and placed at the bottom of the main staircase. In 1988 the trolley was replaced by a new bar, this time a permanent fixture, and offering a much larger range of drinks. It was located in the room that had been the Library, and expanded the area for social activity. A door can be opened onto the terrace, which has a view towards the lake; a lovely place to sit on a Summer's evening for the drink before dinner – or later in the evening.

The Library is now no longer housed in a single room, the books are scattered throughout the college. The founders would probably be sad that the Grace Hadow Library, for which elegant book plates were designed by Reynolds Stone, is no longer there. On the other hand the space for relaxation and informal conversation between members has been increased, which is also something the founders wanted.

Entertainment

In the early years of the college there was a special entertainment on one of the evenings, usually the final one of the course, to which everyone went. On the very first course of all, Margaret Deneke (sister of Helena Deneke, the biographer of Grace Hadow) came over from Oxford to play the piano (see Plate 13, pp 160–161). For many years this entertainment was arranged by the college; in 1975 for example, the entertainment planned for Thursday evenings was frequently given by Helen Anderson, the Warden, who had sung in the chorus at Glyndebourne when she was younger. She talked about her experiences, and gave song recitals. At other times there were recitals by visiting pianists, Christopher Headington and Denis Lee; talks on costume by Atherton Harris; Freda Gwilliam, who had worked with women in developing countries, gave a talk, 'Where shall we go next?' Talks about travel included 'Iran' by Mrs Poore and 'Portugal' by Miss Jones. One evening there was a film about Rhodesia with Avril Dankworth. [37] These were the days when far fewer members had travelled abroad, and these evenings were all part of the college's aim to widen horizons.

If there had been a course which could provide the entertainment, then that was what happened. 'Brush up your Piano', 'Music and Drama Together', and 'Dance Drama' courses all provided entertainments. At one course on 'Country Dancing', Patrick Shulam Shaw, a well known folk singer from Cecil Sharp House, was the guest on the last day and offered to sing any songs requested:

> I asked for 'The Foggy Foggy Dew', but he didn't think the ladies would like that! [38]

The final evening is still a time for all the students to get together, but now it is an informal party with entertainments provided by the students themselves. The 'programme' is co-ordinated by the College Chairmen, and may include songs or sketches devised by the students on a course who have got together, or a 'party piece' performed by individual members. The atmosphere is one of 'fun' rather than 'improving'.

One member who has been coming to the college for 40 years remembers the early entertainments, which she found:

> relaxing … the two sisters Miss Helena and Margaret Deneke, one played the piano and the other sang, long dresses, jewellery, so graceful…

The same member had kept the programme they had been given for the 'Joint Session' on Thursday evening, 19th November 1970, when Dennis Lee (who was Japanese she noted) gave a

Pianoforte Recital
Ravel ... Valses Nobles et Sentimentales
Brahms ... Sonata in F minor Op 5
    i   Allegro maestos
    ii Andante
    iii Scherzo
    iv Intermezzo
    v Finale

This member comments that in comparison "the 20 minutes of 'entertainment' this April was very poor." [39]

Keeping in touch

There are some occasions when members on a course want to keep in touch as a group. It might be by returning to another course taken by the same tutor, but some-times it is through forming a group who continue to support each other, as one member explains:

Denman is a place of discovery, stimulus, challenge, entertainment, friendship, new begin-nings. Yet it is greater than the sum of all these parts. When any group of women come together, they do so from different circumstances and with different contributions and needs. To illustrate this, my writers' course of '84 saw twelve of us gather with pens at the ready. Before long we discovered that of the six widows, one was bravely facing her first outing since her loss, others were still finding it tough going, two were further along the recovery process. Something occurred during our time together that week which bonded us in a way which continues to this day. We write a letter or share a piece of writing and send it round the circle. Some visit or phone each other. Our writing skills were challenged that week and we moved in other ways too. [40]

Another 'club' which formed, after the members had enjoyed their course together, called themselves the 'Denman Derailleurs' – a cycling group. [41]

A 'home' for entertaining

The founders felt that Denman College would be "a home of our own", and just as one entertains in one's own home, Denman has been used as a place for the WI to entertain its guests over the years.

In 1959 the Associated Country Women of the World's triennial conference was held in Edinburgh. Before the conference, during the August Bank Holiday, an informal house party was arranged at the college, to which one representative from each constituent society was invited. Twenty-two accepted the invitation:

Rain caused the garden party to be held indoors, but this gave the visitors opportunity to appreciate the warmth and comforting atmosphere that predominates at the college. The fine design and workmanship of the furnishings made by WI members were greatly admired by delegates, who also enjoyed the delicious tea specially prepared and served with the help of nearby Federation members. One of the overseas delegates summed up the general feeling about hospitality they had enjoyed everywhere by saying, "WI hospitality is something for the world to learn." [42]

Other visitors from overseas have come to see the work of the college. [43] In 1971 14 Danish home economics advisers visited and in the same year 30 educationalists from an international course organised by the Oxford University Department of Educational Studies also came. Visitors from nearer home have included a party of Education Officers from Cambridgeshire, and the Chief Education Officer of Bedfordshire both of whom came in 1977. Members of the government of the day have also been to the college. In 1982 Sir Keith Joseph, Secretary of State for Education and Science, and Geoffrey Holland, Director of the Manpower Services Commission, addressed a conference on work and leisure which was attended by representatives of other women's organisations, voluntary bodies and LEAs. Other visitors have included John Patten, when he was Secretary of State for Education, and John Redwood, when he was Secretary of State for Wales and visited the college with the Chairman of the Federation of Wales.

Other women's organisations have always been interested to visit the college. in 1990 there was a visit from Canadian WIs, and in the same year members of the Scottish Rural Institutes joined WI members for Burns night celebrations made more memorable by the storm that brought down a huge Cedar tree in the grounds. In 1993 there was a delegation from the Federation of Icelandic Women's Societies, and in 1994 NFWI's National Chairman hosted a weekend conference for representatives of the other major women's organisations in the UK.

Food

For most members the opportunity to have meals provided for them is a big treat. When the college first opened, rationing was still in force and students were told that if they were staying more than two nights they should bring their ration books with them.

The college employed a resident cook until 1985, when the catering was put out to contract. This proved cheaper for the college and has also provided a greater variety of menu. The dining room, with its tables for six, has a family atmosphere and members do still help, no longer with the washing up, but with clearing the tables. There are very few complaints; in all the questionnaires returned, only one member commented that she did not like "clearing up in the dining room – rather like school dinners."

In the questionaire, very few (3%) of the respondents rated the food less than satisfactory, and of these about half explained that it was "not as good as usual"; by contrast, over four fifths rated it good or very good! Those who came on NFWI courses were a little less enthusiastic than the rest, perhaps because they had been to the college more often.

Celebrations

The college has always been used for special celebrations.

The first major event was in 1958, when 42 Counties entered a flower arranging competition staged at the college and judged by Constance Spry; 4,570 people attended the exhibition on two days in July. In 1987 there was another flower festival. This time it lasted three days and attracted over 6,500 members who were also able to see how the money raised in the £1 million 'Save Denman' appeal (p 94) was being spent.

There have been 'royal' occasions too. In 1970 HM the Queen Mother opened the new Teaching Centre and in 1979 the Queen opened the Home Economics Centre. Both these occasions gave the WI a splendid opportunity for celebration, and produced some headaches for the organisers:

The whole week was set aside, we had coach-load after coach-load of people pouring through the gates, and we had a huge marquee in the garden with non-stop catering going on – it was quite a week. One of the days was set aside for inviting all the education authorities. We wanted to show off desperately that week to as many people as we possibly could the exciting teaching block and Brunner House. [44]

1.200 members came from all over the country to view the new buildings, and then the official opening day finally arrived:

We got a telephone call after the Queen Mother had actually arrived, but before the major opening, saying that they thought someone had planted a bomb in the Brunner building and immediately we had police everywhere. They were very tactful and came in round the back and got in through the windows to search Brunner House leaving rather a lot of muddy footmarks which we hoped the Queen Mother would not notice... [45]

Not all ran smoothly either for the visit of the Queen nine years later:

[There] was a telephone call from Windsor Castle the night before. Her secretary said, "You do realise that when the Queen cuts the tape she always keeps the scissors?" and we said, "We don't want the Queen to do that," because we had borrowed a beautiful gold pair from Lady Brunner – well you don't get the scissors back – what you get is a silver coin instead. But in fact when it came to it the next day, with a twinkle in her eye she handed back the scissors ... and we got the silver coin as well! ... we had a letter from Windsor Castle thanking us on behalf of the Queen for our hospitality and pointing out that we had the best of both worlds with regard to the scissors. [46]

Special events bring large numbers of members to the college, some for the first time. In 1992, 14,000 people came to two festivals, 'Focus on Europe' and 'Autumn at Denman'. The house and the grounds and sometimes the neighbouring parish church are used to the full on such occasions with flower arrangements, music, exhibitions, stalls... They raise some money, but above all they raise the profile of the college, and ultimately bring new students.

In 1993 Richard Smethurst, Provost of Worcester College, Oxford, was invited to give the first Livingstone lecture (see p 234). There was a lunch at the college followed by the official opening of Willow and Beech, two residence 'cottages', by Lady Anglesey and Lady Brunner. After that, because the college has no room large enough to hold the number of people who wanted to hear the lecture, the proceedings had to migrate to the Examination Halls in Oxford.

In 1995, on the 50th anniversary of the decision to set up the college, 'Denman Fanfare', a musical about the history of Marcham Park specially commissioned from Colin Tarn, was performed in a huge marquee on the lawn. The production, which was seen by 15,000 people, involved over 900 WI members for whom it was a unique experience:

> Two rehearsal weekends, February and June at Denman, and then in July another rehearsal weekend followed by six days presenting Fanfare. ... three shows a day in a marquee with dressing rooms, professional lighting, tiered seating, etc. I ended up dancing a gavotte, being a gentleman in a drawing room scene, dancing drunkenly with a life-sized rag doll... I found out that as far as possible we were to provide our own costumes, so I ended up making a life-sized doll! [47]

Between the performances, those involved were able to enjoy themselves:

> There were many moving moments throughout the week – poetry readings under the trees on a beautiful summer afternoon, poetry and music in the flower-bedecked church, rounders matches in the evenings with the 'big wigs' joining in, wonderful conversation at meals and round the Pimms bar until darkness fell. Overall, the camaraderie that existed the whole time with my fellow thespians was an overwhelming experience and everybody in true WI style was organised, controlled, dedicated and concentrated on giving of their very best to make Denman Fanfare the success it was. I was privileged and proud to be part of it. [48]

Fulfilment of the founder's vision

The vision of the founders was that the college would provide a friendly and welcoming place where members would meet others from all over the country and feel a part of the national organisation. Let today's students speak for themselves: [49]

> Denman is my second home – I am always singing its praises.

> As a widow living on my own, I gained much from the company and the welcoming atmosphere at Denman.

> It was lovely to meet people from all walks of life. I have missed this since retiring.

> Experience of mixing with WI members taking different courses and coming from all over the country.

> Whenever I phone Denman I've always found the staff most helpful.

> I felt that my stay at Denman helped me to gain confidence in going away and meeting new people on my own.

There has been a gap of about 10 years since my last visit and in that time considerable changes have taken place at Denman – all for the better. It is a lovely place for the WI to own, and its good that more members are attending.

Denman offers so much; very good tutors, good varied company who also contribute, peace to study, wonderful surroundings, accommodation and food. What more could one ask?

It is widely acknowledged as a friendly place; those attending on their own soon feel at home and as much part of the group as they would like. Meal times and coffee breaks allow mixing across courses and the last evening sharing of results by exhibition or demonstration is always as eye opener. The real joy for me is in meeting so many women who are interested in life and get the most out of it... Here's a toast to those early visionaries who set up such a treasure for our inheritance! [50]

CHAPTER TEN

"... THE BEST IN LIBERAL ADULT EDUCATION ..."

VISION OF THE FOUNDERS
That it would be a place that offered the best in liberal adult education.

Introduction

Running a short-stay residential adult education college was a totally new venture to the WI, and the programme of courses developed by trial and error. We look at a selection of programmes over the 50 years, to see how the content changed (or did not change).

The programme has always reflected the two aspects of the college's work: the 'open courses' for which any member could apply, designed to offer 'liberal adult education' to the 'countrywoman' who would not find anything similar where she lived; and the training courses which continued the training tradition already well established in the organisation. The college also afforded an opportunity to bring together representatives from the County Federations in order to disseminate new ideas and practices which they were expected to pass on to fellow members when they got home – now referred to as 'cascade' courses.

Table 10.1 shows in summary how the college programme has evolved. It can be seen that the strong emphasis on domestic subjects in the early years has changed, with a much wider range of subjects on offer. **Table 10.2** shows how the total number of courses has increased while the number of training courses has remained nearly constant.

The first college programme

In May 1948, four months before the college opened, every WI received an 'Outline Syllabus' of the courses to be run from 29th September 1948 to the end of the year. WI members were encouraged to apply for places. A letter explained the difference between 'A' (open) and 'B' (NFWI Training) courses and "courses marked 'C' will be for friends of the college whose skill will be of practical use in such ways as preservation, upholstery, etc. Places will be allocated by special invitation." This particular category never appeared again; perhaps it served its purpose in getting the first courses filled by special invitation. The 'Outline Syllabus' was mostly made up of 'B' (training) courses, which were very similar to those which had been offered to WI members for many years. This ensured that the college would have enough students in the first few months.

Table 10.1 – The Changing Nature of the College Courses

Percentages of courses by category for selected years. The categories (except for Country Housewives, Domestic and WI Organisation) are those used in the 1996/7 'open' programme.

	1949	56/7	61	66	74	80	87	96/7
Antiques & Art and Craft Appreciation	0	0	3	4	3	5	2	3
Art – practical	0	5	4	7	7	9	9	9
Craft – general	0	9	7	7	15	11	6	14
Craft – textiles	6	23	29	19	15	15	15	12
Dance, Health & Fitness	0	3	2	3	1	2	7	9
Drama/Theatre	3	5	4	2	1	2	4	2
Flower Arranging	0	6	4	3	2	3	<1	3
Food & Drink	14	12	14	9	6	2	16	8
Gardening & Countryside	14	4	5	4	7	6	4	3
Languages	0	0	0	0	2	2	<1	1
Literature & Writing	6	4	4	6	5	3	5	3
Music & Song	3	2	2	3	3	3	4	7
Personal Development	0	3	3	5	3	3	4	6
Photography, TV, Video	0	0	1	1	1	<1	0	2
Science & Technology	0	0	2	4	2	<1	<1	3
Social Studies, History & Public Affairs	14	7	5	11	14	15	14	9
Sport & Leisure	0	0	<1	<1	<1	1	2	6
Country Housewives	31	4	3	6	5	1	0	0
Domestic	8	4	1	<1	1	0	0	0
WI Organisation	0	5	4	5	4	4	<1	<1
Total Domestic	39	8	4	6	7	1	0	0
All Craft	6	32	36	26	30	26	21	26
Study Tours							4	

Table 10.2 – The Growth of the Programme

Total numbers of Courses Offered in Selected Years

	1949	56/7	61	66	74	80	87	96/7
Open	35	94	144	139	150	193	221	332
Federation	0	0	0	9	0	0	0	153
NFWI	28	20	21	22	23	25	26	30
Total	63	119	165	170	173	218	247	515

With the limited amount of accommodation in the main house, it was only possible to run one course at a time. The first programme consisted of:

Preservation	C
Upholstery	C
VCO refresher school	B
Methods of teaching school (Handicrafts)	B
International – Colonial Empire	B
Country Housewives	A
Market Organisers School	B
Music School	B
Produce Guild Leader's School	B
Country Housewives	A
Christmas Course	A

Country housewives

The only open courses in this first programme were aimed at 'country housewives'; the Christmas course being very similar to the two actually called 'Country Housewives'. The planners had very little idea of what would attract the 'ordinary' WI member, who might have left school at 12 years old, and who was now running a home and bringing up a family. They decided to offer a course that would give her a taste of a range of subjects relevant to her home life and "a bit of culture" as well. In this first 'syllabus' the course was described as:

A general course open to all members which will include subjects such as cookery, gardening, household management and repairs, laundry, country life in other lands, together with an expedition, music and drama etc. [1]

31 students, from 19 Federations, attended the first of these courses. From a report of the course, [2] it is clear that they had some practical cookery sessions for which they were divided into two groups. They also had a lecture on 'Planning the Work of the Home':

... this is not an easy subject for a speaker to tackle with experienced housewives. I would suggest that this subject is dropped. [3]

The report also suggested including a 'Demonstrator on Household Jobbery' in future courses.

Lady Brunner, reflecting on the Country Housewives courses many years later, wrote:

The 'Country Housewives' courses of the early days enabled us to become better cooks and housekeepers – members were unwilling to launch out on specified subjects in a wider field, partly because, if they were to be away from their families from Mon–Fri or Fri–Sun, they must return being better able to make home more pleasurable. But the Denman College Committee's aim was always to widen horizons by including one or two sessions on local history, literature, music, drama and current affairs. So tempted and emboldened, members would quite often book for a specialised course. For it may well have been that the interpolated subject, when reported on to family and WI, aroused even greater interest than improved cooking, gardening and preserving. And for parents whose children were being educated to a degree far beyond what their parents had been, it was a boost. It was seen and could be believed, that learning was a life long process and gave a new dimension even to grown ups. [4]

THE 1949 PROGRAMME

This was the first full year of the college, and already the number of Country Housewives courses had started to fall; they now represented about a third of the open courses offered. Their content was changing too; laundry had already disappeared. We can gain a good idea of the nature of these courses from a diary kept by a Devon member during her visit.

On her first morning she attended two cookery demonstrations, then she had a free afternoon, and then heard talks on 'Fashions in Housekeeping' and 'The Buildings of Oxford'. Next day she made detailed notes of a talk on 'Design in Everyday Things' by a speaker from *Ladies Journal*:

... handles on kettles should fit the hands and jugs should pour well, knobs fit the finger, and a place to put finger under for lifting dishes. There should be a recessed place under the kitchen tops to put your feet... [5]

Although this visit was in 1952 the course programme was very similar to the courses in 1949. This diary records the following piece of history: "After lunch there was a talk on 'Design in the House' ... during this talk Miss Leathart came in to tell us about the death of King George."

At the end of the course the students were asked for their views on it, in those days a very progressive thing to do. It seems that the students liked the 'Design' talk but "would have liked more cookery."

Many of the courses reflect the life of a woman living in a rural Britain which was still suffering from post-war austerity. The gardening courses, for example, concentrated on the vegetable garden. In an article in *Housewife,* there are three photographs of Mary Clarke, the head gardener: "Miss Clarke, head gardener and instructor, shows pupils the fine asparagus kale grown in the grounds," "A practical lesson in the walled kitchen garden" and, most impressive, "the right way to build a compost heap." [6] (Plate 14, pp 160–161)

The cookery courses included 'Pickling and Preserving', but also 'High Class Cookery', "for those who aspire to be more than good plain cooks." There was a course in 'Catering … for Local Functions' – the members of Llanfairpwll WI started something when they "organised the refreshments as part of the Peace Day celebrations" in 1919 (p 28). Other catering courses were "for members who run cafés, boarding houses etc or are in charge of hostels or canteens," and included information about catering licences and book-keeping.

Viola Williams, who was the NFWI Agriculture Organiser at the time, recalls a course in November 1949 on 'Pig Keeping and Bacon Curing':

I was one of the first speakers when Denman started, doing a pig with Sarah Stevens, a Ministry of Agriculture Inspector. We cleaned up the garage, scrubbed up a table, collected the half pig allowed us by the Ministry and in due course cut up the carcass in front of about fifteen earnest (we were all earnest then) members.

Sarah and I had worked together before on war-time jam and our hands-on demonstration seemed to be going well when a member asked "Can you please do a shoulder ham?" In several years of pig I had never done one and Sarah's expression announced that neither had she, so we charged bravely in and mangled out a shoulder ham. We got everyone working hard rubbing in salt and then repaired to the tiny pantry near the present loos. Here we cooked pork pies, faggots and sausages. Talk about hygiene! [7]

In this first programme there were only two craft courses, 'Soft Toys' and 'Smocking', both took place in December. Were the participants making Christmas presents? In the programme for the next year (1950) there were ten craft courses most of which were more utilitarian – 'Soft Furnishing', 'Dressmaking and Patterns', 'Glove Making', 'Children's Clothes' and 'The Making of Underclothes'.

In addition to the Country Housewives courses there were others with a domestic slant. 'Home Management' was aimed at "those members who are taking up housekeeping for the first time" and attracted 14 students; the 26 students who attended 'Family Life' heard talks on 'Foundations of Family Life', 'Family Relationships', ' School and Home' and 'The Family Growing Up'.

Those courses that were more 'cultural' were rather general in comparison with the courses found in later programmes, as this example on a course on 'Books and Music' demonstrates:

'Books and Music'

To include talks on how music began, listening to music. A film on the instruments of the orchestra. Talks and discussions on novels, travel books, children's books and poetry, and a tour of the Bodleian Library. A most successful course on this subject has already been held and members should not feel that they must have a wide knowledge of books or music before applying, as the purpose of the course is to arouse interest and pleasure.

It would seem that the college wanted to reassure the sort of member who had felt threatened by the words 'education' and 'college', that this was an experience they were going to enjoy. The comments from students on general courses like this helped in planning future courses which became more specialised. Joan Yeo said, "We were trying to see how much academic education the WI would take." [8]

On the other hand, 'Feeding the Hungry World', which attracted 26 students, could well appear in the college programme today:

… talks and discussions on World Food Resources and Population, Problems of Production and Distribution, the Future of British Agriculture, the Contribution of the Small Producer and Food as a Factor in International Relations.

From 10th to 13th June there was a course "intended for members on their way to the NFWI Annual General Meeting to be held in London on June 14th and 15th". The students heard talks on 'The Place of London in History', 'The Growth of the City' and 'The London of Queen Victoria', they were also given suggestions for sight seeing. After the years of restricted travel there would be many who were visiting London for the first time.

There were also two 'Holiday Courses' in August "for those members who would like to spend part of their holiday at Denman College. There will be talks on birds and flowers and other country subjects … and expeditions to interesting places in the neighbourhood."

Training courses

There were also 28 'B' training courses (42% of the total). Of these, 12 were intended to provide information to those who were running the different aspects of WI work in the Federations, for example *Home and Country* Correspondents, and Produce Guild Leaders. Five courses were to train members to teach others: 'Methods of Teaching Handicraft', 'School for Demonstrators', 'Ways of Teaching and Speaking', 'School for Speakers' and, interestingly, 'Discussion Group Leaders', a subject that has emerged from time to time over the 50 years, each time as though it was a new idea.

There were two training courses for VCOs and three for those involved in WI Markets, including 'Grading and Packing' and 'Market Stall Controllers'.

Most of the NFWI subcommittees had their own training course in the programme, but as these had no more than the title 'Music' or 'International Relations' the content of the courses is unknown.

THE 1956-57 PROGRAMME

This year is of particular interest because the 'Agendas' ' and course reports for the whole period have survived. The course programmes were called 'Agendas', perhaps because this was felt to be less threatening and school-like than 'Timetable'. Programme 13 ran from March 1956 to April 1957.

During 1956 Betty Christmas, Denman's first Warden, died, having been ill for much of the year before. The college was moving into a difficult period with a series of temporary Wardens (pp 186–189) so it is not perhaps surprising that the programme continued to follow the pattern that had been successfully developed during the first five years.

The Handicraft and Produce Guilds were very active in the Federations, and their work was further encouraged by a grant given to NFWI by the Development Commission. For NFWI Headquarters there was £1,100 to be spent on Handicraft, and £1,400 for Agriculture and Marketing, and a further £2,600 to be disbursed to county Federations for their Agricultural and Marketing work. The extra emphasis on these areas is reflected in the college programme. Craft courses took up 32% of the open programme and the B courses also reflected the additional activity by including training for tutors and judges of Handicrafts and a School for Market Helpers and Producers.

Of the 30 craft courses run during the year, 18 were 'utilitarian': 'Upholstery', 'Soft Furnishing', 'Eiderdowns', 'Pelmets', 'Loosecovers', 'Lampshades', 'Making Underclothes', 'Cotton Dresses', 'Tailoring Processes', 'Glove Making'. During the war years, and the period immediately after the war, many houses had become shabby. Perhaps now was a time to renew both furnishings and wardrobes. The majority of WI members were full-time housewives, many of whom considered making their own furnishings and clothes as their contribution to the family economy.

There were still shortages, and if money was tight an ability to renovate old or worn items was important. The course on 'The Making of Felt Hats', which promised "Members will make one complete new hat and learn how to alter old ones", was fully subscribed. Those who had enrolled were asked:

What colour hat will you make?
Felt capelines for hats will be on sale at the College. Please could you let us know as soon as possible … what colour you would prefer - black, brown or navy or another. If another colour is preferred would you send a pattern of material and the instructor will do her best to match it.

The Chairman subsequently reported that many members had come with the intention of learning to renovate old hats rather than make new ones.

Members also enjoyed learning crafts for the pleasure of creating beautiful things, 'Linen Embroidery', 'Coloured Embroidery', 'Patchwork' and 'Fine Needlework' courses were all filled.

After the craft courses the next most popular courses were for various aspects of cookery. They comprised 12% of the programme, perhaps less than might have been expected. This was probably because practical cookery courses were held in the Home Acres demonstration kitchen which was shared with Berkshire Education Authority (p 214) and was therefore only available for college use for some of the time.

The 'Country Housewives' courses continued, although in this year there were only four (compared with thirteen in 1949/50). There were some new courses provided for 'housewives'; 'Running the Country Home' was "intended for members who have some knowledge of the subjects covered by it: cookery, gardening and flower arrangement." 18 members applied; when they received their 'Agenda' they found further information:

> The practical cookery session will either consist of making Danish Pastry or boning and stuffing a fowl. [In 1956 Danish pastries were quite a new introduction. Cafés had just started to offer these 'specialities'. AS] If you would like to bone and stuff a fowl please let us know by 21st May, and bring with you a bird 1–2 years old, plucked but not cleaned out, as well as a plate and box to carry it home again.

However it seems that only one member responded, which is perhaps not surprising considering the problems that might have been encountered by a member travelling in June by public transport. The subsequent report explained:

> but [as] only one wanted to do this, it was cut out of the practical work and no demonstration was given on this subject and some were disappointed. [10]

'The Country Housewife in her Kitchen', for which 16 students applied, was for the member who wanted economy:

> Tasty and economical will be the key words for this course, which will give opportunities for members to practice baking as well as to see demonstrations on the use of the stockpot and cheaper cuts of meat.

Equally useful for the member intent on brightening up her home was 'Home Decoration' (16 students) where she had "a chance to practice papering and painting the home."

These practical courses were popular. It was suggested that:

> If … a member decided she would come to learn dressmaking or improve her skill in pastry making or preserving, her husband was much more likely to agree to look after himself and the family in her absence than if she proposed taking a course in eighteenth century literature or modern poetry. [11]

That was probably not entirely true, even in 1956, because practical art and craft courses now appeared in the programme and recruited well. There were four painting courses and they were all full, and the two pottery courses were oversubscribed. The 'Puppets and Puppetry' was less popular with only 11 of the possible 18 places taken, but the report was positive:

> Students got far more out of the course than they anticipated. Very few students took the free time available. Mr Hayes was an excellent tutor, he took no free time off himself, he fired the students imaginations. They asked for a 'follow-up' course. [12]

The students on this course gave a performance with the puppets they had made to the other students on the Thursday evening.

6% of the courses in this programme were specifically to help members to run their WI better. There was 'WI Officers and Committee Members', and a course on designing good posters for WI meetings and events. 'How the WI Gets Things Done' had as the highlight a day spent at the AGM at the Albert Hall. Priority was given to those who had never been to the AGM. 28 members attended this course, which was pronounced 'very successful' by the chairman.

Lecture courses could accommodate more students than practical courses, sometimes up to 30. Although some courses included visits, they consisted primarily of lectures, given either by one expert or by a series of visiting lecturers.

'The Story of China and Glass' was "meeting a request for a course about domestic objects." There were 20 students and they were taught partly by Charlotte Bawden (a potter who was a member of the College Subcommittee, and after whom the Bawden Workshop was subsequently named) and partly by visiting lecturers. There was a full day expedition to the Victoria and Albert Museum by coach, which cost 12/6; a picnic lunch was provided by the college. The course report shows that the students would have preferred to have concentrated on either china or glass "and some thought the talk on teapots was irrelevant... Mrs Bawden had expected people to have more knowledge before coming on the course." [13]

Some lecture courses were less popular. Only eleven students chose 'The Problems of Old Age', a lecture course with a series of outside speakers on subjects ranging from 'What are the Problems of Old Age?' to 'Old People's Homes and Housing Schemes'. They paid a visit to some alms houses in Abingdon.

'Local Government', too, only attracted 11 students. It was advertised as being useful to newly elected parish and rural district councillors, or those who intend to stand for election. The Agenda included 'Local Government Finance', 'Health and Social Welfare', 'The County Council' and 'The Reorganisation of Local Government'. The Chairman reported:

> ... the course would have been better with double the number of students. The discussion was rather overweighed by a preponderance of Parish Councillors .... a joint session on local government was suggested by this course but I do not know whether the others would have appreciated it. [14]

The Folksong and Guitar recital, arranged at the 'joint session' for that Thursday evening was probably a more entertaining option for the last night 'party'.

The 1956 programme included the first appearance of a subject area which was to prove popular. 'Looking Your Best', although planned for only 18 students, had 24 attending to hear talks on 'Health and Good Looks', 'Care of Hands and Feet', 'The Foundations of a Good Wardrobe', 'Accessories', 'Hair Styles' and 'Make Up'. They were able to take on the extra students as the 'Drama for members under 25', which was on at the same time only attracted 9 for the possible 18 places. The Chairman reported, "members were so pleased with being given basic instruction and … welcomed time spent on hair styling and make up." [15] Courses of this type are still popular, they are often chosen by a member who lacks confidence and is on her first visit to the college. The 1990s' title is 'Looking Good, Feeling Great', which captures the essence of such courses.

A/B courses

In this programme there were five courses, designated 'A/B', which were planned by the relevant NFWI committee and funded from NFWI. Some of these were of a rather erudite nature; 'The United Nations and Ourselves' was organised by NFWI International Subcommittee and was for:

> … all members who wish to learn something of the work of the United Nations, particularly the specialised agencies such as FAO and the Children's Fund and how the work is helping the underdeveloped countries. There will be discussions on how individual WIs can help.

The records show that there were places for 33 students but only 16 attended.

'What Every Housewife Doesn't Know' was the enigmatic title given to a course organised by the Public Questions Subcommittee. The description explained a little more:

> With the home as its central theme this course will try to bring new ideas and fresh insight to the housewife and mother on the problems of present-day housekeeping, shopping, decoration and design in the home and other family matters.

If, having read this description, a member expected something like a Country Housewives course, she might have been in for a surprise. This was quite a challenging course:

Day 1
- 'The Price We Pay' – regulation of prices, advertising, monopoly etc – Mr Ward Perkins, Fellow of Pembroke College, Oxford
- 'Keeping Standards High' – quality of household goods and how we can help – Mr R Diplock, secretary, Retail Standards Association
- and in the evening a 'Housewives Quiz' on 'How much do you know about fabric today?'

Day 2
- 'What Everyone Should Know About The Law' – Mrs Horsfall-Turner, under-secretary, Law Society
- an afternoon visit to a Dr Barnardo's Home
- 'Educating Children in their Duties as Parents' – Mr Ingleby – Marriage Guidance Council
- and in the evening, 'The Care of the Feet' – Mrs Buxton – Officer in charge of the Foot Health Education Council.

Day 3
- 'Making the Most of the House that you Live In' - Miss Ledeboer - Chairman of the Housing Centre
- to be followed by an 'active session' and the Thursday afternoon visit to Oxford, a final discussion and in the evening joint session with other courses to see a film. [16]

'Holiday' type courses

In August there were full-week courses planned for those who wished to make them their holiday. From 16th to 23rd July there was 'Clay Modelling and Pottery' (13 students) at the same time as 'Digging for History' (with 22 students) and "As this is a holiday course there will also be an optional expedition to Stratford-on-Avon to see a play."

Holiday courses continued in the following years and we have a detailed account of one in 1958 which was almost twice as long, 'Cotswold Country, its History and Famous Men'. It was open to husbands and wives and one member recalls, "This was our Summer holiday instead of the planned Scotland one. We had a mini coach, Miss McCall leading in her car plus my husband as map reader … we got a lot done in the 12 days." [17]

With the letter from which this is quoted, were the course Timetable (by 1958 they had stopped using 'Agenda') and a receipt dated 1st August 1958, showing that they paid on arrival. It cost Mr and Mrs Norman £32.2.0 (£22 accommodation, £4 tuition, £5.12.0 buses, 10/- theatre).

The programme included introductory talks on the Cotswolds, and visits to such places as Burford, Fairford, Painswick, Sheepcombe, Kelmscott, Broadway, Chipping Camden, Minchinhampton, and Firkins (where Mrs Norman noted, "Socialist Warden Miss McCall took us to Sir Stafford Cripp's home at Firkins and showed us the village swimming pool built by him."). Cecily McCall was known to be a socialist. Before becoming Warden, she had been NFWI Organiser to the Education Subcommittee, but resigned this post to contest, unsuccessfully, a seat in the 1945 General Election. They also went to Oxford by river from Abingdon, visited the Royal Agricultural College and went to Stratford to a play at the Memorial Theatre:

We got back at 1.30 am, crept round the Old Croft, someone put the kettle on, one found some biscuits, another a tube of Nestlé milk (not to use the jug of milk put out for the morning tea) men on one bed wives on the other, all correct, enjoying company. We made many friends there… [18]

Training courses

18% of the courses in this programme were training courses. There were the usual training schools for new VCOs but this year there was also a conference on 'The VCOs and the Institutes of Today' described as "a course for experienced VCOs to discuss aspects of their work in the light of changing rural conditions." Both the National Chairman and Lady Brunner attended.

There were courses for those who wished to teach gardening, cookery and folk dancing. But in this year, with the special funding from the Development Commission, handicraft received extra emphasis. There were two 'Staging and Display' courses in order to help the Federations with their own county exhibitions in the run up to a national exhibition. There was a week's course on 'Methods of Teaching', and a special course to train teachers to take craft open courses at Denman. As a result of this training more tutors were added to the team of travelling tutors who ran classes all over the country. [19]

55 schools were taken in 25 counties. They were to help members who were getting ready to enter for the National Exhibition to be held at the Victoria and Albert Museum in 1960. In October 1959 NFWI received 3,239 entries sent in by county Federations, from which they selected the 543 entries which appeared in the Exhibition.

'Education Through the WI Movement' was a course for VCOs, county subcommittee members and those on Federation speakers panels. Lady Albermarle (the National Chairman) opened the conference by talking about 'The Place of Denman College in the Work of the WI Movement' and this was followed by "group study on ways of tackling different types of subject in the institute and county." [20]

'The Ceylon Conference' allowed representatives of Counties to hear from the delegates who had been at the ACWW Triennial Conference in Ceylon. They were expected to go back and give talks to WI meetings.

THE 1961 PROGRAMME

The previous year had been designated 'Denman College Year' with the twofold purpose of "further popularising the College and of raising a capital sum to reduce the necessity of too large an annual grant from Headquarters Funds." [21] The Denman College Year Fund was subscribed to by 6,580 WIs (i.e. 77% of WIs) and raised £39,243. Perhaps the 5% increase in the number of students attending the college was a result of this extra publicity. Over the years it would seem that raising money for the college has the spin-off of increasing the numbers who come – if only to see how the money has been spent.

The 1961 programme reflects some of the innovations introduced by Cecily McCall, who was Warden from 1957 to 1958 (Chapter 13):

She believed that the College had become inward-looking, and that change was being resisted for the sake of "keeping things as they always have been". Her first job, as she saw it, was "to let in the light". She then wanted to widen the whole range of courses so that the College became a spearhead for the further education of women. [22]

The programme included two 'Mother and Baby' weeks. This was the third year that such courses had been run, and the records show that a total of 19 babies (i.e. children under three years old) with their mothers attended. The mothers could choose from 'Reading for Pleasure', 'Fine Sewing – Children's Dresses' and 'Pottery and Clay Modelling'.

There were also 'Family Weeks' which had been introduced two years previously for the first time, when members could bring their husbands, and children between the ages of eight and 15. The children camped in the grounds, and in 1961 35 boys and girls attended (p 106). In addition, 42 courses (30% of the open courses) were marked with an asterisk which meant, "to which husbands are welcomed with their wives." [23] This was a considerable increase on the previous year when the idea had been introduced and only seven courses had welcomed husbands. Was this all part of the "letting in the light"?

The courses open to husbands included 'Going Abroad – Spain', 'Old-time Dancing', 'Making the Most of a Small Garden', 'Pleasures of Poetry' and 'Bird Watching'. A tale is told of one husband who, having been asked if he had told his colleagues at work where he was going, replied, "No fear! Coming to a women's college would have been bad enough – but *bird* watching would have been too much!" [24]

There were also 15 weekend courses, from Friday evening to Sunday lunch time; there had been very few of these in the earlier programmes. They offered the chance to come to the college to more members, especially those in paid work.

January and February, with the threat of bad weather, have always been months when fewer members wish to come. In order to offset this the college has on occasions been offered to outside organisations in order to bring in some extra income (p 200). In February 1961 the programme records one such booking: 'Colonial Officers' Liaison Course (not for WI members)'.

Craft courses, making up 36% of the open courses, continued to be a dominant feature, although the proportion that can be classed as 'utilitarian' had dropped to 29%. New crafts introduced included: 'Machine Knitting', 'Tatting', 'Lacemaking', 'Fabric Printing' and 'Tie and Dye'.

In the past, craft work in the WI had tended to concentrate on the skills involved rather than design. There was now a desire to correct this; courses such as 'Colour Design in Embroidery', which offered "Demonstrations and practical work on the main principles of design, experiments with design motifs and the use and value of textures &c", were leading up to the introduction, in 1968, of the NFWI Design Award.

(1) Right: Betty Christmas, (the first warden of Denman College) photographed at Ontario Agricultural College, Guelph, Canada, beside the portrait of Adelaide Hoodless. She made this visit in 1945 when she was General Organiser at NFWI.

(2) Below: Lady Denman (centre) with Elizabeth, Lady Brunner (left), and Sir Richard Livingstone (right) at the opening of Denman College.

(3) Above: The Staircase in the 1950s.

(4) Left: Grace Hadow with her brother Sir Henry Hadow, taken in 1930.

(5) Above: The Queen Mother opens the Teaching Centre and inspects students work in the Bawden Workshop, 1970.

(6) Right: Dame Florence Horsbrugh, Minister of Education, inspecting a pair of Wessex Saddleback pigs during her tour of the College after opening Home Acres in 1952.

(7) Above: The Queen is handed the borrowed gold scissors by Bursar David Austin, prior to cutting the ribbon to open the Home Economics Centre, 1979. Behind her to the left Hilda Jones, Principal, to the right Anne Ballard, NFWI General Secretary, Kate Foss, Treasurer, Patricia Batty Shaw, National Chairman.

(8) Left: Richard Smethurst and Lady Brunner at the Livingstone Lecture, delivered in the Examination Schools, Oxford, 1993.

Fourteen percent of the courses were about food. Cake icing continued to be popular with seven courses offered, which allowed a member to progress through various levels from elementary to advanced. Some of the courses reflected the new equipment which was beginning to appear in the nation's kitchens:

Cooking with New Equipment including Deep Freeze

Methods of cooking to make full use of newer equipment will be the basis of the course, but this will be linked with menu making for varied occasions. There will be a special session on deep freezing and the use of frozen foods.

Others reflected a change in life style: 'Packed Meals, Picnics, and Food for Television Watching', and a weekend course (which was open to husbands):

Cooking for Husbands and Wives

A course specially planned to include dishes for husbands to prepare when their wives are away from home. Quick methods of preparation and cooking will be a feature of the practical sessions, which will also include an exercise in open air meals. Some of the newest types of cooking utensils and aids will be in use.

Only 4% of the courses were now about home management. 'What Every Housewife Doesn't Know' was still on the programme; so were the Country Housewives courses which had become more active.

My course was wonderfully varied, consisting of gardening with flowers and herbs in the grounds, painting and decorating and some elaborate cooking. We made wonderful cakes, one of which we shared and one we donated to the camp. [25]

In her account, Joyce Cormack is actually describing a Country Housewives Course which she attended in 1959 (the programmes were very similar in 1962). This was a family week and the 'camp' referred to was where the children were staying; they probably devoured the cake with relish.

Women's lives as reflected in this programme seem to have more time for leisure. The gardening courses included less about growing vegetables and more about flowers, 'Rose Growing' and ' Flower Arrangement and Growing for Cutting'.

For the first time there were courses on photography, one on 'Simple Photography' and one on 'Colour'. 'Keep Fit' was also a new venture, and the music courses included 'Music for Wind and String Players'. There were also two courses for 'Car Owners'.

Literature and writing courses included 'Pleasures of Poetry', 'English Novelists' and 'Shakespeare's England' – and also two courses for writers, 'Writing for Pleasure and Profit' and 'Writing for Children'. In both of these courses the programme notes that:

Time will be given for writing and the tutor will comment on work individually.

The courses in the area of social studies included one for WI members who were magistrates, 'Ourselves and the News' which included a visit to the Oxford Mail, and a course on researching and writing a local history of your village.

Training courses

15% of the courses in this programme were training courses, a quarter of which were for VCOs; others were for training judges and teachers, market controllers, Guild secretaries, and drama producers.

The NFWI Drama Subcommittee had run a play-writing competition during the year which attracted 293 entries. The winners received bursaries for a play-writing course held in the autumn when the winning entries were performed by drama teams from Oxford. Margaret Rawlings, the final round judge,

> gave a short talk on the merits of the three plays. Forty three members attended the course and all but two of them were competitors. [26]

Two courses were organised by the International Subcommittee, 'The Implications of the Nuclear Age' and 'Sharing the World's Larder' which was:

> concerned with feeding the undernourished peoples of the African and Asian countries. Both courses, for which the programme was arranged with the kind co-operation of the British Association for the Advancement of Science, were fully booked and proved most useful. [27]

THE 1966 PROGRAMME

For the first time in this year Federations were invited to take the college and choose the courses they would like to have organised for their members. Cumberland, East Kent, Lindsey (Lincolnshire) and Suffolk East and West took up the offer.

The college was now receiving plenty of applications and there was a rationing of places; members were allowed to apply for no more than three courses in the year, and these to be on different subjects. The only exception was if a member was working for a craft test. There were some courses open to husbands and there was one 'Mothers and Babies' week, although 'babies' were not now included:

> Members can bring children between two and five years of age. Mothers attend whichever courses they prefer while the children are looked after by an experienced nurse. Special meals are provided for the children. [28]

There was also one 'Family Week', when members could bring children between 11 and 15; and a 'Mothers and Daughters and Sons' week, when members could bring their daughters aged 15 years and upwards and their sons aged 15 to 20. The young people slept in dormitories; the days of tents in the grounds were over.

Comparing the courses on offer in 1966 with those of five years before the most marked change is a decrease, from 36% to 25%, in craft courses, although these still remained the biggest single category. In 1966 the description 'craft' formally replaced 'handicraft', "This being more literal, since much work today is done by machine." [29] The types of courses were not very different, a new venture was a 'Sewing Weekend' intended to provide members with a

> … peaceful weekend before the rush of Christmas, when they can do their own sewing, embroidery, handknitting &c. While they work, members will be read to and have music played to them.

Cookery had declined from 14% of all courses in 1961 to only 9%. There was more emphasis on cooking for parties: 'Parties – Only One Pair of Hands', 'Cooking for Special Occasions', 'Gateaux and Tortes' and 'Home-made Wines and Party Drinks'.

The most noticeable change was the increased number of courses in social studies, history and public affairs from 3% in 1961 to 11%. The courses on offer seem to reflect women looking more outside their home and considering the wider community. 'Learning to Live' was a course about contemporary education; 'Local Government' covered the responsibilities and organisation of local government; 'Us and the Community' was about the rôle of voluntary organisations in meeting community needs.

Courses that looked even wider, to the International scene, included 'Religions of the World'; the course description explained, "with the growth of internationalism there is an increasing need to understand the beliefs of non-Christian peoples…" 'World Neighbours' was introduced by:

> … there is a growing interest in the influence of women in other countries. This course will consider the development of countrywomen's organisations, and will include reports on the progress of the WI projects resulting from the Freedom from Hunger Campaign.

Owing to increased mechanisation and the reduced number of small farms, the total number of people in Britain engaged in agriculture was decreasing. Fewer people who lived in rural areas were now directly concerned with agriculture, and the WI membership and its interests reflected this. A theme at the AGM in 1965 had been 'The Countryside Tomorrow' and some of the courses began to reflect a greater interest in conservation matters in comparison with agriculture and farming. In 1961 this had only been evident in the training courses, but now it was appearing in the open programme also. One such course was 'The Changing Village':

> Changes in the last 50 years have altered the character of the countryside, and affected the lives of country people. The course will consider the nature of these changes, the problems that have arisen out of them, and the steps that are being made to solve them.

The section on personal development now included not only 'Public Speaking' but also courses on 'Money Matters', 'Buying a House' and 'The Law and You'. 'Living Alone' was a course for:

all members who live alone … and the special contribution that people who live alone can make to the community.

Many of the courses were more specialised. Among the antiques courses were a course "for those who enjoy and perhaps collect Persian rugs" and one on 'Antique Clocks and Watches'. Music included 'An Introduction to Opera'; literature had courses on 'TS Eliot', 'Biography and Autobiography' and 'The Literature of the Seventeenth Century'.

'The Seeing Eye' was a new style of course:

> The world we live in is full of interest for those with eyes to see. This course is designed to help members to understand and appreciate beauty in a village street or town centre, in old furniture or modern painting, in the shape of a leaf or a lamp-post.

There were still no language courses, the first were introduced the following year when both French and Spanish for beginners were offered.

Training courses made up 7% of the college programme, a significantly lower percentage than in 1961. As is shown in **Table 10.2** the total number of training courses has remained fairly constant throughout the 50 years, but as the number of open and Federation courses has increased the proportion of training courses has decreased. In 1966 a quarter of the training courses related to the work of VCOs and running the organisation, and a quarter were offering training to those involved in judging, staging, and demonstrating crafts and other skills.

NFWI had recently appointed a 'technical adviser' to work on correspondence courses and postal judging courses. The huge size of the organisation and its wide geographical spread has always posed problems as to how to make all the possible opportunities available to all members. The introduction of correspondence courses was an attempt to address that need, and those on offer were shown to County representatives on the 'B' courses. 'The Countryside in the Next Decade' was a course following up a conference on 'The Countryside in the 1970s'; it enabled WI members to discuss what part they could play, and to hear about the 'Education Programme by Post' which had just been produced, entitled 'Our Countryside' and compiled by Dr Bruce Campbell, "a well-known naturalist and broadcaster." [30]

There were courses for those running Produce Guilds and WI Markets, but overall there was a reduction, compared with earlier years, in the number of courses which trained WI members to teach others.

There were courses to train members to do a whole variety of jobs in the Federations. 'WI Publications and Selling Them in the Federations' was a course for Publications Officers to help them with "stocking, storing, and selling". County Press Officers, County Secretaries and Advanced Drama Producers all came for further training.

THE 1974 PROGRAMME

The facilities at the college were now considerably enhanced by the new building opened in 1970 by the Queen Mother. Her visit had produced a great deal of publicity both amongst WI members, and outside, and the college profile was high.

The new Teaching Centre with its specialist accommodation: studio, light craft room, Bawden Workshop and lecture room, allowed for a wider range of courses. The Brunner buildings provided modern accommodation and it was now easier to accommodate a wheelchair user:

> The College is glad to welcome handicapped members wherever possible. If a handicapped member applies for a course she should write to the Warden explaining fully the nature of her handicap. As a general rule, she should be accompanied by a friend during her stay at the College. [31]

In 1972 the NFWI Executive Committee had initiated a discussion with the Consultative Council asking if Denman College was fulfilling the needs of members in the 1970s. They asked if the college should concentrate more on "courses of general interest that stretch the mind?" Should there be more time allowed for discussion on courses? Was the Family Week still needed and what age children should be allowed? How could the needs of working mothers be met? [32]

As a result of these discussions extra weekends were put into the programme to accommodate members who had paid jobs. There was more flexibility in the programming, with some courses running from Wednesday to Sunday, although most were still from Monday to Friday, or Friday to Sunday. There were occasional Monday to Sunday courses if the subject required it; 'Tailoring Processes', for example, needed this extra time – the course description read, "a suit or overcoat will be made though not necessarily finished" and there are stories of members sewing late into the night in order to have a garment finished to show off on the final evening.

The reorganisation of local government boundaries had affected the WI who had redrawn their own county Federation boundaries to fit in with the new local government ones. This probably explains one course in the open programme:

The New Look in Local Government

Sweeping changes have just been made in the local government of this country. The course will examine the new structure in its various aspects and consider how the individual in all walks of life will be affected by the changes whether he or she is an active councillor or a passive citizen.

Lady Denman would not have liked the reference to a 'passive citizen', but she would have approved of the course.

Open courses

31% of these were craft courses, but textiles are no longer so dominant; they now only represent half the craft courses, the rest being general crafts. Now that the Bawden Workshop was available a far wider range of courses could be offered including not only 'Pottery' and 'Wood Sculpture' which were in previous programmes, but also 'Glass Engraving', 'Rushwork', 'Baskets for Pleasure'. 'Hedgerow Basketry for Beginners', 'Corn Dollies for Beginners', 'China Mending', 'Paper Sculpture' and 'An Introduction to Book Binding'. To help the latter the college had "invested in expensive equipment needed to teach bookbinding." [33]

The textile craft courses included the standards: 'Dressmaking', 'Tailoring', and 'Making the Best of Your Sewing Machine', but there was also a course in 'Machine Embroidery' which reflected the modern sewing machines that members were now buying. The decorative crafts of 'Lacemaking', 'Tatting' and 'Macramé' were also represented.

The Berkshire Rural Domestic Economy Centre at Home Acres closed in 1967, when the service was relocated to the new Further Education College in Abingdon. Now students wishing to take a practical cookery class had to travel into Abingdon, so the number of courses available was limited. Cookery courses given in the college could only be demonstrations (p 216). As a result only 2% of the courses in the programme are cookery. These however do reflect changing demands. Help with entertaining is still offered in 'The Small Dinner Party' and 'Home-made Wines and Party Drinks', and there was even a course which recognised that sometimes women go out and buy a meal, 'How to Choose from the Menu and Wine List'.

In this programme for the first time there were three courses on languages – Spanish, Italian and French – these were all 'brush up' courses where members could "practice talking to each other and the tutor, a basic knowledge of the language is essential."

Another increase since 1966 was in the number of lecture-style courses in social sciences, history, and public affairs. Many of these were planned as a series: 'The Age of the Tudors', 'Great Cities of the World', 'Design and Living – New Towns'. Hilda Jones, who was Director of Studies at this time, remembers that "these were all great fun to plan and very exciting for the members who came on them." [34]

In 1971 the non-sectarian, non-party political rule had been changed (p 29). The Annual Report had commented:

> ... following the new interpretation of the non-sectarian non-party political rule the college was able to concern itself more closely with matters of religious and political significance. [35]

Perhaps 'Is There a Christian Ethic?' and 'The Morality of Science' were reflecting this new freedom.

There was a shift in interest from practical gardening, which only had three courses in this programme, to 'countryside' matters. Five courses were about natural history and other courses looked at changes in the countryside, 'The Changing Face of Agriculture' and 'The Environment – Limits to Growth'.

Courses related to running the WI remained at the same level as before (4%). There was a course, 'Marketing for Pleasure and Profit', to encourage members to get involved in WI Markets. There was a special course to introduce the new arrangements since the Craft and Produce Guilds had been dissolved in 1973. Their work was now integrated into a new department of Home Economics, and members were still needing the changes to be explained.

Sports activity had played a very small part in the programmes until now, but a new course was 'An Introduction to Orienteering', though potential students were reassured that it would include "practical work of not too strenuous a nature."

Training courses

Perhaps as a result of the 1972 review already referred to, NFWI decided to introduce, as a new initiative, the first Denman College workshop/conference. The theme of the workshop was 'European Architectural Heritage Year 1975' and the purpose was to use the college as a means of disseminating information which would lead to concerted activity all over the country. This workshop is further discussed in Chapter 14.

23% of the courses were training. The workshop referred to above was the most important innovation, the other training courses were much as before with a quarter, being VCO related. There were fewer courses for teachers and trainers, but there was some training for demonstrators and those who cater for shows.

THE 1980 PROGRAMME

The Queen had opened the new Home Economics Centre in 1979, and this was the first year in which WI members could come on practical cookery courses in the newly equipped kitchens. 24 courses (12% of the total) were offered and they ranged from the basics in 'The Skills of Cookery' and 'Cooking with Confidence' to 'Cookery for the Working Housewife' and 'French Regional Cooking'. 'Healthy Living' was a course which showed that members were becoming more aware of nutrition and health:

> [This course] will help members to compete with the stresses and strains of life today. There will be talks and discussions on nutrition and diet, physical and mental relaxation. Some practical movement work will be included.

Hilda Jones retired as Principal of the college after twenty years of being involved in programme planning, so this programme represents the culmination of her long experience. The Education Co-ordinating Group (Chapter 13) had now taken over the co-ordination of all the education work of the organisation and contact with others in the adult education world was being fostered.

The National Federation hosted a conference at the college, 'The Developing Partnerships in Adult Education', which was attended by local education officers, and representatives of other voluntary organisations:

> The Conference was most timely as overall reductions in public expenditure due to the national recession had a disproportionate effect on local adult education provision. Information collected from the Federations showed that WIs suffered from rising costs of tutors, demonstrators, and halls; some Federation grants were cut; increasingly members attending LEA classes were forced to travel long distances and the decline in the number of Rural Home Economics Instructors made it difficult for members in some areas to obtain instruction.

> Discussion during the weekend also centred on ways of improving communication and co-operation with LEAs and subsequently led to constructive and interesting follow-up work in some Authorities. The Group hopes to build on this achievement and work with WI County Federations during 1981 to pinpoint and develop the potential for adult education of a practical working partnership between statutory providers and other agencies. This intention was strengthened by statements from the Department of Education and Science supporting improved co-operation between statutory and voluntary sectors. [36]

Most of the open courses were 'one offs', single episodes of learning. However on a few courses students started to request a follow-up course in order to help them to progress further. 'Writing for Pleasure and Profit' was one such course and a 'Stage Two' was run. Language courses also built on what had been learned before. 'Parlons Francais' and 'Wir Sprechen Deutsch' were joined by a 'Welsh Course for Beginners':

> ... a repeat of the successful course held in 1978. It will concentrate on the presentation of basic sentence structures and everyday vocabulary.

The number of practical art courses increased to 9% of all open courses and included courses on basic skills in water colours and oils as well as specialist areas such as 'Chinese Brushwork' and 'Calligraphy and Illumination'.

Training

Training was now available at the college for those members who wished to take the WI Basic Certificates in Home Economics, in particular those who were unable to attend a suitable course in their own area.

The NFWI was able to interest sponsors in supporting courses at Denman. In a fully sponsored course, the sponsor provides enough money to be able to pay for representatives from all Federations to come to the college, and to cover their travelling costs. Kellogs organised and financed a Nutrition Conference in the newly opened Home Economics Centre. Those Federation members who attended were expected to use what they had learned when they returned home. This 'cascade' conference was very successful and was repeated for a number of years.

Another sponsor was the Ralph Vaughan Williams Trust, which supported the 'Making Music in the Institutes' training scheme, launched at a weekend course at Denman:

> The Scheme aims to provide a new music perspective and training in more than choral work. It also encourages innovation and suggests novel and varied ways of developing and enriching WI musical activity. [37]

This seems to have been an initiative that did not flourish, for in 1981 The Michael Tippett Musical Foundation offered to support some WI members to study the Open University 'Elements of Music' course. Unfortunately this offer could not be taken up due to insufficient applicants registering for the course. [38]

There was another example of Denman being the venue for NFWI to present new ideas to Federations in June 1980, when 48 Federations sent representatives to a 'B' course – 'Sports and Leisure Activities', "for discussion and exchange of ideas in the future of WI Sport and Leisure." For several years Green Shield had sponsored a national tennis tournament; now Tesco had just taken over the sponsorship and given grants for tennis coaching, and this was the opportunity for the Federations to find out how they would be involved.

THE 1987 PROGRAMME

This was a 'low' year for Denman; fewer students came to the college (3,549) than in any year since 1968. As a result of the crisis in 1984 (p 94) there had been some uncertainty about the future of the college and whether the organisation would raise the money required to 'Save Denman'. It would seem that WI members held back from booking to come to the college, even though the Appeal money was coming in.

There were other reasons for uncertainty. The college had been through a period of instability when one Principal followed another in rapid succession (Chapter 13). In 1987 Bernard Batchelor was acting Principal; the programme had been compiled by staff who were not familiar with WI members and contained a number of new courses, some of which were 'different'.

This was not the only change. The programme was published in two parts, January to June and June to December, and its format was altered. Instead of the handy little book that everyone recognised, there was an A4 insert in *Home and Country* with some separate leaflets also available. The arrangements for booking were changed, too, and some members, familiar with the system that had been in place for many years, were confused. There were some improvements, however. The introduction of pictures and graphics (almost overdone) made the leaflet lively, and in the June to December part the tutors' names were included, something that members had been requesting for some time.

Contrary to expectations, the half-yearly programmes appeared to produce less rather than more applicants, so the experiment was not repeated.

'Country House' weekends were introduced. In some ways these reflected the holiday courses found in earlier years and the descriptions stressed the 'gracious living' aspect:

> Enjoy the lifestyle of living in a country house coupled with a day's visit to Henley Regatta. Hats are 'compulsory'.

> Continuing the tradition of previous country house weekends join us for good food, wine, a day at the races and a relaxed and entertaining weekend. Relive the experience of the 'upstairs' life in a Georgian House.

Such weekends cost more, but they had echoes of WI members having a 'big house of their own' to enjoy. They could not be considered 'educational' in the normal sense of the word, and the Charity Commissioners might have considered that the charitable objectives of the college would be compromised if too many courses of this nature appeared in the programme. On the other hand such weekends could be used to fill the college at a time when it would not be possible to recruit for any other courses. Weekends of a similar nature are still included in the programme today, at New Year for example, and they serve a social need for members who might otherwise be on their own.

Study tours

In this year there were a number of study tours, with regular Denman tutors. The most popular, which was repeated three times, was to Cornish gardens:

> … a week's study tour visiting the cream of Cornish gardens, famous for their magnificent magnolias, camellias and rhododendrons growing in sub-tropical glory. In addition to the visits evening lectures will include garden history, the great plant collections, plant profiles and garden designs.

There were two visits abroad, one to Yugoslavia, and one to Holland.

The development of 'study tours' and 'country house weekends' was not peculiar to Denman; quite a number of other short-stay residential colleges were introducing such things into their programmes at this time to help to bring in more money (Chapter 15).

Open courses

For the first time there were more courses concerned with food and drink than textile related ones. The food and drink courses reflect increasing interest in the cuisine of other countries: 'Hot and Spicy', 'West Indian Cooking' and 'South Sea Island Cooking' were supported but 'Traditional Scottish Dishes' was cancelled through lack of support.

Among the craft courses were old favourites like 'Making the Most of Your Sewing Machine', 'Basic Dressmaking' and 'Fashion That Fits', but new crafts were appearing such as 'Cathedral Patchwork', 'Colour Pattern and Picture Knitting', 'Silk Ribbon Flowers', 'Lace Collage' and 'Stumpwork'. Some new general craft courses also appear, 'Stick Dressing', 'Pewter Work' and 'Raku Pottery'.

The number of literature and writing courses increased, as did drama and theatre, but the most dramatic increase was in the number of 'Dance, Health and Fitness' courses, four in 1980, 16 in 1987. These courses included 'Fitness in Middle Years', 'Age Well', 'Health Care and Maintenance', 'Alternative Medicine', 'Yoga and Massage', 'Alexander Technique' and 'Yoga and Self Awareness'.

Although many of the 'old favourites' like 'Oxford' and 'The English Country House' continued to appear, they were joined by lecture-style courses on such new topics as 'Magic to Star Wars', 'Ghosts and Ghouls' and 'Astrology'. The Trustees were far from happy about this last and it never appeared again.

Personal development courses covered a broader range, including 'Managing Retirement', 'Self Defence for Women' and 'Women and Money'. 'Making the Most of Your Word Processor' indicated a movement by women into a technology that embraced more than the sewing or knitting machine. Before long a course would be offered on designing on the computer for the knitting machine.

Sport and Leisure courses also increased in number. 'Distance Walking' and 'Croquet' joined 'Inventing Games' and 'Bridge'.

Training courses

Of the 26 courses offered, six were training for VCOs, Chairmen or Treasurers and five were WI Markets courses, but there were only two for training tutors or demonstrators. However in this year NFWI had formed an Education Subcommittee and appointed a Training Officer, and the development of a training framework for the organisation began. It was to take nearly ten years before it reached a fully realised form (see Chapter 13).

THE 1996 PROGRAMME

After the low of 1987 the fortunes of the college looked up. The success of the £1 million appeal had secured the future. Pauline Brown became Principal with Graham Jones as her deputy. Three years later, after Pauline's resignation owing to ill health, Graham himself became Principal. Thus the college moved into a period of stability. The management committee decided to work towards continuous use of the premises, and the number of students increased rapidly to over 6,000 a year.

As there were now usually five courses running simultaneously, even those who had little option over when they could come to the college were able to choose from a wide range of subjects.

In the programme for October 1996 to September 1997, the last full year before this book, there were 332 open courses and in addition 26 Federations came to the college and had courses organised for them. Thus the college organised over 500 courses in the year and there were also 30 training courses run by NFWI subcommittees.

The programme probably shows a better balance and a wider spread of subjects than at any time previously. There were a number of 'Theme Weeks' and weekends. The 'Churches Theme', had courses on 'Church Choral Music', 'Church Flowers', architecture and needlework. 'Flowers Through the Ages' was a series of courses organised jointly by Denman College and the National Association of Flower Arranging Societies. There was 'A Spanish Fiesta!' with courses on Spanish music, wines, dance, history and beginners language, a 'Royal Week' and a 'Craft Taster Week'. There is an 'added value' that many students find from attending when all the other courses are on a similar theme, as there can be shared sessions both formally and informally.

Craft subjects still made up the largest proportion of the courses at 26%, a figure that has remained fairly constant throughout the 50 years. Of the 40 textile courses only seven can be classified as 'utilitarian', but they include old faithfuls like 'Making the Most of your Sewing Machine' and 'Dressmaking'. There are some which show a different emphasis, like 'Curtains, Cushions and Blinds' and 'Machine Knitting – Cut and Sew'. Other subjects reappear after an absence, for example 'Learn How to Make Hats', which offers traditional methods, and 'Make Your Own Lingerie', which sounds more glamorous than the 'Underclothes' of the past.

Many of the textile courses were quite specialised, concentrating for example on specific kinds of needlework such as 'Danish Hedebo' and 'Amish People and Quilts'. The members of 50 years ago, who were warned that the sewing machines at the college were electric ones and that if they preferred they could bring their own hand models, would have been amazed at:

Janome – New Home Sewing Machine Course
Learn to get up-to-date with all that is available in the computerised Janome Memory Craft sewing machines which will be provided for your use.

The general craft courses now outnumbered textile courses, continuing a gradual trend in that direction throughout the 50 years. Many of the crafts which appeared regularly in past programmes such as woodcarving, basketry, upholstery and chair caning are still there. The WI continues to uphold the traditions of the Handcraft Guild of the early days.

Appearing more recently were some popular 'hobby crafts' like 'Découpage', 'Swiss Straw Lace', 'Parchment Craft' and 'Miniature Furniture'. These courses provide instruction on crafts which have become absorbing hobbies for some members and a source of income for others.

There was a threefold increase in the number of Sport and Leisure courses. This reflects the increased emphasis put on these activities by NFWI in recent years. Regional Sports

Advisers, aided by grants from the Sports Council, have been stimulating interest amongst WI members. Denman courses included 'Golf for Beginners', where students play on a local golf course, and 'Swimming', where a student can choose from 'For Absolute Beginners', 'For Advanced Beginners' and 'For Improvers'. A school nearby allows the college to use its swimming pool during the summer holidays.

There is also a marked increase in the number of Dance, Health and Fitness courses. Folk dancing and English and Scottish country dancing are familiar from the past, but the members in 1948 might have looked askance at:

> Middle Eastern Dance is a beautiful, graceful art form. An excellent and exciting way to keep fit allowing your own personality to shine through.

There is also a whole new area of alternative therapies on offer, Aromatherapy, Reflexology, Shiatsu and Tai Chi, which members in the past would not have recognised, although Yoga would be familiar. They would also have been surprised to find.

> ITEC Massage Part I. Working towards the ITEC diploma, a professional qualification in holistic massage. It will encourage intuitive skills and will be suitable for those working with family and friends as well as those who are aiming to practice professionally.

The number of music courses has nearly doubled. The range extends from traditional courses studying the work of a composer, 'Brahms' or 'Elgar', to popular music, 'Magic of the Musicals' or 'Music is Fun'. Practical music making included 'Handbells in Harmony' and 'Learning to Play the Harp':

> Learn to play simple tunes and chord patterns as a means of accompaniment on the harp. An ability to read music is not essential. Harps are available for hire.

Personal Development courses have increased from nine courses (4%) in 1987 to 20 (6%) in 1996. 'Speaking with Confidence' and 'Personal Finance' are titles familiar from the past, and 'Confidence in Colour and Style' is the most recent version of the 1956 'Looking Your Best'. New in the 1990s is 'Counselling Skills':

> Two linked courses with additional study at home, giving students the opportunity to obtain the City & Guilds qualification in Basic Counselling Skills. Students will receive training in Counselling Skills which will enhance relationships in a variety of work and personal situations.

The college has improved its facilities for those members who have a disability. There are bedrooms adapted for wheel chair users, loop system for those with impaired hearing, a tactile map of the college buildings, paths, trees and features in the grounds, and special courses put on from time to time. 'Oxfordshire Life – for both the sighted and visually impaired' is an example of one of these. Both guide dogs and hearing dogs have been to the college with their owners.

Food and drink courses have decreased to only 8% of the programme. They still include some basic instruction, 'A Beginner's Guide to Cookery', 'Breadmaking Stages

I and II', but also some more specialist courses, 'Balti Indian Cookery' or 'Cordon Blue – Cookery for Friends'. There is, however, an increase in the number of wine courses.

Science and technology courses have never been very popular, in spite of special promotion at intervals over the years. However in 1996 they had increased to 3% including the very popular Advanced Driving courses:

> Understand mechanics, learn to change a wheel, reverse, tow a trailer, drive cross country, advanced road driving and about personal safety – to be the complete driver. Cars kindly provided by Vauxhall… Some students will have the opportunity to take the Advanced Driving Test on Friday morning.

A course which would have stunned the members 50 years ago was 'Introduction to the Internet, Word Processing and Spreadsheets':

> Find out what's on the internet and how to negotiate the information super highway. Use the computer to create documents and perform calculations automatically.

Those members who came in 1952 on 'A Course for Farmer's Wives and Daughters', which included 'practical help with farm accounts', would probably have appreciated the spreadsheets.

The increase in the number of courses in other categories means that the percentage in the Social Studies, History and Public Affairs section is reduced to 9%, but some of the courses found there would have been familiar to Sir Richard Livingstone, 'Life in a Medieval Monastery', 'Rothschilds and the National Trust', 'Oxford and its French Connection', '18th-Century History'. Generally speaking, however, the more serious 'lecture courses' have declined in favour of more active participatory courses. Perhaps we can all get 'culture' through some of the television programmes available today that our predecessors did not have.

Languages still only take up 1% of the open programme but there is now more progression possible. In German for example, 'German – A Second Stage':

> Intended for anyone who has learned German in a class or privately for between one and two years. Set in a friendly atmosphere our emphasis will be on practising the spoken language using a little booklet which depicts the life of a German family at the turn of the century.

Students who would like to progress further are offered the opportunity to take part in a new venture – the 'Denman Open Study Programme', run in partnership with Abingdon College. This provides:

> the opportunity to study for qualifications with like-minded members in the peaceful and caring surroundings of Denman.

The student could choose either GCSE or A level German, and would be working with the same person who had tutored the course outlined above. The student would come to Denman for a day school every six to eight weeks and then study at home using home study packs, but with the tutor available to give telephone help.

Training courses

The number of courses remains much as it has been throughout most of the 50 years and they follow a very similar pattern. VCO and related training and WI Markets training dominates; many of the other NFWI subcommittee 'courses' are run as 'conferences'.

1n 1996 there was tutor training and also training for assessors for the newly introduced qualifications in Home Economics which will be described further in Chapter 14. A special grant from the Department for Education and Employment supported a 'Rural Adult Guidance Workshop', and further grants from the Chartered Institute of Marketing Charitable Trust supported training for Federation Marketing Advisers.

Fulfilment of the founder's vision?

The vision of the founders was that the college would be a place that offers the best in liberal adult education. The college programme has changed over the 50 years, reflecting the changing nature of the WI members who come. The average age of the WI member is now higher than it was in the early days of the college, and 'Mothers and Babies' courses and 'Family Weeks' are things of the past. Today's member is more interested in a course to provide added interest and activity to retirement, or relaxation from paid work, and less concerned about domestic matters.

Let today's students speak for themselves: [39]

I left school without taking 'O' levels... I hadn't realised just what a large part Denman has played in my thinking, in my education and learning and in my enjoyment of life.

I feel Denman has gone from strength to strength in recent years. On every visit there is some improvement, and always new courses being tried.

I have found it an interesting exercise listing the very varied courses I have done, and how they fitted in with, and enhanced other aspects of my life. [40]

There should be a health warning; "This can seriously change your life," said Vicki Fattorini... She was referring to Denman College, where she first attempted a course six years ago, on 19th-Century literature. This so whetted her appetite for further education that she enrolled for an Open University Foundation course. [41]

My first visit to Denman, earlier this year, was one of the greatest delights of my life (and there have been many); to learn with like minds and be so cared for is invaluable. My second visit proved just as wonderful and I can't wait for the third.

Each time I have been I have been encouraged to explore aspects of whichever craft I was interested in that I didn't know I was capable of.

I hadn't done much history, then I attended a course about William the Conqueror at Denman and got enthusiastic. I am now working on an access course at the local University 'Relating the Past to the Present' … what about the FUN AND FRIENDSHIP!

With such a variety of courses there is something for everyone.

[I have] gained a knowledge of science because I am on the arts and crafts side.

I am an art teacher and frequently lament the decline of handicraft skills among young people. Art schools follow a more academic path and I am grateful for Denman providing strongly in this area.

CHAPTER ELEVEN

"... THE VERY BEST LECTURERS AND TEACHERS ..."

VISION OF THE FOUNDERS
The College would provide the very best lecturers and teachers
who would offer women a chance of learning
whatever their previous experience or stage in life.

"Denman College sells good tutors." [1]

The students come to the college "to have expert tutors". This was the 'highest scoring' of the reasons for coming to Denman offered to respondents in the questionnaire (**Appendix 2**).

Who are these 'expert tutors'? Like most other short stay residential colleges, Denman does not have any permanent teaching staff of its own. Each course is taught by a tutor (or, sometimes, by a team) employed for that particular purpose, usually someone from outside the WI. As this is the college of a national organisation, attracting students from all over the country, it is able to attract tutors from all over the country as well. Many members come because they know that they will get something special that they would be unlikely to get at their local adult education centre.

How does the college obtain 'the very best lecturers and teachers'?

When the college first opened there was an expectation that some of those tutors and lecturers who were already known to the WI would be prepared to teach there. For the residential courses that NFWI had organised previously, they had been able to obtain the services of some very eminent people. At a residential school held in Oxford in 1946, for example, the speakers had included Ralph Vaughan Williams, Thomas Armstrong, Susan Richmond, Rebecca West, and Stephen Dykes Bower.

Sir Richard Livingstone had suggested that Oxford University might provide speakers, a possible source being the Oxford extra mural department. [2] Sir Richard mentioned C.S. Lewis as a possible speaker, but there is no record of him ever having come to the college. Using the personal contacts of Sir Richard and of members of the national committees, and building on relationships from the past, the college started to recruit tutors.

As we have seen, the courses in the early years were of two types, the 'lecture' courses, which often brought in one or two 'big names' to give single lectures, and the 'practical' courses which were more frequently taught by tutors trained by the WI.

Recruiting for the lecture courses was easier than might have been expected. Once the outline programme for the year had been agreed by the programme planning committee, and the various suggestions for new subjects had been incorporated, it was the job of the college to find the tutors and engage them.

Shirley Angelsey, who chaired the Denman College Subcommittee in the late 1950s, remembers:

> You really could get anyone you wanted … in those days the top people in their field were excited by the thought of speaking to countrywomen who hadn't had educational opportunities – people gave their time more readily than now. [3]

Hilda Jones, who put together the College programme for 20 years, from 1961 to 1981, first as Director of Studies and later as Principal, said, "I always went to the top for tutors – after all we were a national college and had students from all over the   country." [4] She recalled Oxford always being a good source; she had contacts with many of the Oxford Colleges, and also with the (then) Oxford Polytechnic, the Bodleian Library and the Ashmolean Museum. Some of these contacts, which were built up by Hilda in the 1950s and 1960s, are still used today.

The college did indeed welcome some well-known national figures; among those who visited during the early years were Lord Beveridge, who spoke at a course on 'Social Legislation', Neville Coghill, who talked about 'The Choice of a Play', and Patrick Moore, who taught 'Astronomy':

> We were fortunate in having so many well-known and distinguished lecturers, as well as rising young artists, like David Gentleman, who accepted our invitation to come to Denman. [5]

Others lecturers from the 1950s and 60s included Lawrence Bradbury from the Tate, and scientists Raymond Priestly and Dame Kathleen Lonsdale (see also Chapter 14).

On the whole, university lecturers, and particularly professors, have been used more for single lectures than to be the main tutor for a whole course. Many have proved most successful in putting over their subject in a way which is accessible to an audience with a mixed background, though not all have been very good time keepers:

> Members were interested in Dr Leyton's talk on 'Land and Life' but were too tired at 8pm on the first night (we started late because of washing up, the epidiascope went wrong in the middle, and he talked for one and a half hours). [6]

Members have been impressed by the opportunity to hear well-known people.

One of our literature weekends I shall never forget because ... I managed to get Stevie Smith the poet to come and talk to the students, it was the most memorable hour ... members went away thrilled to have met someone of such stature. [7]

Not all of those at the top of their profession are necessarily good at putting over their subject to lay people. Sometimes it was wise to do a little discrete enquiry before issuing an invitation. Jan Bateson (who was acting Warden in 1959) wrote to Helena Deneke (p 69) asking her advice as an Oxford academic and a WI member:

Miss Reeves (St Hugh's) has been suggested for historical talks – do you know her? It is essential that these talks should be put across in an attractive way. [8] [Helena Deneke also gave advice on possible tutors for courses on 'Russian History', 'The Civil War in the Cotswolds' and 'Warren Hastings'. AS]

This highlights a particular skill which all successful Denman tutors display, that of realising that in part they are 'entertainers' and that they are speaking to adults with a variety of knowledge and skill. They must neither patronise nor destroy confidence.

In the late 1980s Lady Brunner perceived some changes:

During the last 15 years the lively interest shown in the earlier years, in education and its involvement in almost any aspect of public and individual life, seemed to totter! No one succeeded Sir Richard as an outside source of inspiration. The humility with which the pioneers approached the establishing of the college faded away. There was noticeably less support from Oxford University in lecturers and tutors. [9]

To some extent this is due to changes in academic life. It may also be due to Denman's inability to pay large fees. But it is also because of the changing nature of the courses, referred to in Chapter 10; lecture courses have largely given way to those of a more participatory nature. The college does still attract people who are at the top of their professions, but they tend now to be part of special courses. An example of this is the 'Genetics Now' course which was held in October 1995, when the lecturers included Professor Sir David Weatherall, Honorary Director of the Institute of Molecular Medicine, Oxford, Dr Ron James of PPL Therapeutics, Edinburgh, Professor Sir Alec Jeffreys of the Department of Genetics, University of Leicester, Professor John Durant of the Science Museum, Dr Martin Richards of the Centre for Family Research, Cambridge, Professor Richard Flavell, Director of the John Innes Centre, Norwich, Dr Erika Hagelberg of the Department of Biological Anthropology, Cambridge, and Dr Kenneth Boyd of the Institute of Medical Ethics, Edinburgh. [10] Here were some of the country's leading scientists who were prepared to come to Denman to share the excitement of their work with WI members, academics from all over the country and not just from Oxford.

When courses on international subjects are planned, various embassies have provided experts. In 1970, for example, 'Background to Norway' was timed to allow those who were attending the ACWW Triennial Conference in Oslo to come for some briefing. On that course 'The Political and Social Systems of Norway' was delivered by John Grieg, from the Norwegian Embassy, 'The Geography and Geology of Norway' was given by

Dr Reading and Dr Hobday of Oxford University Dept of Geology, and a lecture on 'Norwegian Art' was given by John Boulton Smith of the University of London Department of Extra Mural Studies.

Teachers for the practical courses

Just as the lecturers in the early days of the college were drawn from those already known to the WI, so were the tutors who came to teach practical courses, including 'Country Housewives'.

Two old friends of the WI who came to the college a great deal in the early years were Miss Hutton and Miss Bode. Miss Bode was Principal of Radbrook College, the domestic science college where the 1943 conference was held (p 67), and Miss Hutton was one of the staff who taught there. Both retired from Radbrook in 1948 and immediately became tutors at Denman. Their specialities were sweet making, cake icing and 'Household Management'; they continued to teach at Denman until 1970 when they were in their nineties!

> We had to make a survival team to keep them going, they were so slow. Miss Hutton ... the driver in a very antique Morris Minor had a wooden leg. [Miss Bode] would service Miss Hutton by having everything ready for the next course. They were remarkable, we didn't have the heart to tell them they couldn't come any more... [11]

> Miss Hutton's artistry in cake icing won her many awards in national contests. Always modest and unassuming, no one was more surprised than she when her decoration of a small basket of primroses exquisitely modelled in sugar, standing beside many more imposing confections, won the Gold Medal at Hotel Olympia. [12]

At the party given for them by the college when they finally retired, Miss Hutton was persuaded to wear all the medals she had won, they made an impressive total – 2 bronze, 3 silver and 1 gold.

Another long standing friend of the WI was Doris Cumming, the Rural Domestic Economy Instructress for Berkshire County Council (not only that but also the chief RDE Instructress for the whole country). Already well known to the WI, she was used frequently as a tutor, especially after the opening of Home Acres (p 214) where she was on the spot as she lived in the Home Acres flat. Miss Cumming explained her work:

> The special nature of rural domestic economy is difficult to describe, but it is mainly concerned with the products from farm, garden and holding. The country woman can make a real contribution to family prosperity when she makes use of the facilities at her disposal... [13]

Sometimes she would be the sole tutor on a course and at other times she would contribute one session, as when, in 1956, she gave a demonstration of cooking with the fruits of the countryside as part of a natural history course entitled 'The Countryside in Autumn'.

The other person who lived in the grounds and was employed in teaching was Mary Clarke the Head Gardener. She gave practical instruction and demonstration in the garden and wrote a booklet, *The Country Housewife in the Garden*, published by NFWI. The introduction read:

> It is the gardener's job to keep the housewife supplied with vegetables every day of the year. For the Country Housewife this should be easy if she takes some part in, or acts as guide in the planning and working of the garden, so that she is able to have a good variety of vegetables all the year round. [14]

The booklet goes on to provide the reader with details of the kinds and varieties of every possible sort of fruit and vegetable with details about their planting.

There has always been a ready pool of tutors in craft and home economics drawn from the WI itself; the Craft Advisers and Home Economics Advisers appointed by NFWI over the years have all tutored at the college. Another ready source of tutors has been those WI members who have trained as tutors within the WI system. Today there are numerous craft and home economics tutors who teach both at Denman and in the Federations as travelling tutors.

After a period of decline in the use of the travelling tutors appointed by NFWI, there is now once more an increased emphasis on their work. New ones are being trained and the service is being promoted. A grant from the Institute of Marketing Charitable Trust has made it possible to pay for the travel of these national tutors who go to Federations without a specialist tutor of their own. The traditions begun in the 1920s and 30s still continue.

Finding new tutors

Hilda Jones recalls that she sometimes had problems in finding a tutor for some of the more innovative courses. When the committee suggested a course on 'Atlantis' she had a real hunt to find a lecturer. In the end she learned that Professor John Luce had written a book on the subject. She tracked him down (in Ireland), wrote to him and he agreed to come for the weekend course.

When Hilda had persuaded people of this sort to come for the first time she briefed them personally, and once they arrived at the college she looked after them very well:

> Getting lecturers and keeping them – gave quality and continuity, we spoilt our lecturers like mad, treated them as if they were the most important people in the college – which they were – they were the *raison d'etre* for members coming. We retained them because we looked after them well. They were nearly all entranced with the college, and the response they got from members who had an intelligent desire to learn, [they would comment] "it is a joy to talk to members" … [15]

Once tutors were 'hooked' Hilda would invite them to suggest courses which they would like to teach in future programmes, asking them to write the 'blurb' to put in the programme. Professor John Luce was 'hooked' and came back every year for many years; he "would not miss his visit to Denman". One of the courses which he suggested after 'Atlantis' was 'Homer and History', and the 'blurb' which he produced was much fuller than the descriptions of many of the other courses in the programmes:

> Archaeological discoveries from Schliemann's time on have thrown much light on the historical background of the events described by Homer. The course will survey the culture and society depicted in the Iliad and Odyssey, and will examine particularly the Trojan War. It will discuss the extent to which Homer's picture of the 'Age of Heroes' corresponds with the realities of Late Bronze Age Greece. Various aspects of the subject, such as the site of Troy, the topography of Ithaca, Homeric weaponry, will be illustrated with slides. [16]

"Always start at the top" was Hilda's maxim, and she supports this by describing how she got Tim Rice to come to talk about the planning and work he had done on the musical 'Evita'. Professor Lionel Butler was another early lecturer at the college who obviously enjoyed being 'spoilt' and went on to come regularly for many years.

Today the College still has its 'regulars'; tutors who come frequently to the college can develop a 'following'. This can have advantages, because the college knows that there are members who will book for that course because of the tutor, and disadvantages, if new people joining the course feel somewhat discriminated against by the 'matey club' who keep remembering past occasions.

There is a constant need to find new tutors. Occasionally a Federation may recommend someone they have used. One tutor may introduce another tutor, if for example they are unable to take the appointment themselves. Other short-stay colleges may also be a source for new tutors; many of those who tutor at Denman work for other colleges.

Over the years the college has built up a network of contacts, and in addition there is always a steady flow of unsolicited requests from potential tutors. On receipt of such a request, if the Denman staff think that the person has something of interest to offer, they send a copy of the current programme, tutor's notes, specimen course agenda and CV form. The potential tutor is invited to return the completed CV and an outline of what they might offer. They will then be invited to come to the college to see the facilities and have an informal interview. First and foremost the college has to be satisfied that they are competent in their subject and have adequate experience of residential intensive learning. They have to be the sort of people who will create the right atmosphere and who will have sympathy and understanding of the Denman student's needs and WI ethos.

Tutor fees

It is difficult to find out what fees were paid to tutors in the early days of the college. In 1956 records show that the tutor for 'Watercolour Painting' was paid £27.0.0 for a four day course, and the tutor for 'Shakespeare and His Plays' got £39.7.0 for a seven-day course. [17] However the payment of tutors does seem to have been somewhat haphazard. In that same year one tutor had a fee of 16 guineas suggested before coming to the college, but when she received her payment it was not so much. In the letter she wrote to the Warden she was justifiably indignant:

> .... the fee was slightly lower than usual, Miss McWilliam (Bursar) explained that Denman College was in some financial difficulty. I should have thought, in that case, that it should find ways of raising money other than suggesting arbitrary cuts in payment to tutors.

She goes on to suggest that the college should fix fees that bear some relation to fees for comparable work elsewhere, e.g. WEA. However she ends her letter:

> I very much enjoyed taking the course. I am always very impressed by the keenness of the students and the very stimulating atmosphere of the college. [18]

In the 1960s and 70s the fees paid to lecturers on the lecture courses was often higher than those paid to the tutors on the practical courses. Much was at the discretion of the Warden. In 1972 a report on the tutor's fees showed:

> Lecturers: £9 a session (with discretion for free-lance lecturers to go to a £10 maximum)
> N.F. Craft Instructors: Mon/Fri course £25
>   Weekend course vary from £25–£35

> Tutors normally paid at £40/£45 for Mon/Fri:
>   Mon/Fri course £50
>   Weekend course vary from £25–£35

Full week: fees depend on whether tutor is single handed or has assistant, and on numbers in class e.g.:

> Full week Music & Drama, 2 equal tutors, total paid £100 divided 50/50
> Full week painting; 20 students £75 single tutor
> Full week pottery}: 12 students £45–£55 single tutor
> Full week carving}

The other thing to remember is that we do take into account the number of students on a course to some extent. When we have 20 students on a full week's course we take £96 in tuition fees, compared with only £57.60 for a course such as pottery or carving, which can only take 12 students, so we can afford to pay the tutor rather more for a larger class. [19]

At the same time the tutors on 'B' courses organised by the Speech and Drama Subcommittee were paid £60 for a four day course and £94 for a six day course, plus full travelling expenses. If more than one tutor took the course, the fees were divided pro rata. [20]

Since the 1980s the college has linked its fees to those paid in further and adult education. Now the fees are reviewed annually and those agreed for 1996-7 for all tutors, irrespective of subject, are shown in **Table 11.1**.

Table 11.1 – Tutor's Fees 1996–97		
Type of course	No of periods	Fee
2 night - Mon–Fri	8	£ 165
3 night - Mon–Thu		
or Thu–Sun	13	£ 268
4 night - Mon–Fri	16	£ 330
5 night - Tue–Sun	21	£ 433
6 night - Mon–Sun	28	£ 580

Changing educational methods

As we have seen from descriptions of some of the early courses at the college, the 'lecture' courses were just that, the students sat and listened and sometimes watched. The course chairmen were supposed to encourage student participation and to get the members to discuss what they heard and what use they might make of it.

In 1955 the Education Subcommittee showed concern about the educational methods being used on courses at the college, the 'lecture' courses in particular.

> It was agreed that there was a general need for WI members attending the college to have some active work, whether the subject of the course was one which was normally regarded as practical or not. It was agreed to give continued consideration to this question and to recommend that Miss Dickson be asked to raise it at the Annual Conference of Wardens of Adult Colleges. [21] [Miss Delphine Dickson was Tutor at the college and at this time was acting co-Warden. AS]

Miss McCullough, who was the HMI appointed to NFWI in the 1960s, strongly advocated banning the lecture. Hilda Jones recalls that when the new Teaching Centre was being planned Miss McCullough wanted the design to be entirely open plan. Although her advice was not followed, there was a real effort made to include more active involvement for students on lecture courses, for example by including visits.

In order to help the students to get more out of their short course, the college asked tutors to provide lists of suggested books that the student could read beforehand. This was mostly done for the more academic subjects like social history, science and literature. The practice continues today and lists are sent out to students a few weeks before the course. "Not everyone reads them, but it sends out messages." [22] Tutors are also encouraged to suggest what a student might do subsequently.

The college has always been aware of the problems of the lack of continuity in short-term residential learning. There have been various initiatives to try to address this issue. In the mid 1970s Hilda Jones introduced a variety of 'series' which encouraged members to return and find out more about a subject. In 1980, for example, the programme included 'Great Rivers of the World – The Rhine', and 'Great Museums of the World – The

Hermitage in Leningrad', 'Regions of France – Burgundy', 'Vanishing Peoples of the World - The Aborigines'. There are still some series today, though fewer than in the past.

Another way of expanding the learning experience is by having 'themed' weeks or week-ends. These started in the 1960s when all the courses would be related, for example 'Modern Dramatists', 'Modern Poets' and 'Modern Novelists' would all be held at the same time, with one or two lectures for all the students together. In 1980 'The Regency 1798-1832', was a week with three courses looking at different aspects of the period: social history, literature, and the arts, architecture, painting and music. There are still 'Theme Weeks' in the current programmes (see the **Postlude** on p 240).

Tutoring students with a range of experience

When tutors come into the first session of a short-stay course, they are meeting their students for the first time. They will probably discover a very wide range of previous experience within the group. On a recent course on 'Stonehenge' one tutor found amongst the students a women who had written a book about stone circles, someone who was doing research on the topic and a woman who did not know where Stonehenge was. [23] What a challenge to a tutor to keep them all satisfied! Tutors who are faced with a student who is not at the same level as the others have to do their best to see that all gain from their course. All the students have arrived expecting to learn and enjoy the course; they are in residence. Unlike the student attending a weekly evening class they cannot decide not to come back to the next class. They could decide to go home, but in Denman's experience this is exceedingly rare.

This is less of a problem in practical courses because they are always for small numbers and the equipment is such that individuals can all work at the same time and the tutor can give them individual attention. Sometimes the course is advertised in such a way that potential students know what level to expect. In the 1952 programme, for example, a course on 'Linen Embroidery' was described:

> This course is planned to help those members who already have experience in this craft and is specially intended for members working on their 'A' test.

A course in 1987 on 'Chinese Brush Work Stage II' was described:

> The course will enable the students to use what they have learned previously to work more skilfully and confidently in various subjects including figures in Chinese costumes and in the ink-water technique. [24]

A continuing problem for tutors is that, although they may have put a carefully worded description in the programme, there is no guarantee that the students will all be at the required level. This problem was probably less likely to arise with the 'Linen Embroidery' quoted above, which is specific about how the level of attainment is measured, than with 'Chinese Brush Work Stage II', where the student decides for herself if she is ready for Stage II.

One tutor in patchwork explained how she had an elderly member on her course who lived on her own and had "just come to be with others". The tutor found that the rest of the students were sympathetic and understanding, and she was able to find a simple patchwork task that this member could do "so that she had something to take away at the end", whilst she got on with tutoring the more advanced course. [25] Most adult education tutors will be familiar with this situation; there are always some students who come for reasons other than learning.

Tutor's view of the college

That Denman is a place that tutors like to come to seems always to have been the case. The 'hooking' of Professor Luce (p 149) is a good example, and the fact that the college is always able to find tutors despite offering rather small financial rewards provides additional evidence. This is equally true for today's tutors, as can be demonstrated more unequivocally from the results of the questionnaire (**Appendix 3**). These indicate that the tutors particularly valued the interest and enthusiasm of the students and the support and efficiency of the college administration.

The students may come because they want good tutors, but the tutors come because they find enthusiastic, hardworking, committed students. Here are comments from four tutors that illustrate this:

> Many students feel quite inspired by a visit to Denman College. This places a particular responsibility on the tutor to offer an excellent standard, and indeed to "pull out all stops" to make those few days special.

> The commitment of the students is much stronger than at most Adult Education Institutes

> There is an unusually high determination among students to work hard, to get as much out of the course as possible, which makes tutoring rewarding.

> A very wide range of student ability and experience, but enormous enthusiasm and goodwill. [26]

One tutor recalls the response of a colleague who, on hearing that he was coming to tutor at Denman, said, "As it's the WI you will have to lower standards a bit and make allowances". "NOT SO, the women who come are lively, interested, committed, hardworking, want to probe deeper, work hard and with enthusiasm, if anything they are more committed than students in other short stay colleges." [27]

A number of tutors comment on the particular nature of the students at Denman. One tutor, who has been teaching art courses at the college for 20 years, says that she finds teaching Denman students different from those in other colleges where she works.

> The women who come are very human, no pretensions. They often come from judgemental backgrounds and their concepts are thus limited, they are not ready to be challenged; they want to learn but you have to start by building on their strengths and not by going straight into

the challenge. I aim to shift these students from straight copyist techniques to internal concepts, to encourage them to have more abstract ideas of their own. This internalisation – an ability to use and explore their own ideas with certainty – gives increased self esteem.

She explained further that the students, particularly older women, are often very constrained, they find it difficult to 'let go' and want to be told what to do. They have served the needs of others all their lives and find it hard to do something for themselves. She recognises some changes over the 20 years; she thinks today's student has a greater capacity for risk taking, and wonders if perhaps the exposure to media graphics has helped. "Students are more prepared to leave the safe territory than in the past, but there are still many members who prefer to take the 'safer' way with hobby crafts such as découpage." [28]

This tutor feels a real sympathy with the students and says "I love coming here because you want to give – you get a satisfying sort of tired. I can't speak highly enough for what it does for women." That view is echoed by other tutors:

A lot [of students] come with low self esteem, and return home after their wonderful Denman experience knowing that they *can* achieve, and that is very special and I love tutoring here. [29]

I am constantly amazed how nervous and lacking in confidence many students are when they arrive at Denman. It's lovely to see them 'blossom' in only a few days, gain confidence and assertiveness and be a much more outgoing person when they leave – they really have a sense of achievement! [30]

The support of the college administration is also highly valued. A tutor writes, "a genuine friendliness emanates from *all* the staff – domestic, administrative etc. and transmits itself onto the ambience of the courses." [31]

The support given by the college both before and during the courses is appreciated. "The staff are always on hand to assist"; "very efficient backup and support by a larger than average team." The special role of the College Chairman is also noted, and how this adds to the "family atmosphere".

The accommodation, for both teaching and social purpose, is considered adequate, and many tutors appreciate having the Nugent Harris Room as a staff room where tutors can meet together with other tutors, Denman staff, and sometimes with members of the Management Committee. Several tutors commented on how they appreciated having this room, though not all choose to go there for coffee; one tutor said, "I like my ladies and I want to talk to them." [32]

Tutors, like the students, enjoy the atmosphere of the college:

The college ambience is that of 'stately home' combined with feeling of 'own home', and of friendship and understanding which is the result of like-minded people working and relaxing together. [33]

A new tutor, after her first visit, reported, "The ethos I have picked up is one of real 'care'. The attention to detail in the accommodation – there is a real desire that everyone should enjoy their stay."

The students come to the college to get expert tutors, and they are not disappointed. In their response to the questionnaire the students showed that they were most satisfied with the standard of tuition (**Appendix 2**), those on the open courses being 'numerically' the most satisfied. Out of the 493 responses only nine had any complaint about the standard of tuition.

The overwhelming response of students was enthusiasm for the tutors, with comments like "excellent teaching", and "brilliant tutor" being frequent. Students often acknowledged their increased confidence and determination to take what they have learned further.

Fulfilment of the founder's vision?

There is no doubt that this vision, "that the college would provide the very best lecturers and teachers who would offer women a chance of learning whatever their previous experience or stage in life," has been met:

> Confidence in what I am doing, trying out ideas that I would not have dreamed of trying before. I would like to do more; perhaps even City and Guilds.

> All the tutors are at the top of their chosen skill and one goes home enthusiastic to continue and explore possibilities.

> … one of the best tutors … his enthusiasm and encouragement bring out hidden talents in his students. [34]

CHAPTER TWELVE

"... WIDEN HER HORIZONS ..."

VISION OF THE FOUNDERS
That here a member might widen her horizons, and be led on to something
she might not even have considered learning.

---

*In this chapter, in contrast to those around it, there is no attempt to trace the historical development of the vision. Instead the results of the questionnaire (**Appendix 2**) are used to show how the vision is being fulfilled for the members today.*

Most women who join a local WI do so because they want to make friends and join in the social activities of the group; they are unlikely to join for 'education'. It is only through being offered a variety of opportunities to 'widen her horizons' – and taking them – that a member comes to appreciate just how much she has learned through her WI membership.

In 1985 the author asked the hundred or so members who were attending a conference in Dorset to fill in a short questionnaire. They were asked what they felt they had learned as a result of belonging to the WI. The answers included the expected list of crafts; there was one member who said that she had learned 'upholstery and tolerance'. But 20% said they had gained confidence to speak in public. When asked what they would like to learn, the answers varied from DIY to bird watching, from photography to hot air ballooning. In true outreach fashion, the WI draws women in for friendship and then leads them on to learn and experience things they would never have considered possible. [1]

At her local WI meeting a member will hear about the opportunities available to her in both her Federation and at Denman College. She may first hear about Denman when she learns that her Federation is taking a Federation weekend at the college, or she might see the college programme on display and decide to book, or she might win her WI's bursary.

Throughout the 50 years of the college's existence about half the people who came were attending the college for the first time. About a third of those who come now have some sort of bursary from their WI. This proportion has increased over recent years; in 1987 only a fifth had a bursary. [2] **Figure 12.1** shows how the total membership of the WI nationally and the number attending the college have changed over the years.

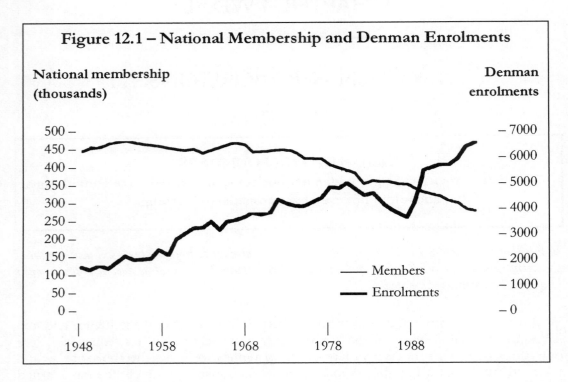

Figure 12.1 – National Membership and Denman Enrolments

2.5% of the membership attended the college in 1996, over half of whom were coming for the first time. The college is attended by about 6,000 WI members every year, of whom about 3,000 are going for the first time. During a woman's membership of the organisation, which probably lasts about 20 years, some 60,000 women make their first Denman visits, representing a quarter of the membership.

What do members expect of the WI?

In September 1994 the Cheshire Federation commissioned a survey to investigate the views of members and to find out what sort of organisation they thought they belonged to. [3] I have chosen to use this survey because it is more up to date than the 'Survey of Attitudes to Women's Institutes' commissioned by NFWI and carried out by Strathclyde University in 1980. 1,162 members completed questionnaires, a 54% response. When asked what they felt was the main benefit of membership, 95% felt that it was 'making friends' whilst 32% felt it was 'improving education'. 76% of the respondents rated Denman College as a 'useful facility'; when they were asked to make suggestions for improving the range of facilities and activities, 'training and education' came top of the list.

The conclusions drawn by the market researchers who conducted this survey were that members consider the main benefit of belonging to the WI is friendship, but they do also acknowledge that the WI educates and builds confidence. [4]

The fact that three quarters of members thought that Denman was a 'useful facility' indicates considerable support even from those who have not been.

The single most strong indicator for going to Denman is length of membership of the WI. **Figure 12.2** illustrates this graphically. Of those members who had never been on a course and who completed the questionnaire (**Appendix 2**) only about one in six said that they were not interested in going, though if we also include those who said they did not know enough about the college, the figure rises to one in five. A quarter of the respondents said that they hoped to get to Denman College sometime.

It would seem that WI members expect some level of 'education' from the organisation, and whether they have been to Denman or not they approve of the WI having its own college.

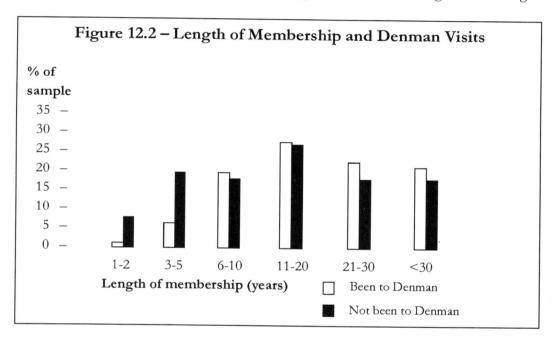

Figure 12.2 – Length of Membership and Denman Visits

Who are the WI members who come to Denman (and who are those who don't?)

They are older women – Almost half of those who come to Denman are in the 56 to 65 age group and well over three quarters of them come from households of one or two people. These are women who probably have fewer caring responsibilities and more disposable income than younger women, and they may be retired with more free time.

Just under a quarter of the students are in the 45 to 55 age group, and of those half come from households with three or more people in them. This group of women have heavier caring responsibilities and half are in paid work, thus they may find it more difficult to get away.

They live in rural areas – Three quarters of the students described themselves as living in a rural or semirural area. These women are likely to have fewer opportunities to get specialist adult education classes near where they live.

They have left school at 16 or under – just over half of the students coming to the college left school at 16 or under – 9% at under 14. 28% of the students have no formal qualifications, 30% have O level or its equivalent. The college is able to offer learning opportunities to groups who had not had them earlier in their lives.

With regard to participation in adult education, WI members are far from typical of the population as a whole. A NIACE survey [5] has established that 41% of women have not participated in any form of education or training since leaving school. Of WI members who have not been to Denman, this figure is reduced to only 16%. If we were to include those members who have been to Denman, the figure would be lower still, since all of them, by definition, have participated in adult education!

It is interesting to see how these figures break down by school leaving age, which the NIACE survey identifies as the best predictor for participation. **Table 12.1** summarises the findings:

Table 12.1 – Percentages of Sample who have never done any Adult Education		
Terminal age of education	NIACE sample†	WI members*
Under 16	56	23
16-17	38	15
18 and over	14	10

* Based on sample of members who have never been to Denman College
†Men and women

It can be seen that the WI member who left school at under 16 is twice as likely to have been a participant as a member of the general population. If she remained in education till she was 18 or more, however, she is scarcely distinguishable in this respect. Whether this is to be interpreted as saying something about the sort of woman who joins the WI, or whether it implies that WI membership encourages participation in adult education cannot be determined from the information that is available!

Denman is providing opportunities for the older woman learner, and the woman who left school at the minimum leaving age.

How do students hear about Denman College?

The satisfied customer is always the best advertisement – a third of respondents had heard about the college from another member who had been. A quarter said they had heard from the president or secretary of their WI. A smaller number had heard from the Federation Denman representative (10%) or at a Federation meeting (10%), while a few (4%) had first

(9) Above: The teaching centre, with its interesting hexagonal design, taken before the foyer was extended.

(10) Right: Home Acres. Converted huts left by the RAF c1955. Run jointly with the Berkshire Rural Domestic Home Economy Centre.

(11) Top: Tea break for canners in the 1940s. Did any of these members have their certificate in competence to can?

(12) Above: Tinkering class at Scaynes Hill WI in Sussex circa 1920.

(13) Left: Margaret Deneke playing to members for the 'joint session' on a Thursday evening in the 'Big House' atmosphere of the drawing room – early 1950s.

(14) Above: Gardening course in the walled garden in 1949. Mary Clarke, Head Gardener and Instructor, "shows pupils the right way to build a compost heap".

(15) Right: Family Week in 1959. Joyce Cormack's twins, Hilary and Felicity, are in the centre.

(16) Top left: Poultry course in Home Acres 1950s.

(17) Top right: Course on Beekeeping 1960s.

(18) Above: Car maintenance 1970s.

(19) Right: NFWI Training workshop 1990s.

(20) Below: Use your sewing machine 1980s.

(21) Left: Painting on China 1990s.

heard of the college by reading articles in *Home and Country*. Coming to Denman can become a family tradition; several respondents wrote that they had first heard of the college from their mothers, or even in one case from 'mother and grandmother'.

Members also learned about the college by coming on a day visit with their WI, from a VCO, or by reading an article in a newspaper. Many local newspapers give the WI a special column; in the North Yorkshire *Ackrill Press* for 1st November 1996 one could have read:

> Have you every heard of Encaustic art? Neither had I until I visited Denman College in October, and found ten WI members had signed up for a course on that mysterious subject. Yet another old craft revived and being enjoyed by WI members… [6]

One member first learned about Denman "from an article by Mary Stott in the *Manchester Guardian* about 1950." That she could still remember it shows what an impression it made.

Why do students come to the college?

The questionnaire invited students to rate a selection of reasons for coming to the college. The results are presented in **Table 12.2**.

Table 12.2 – Reasons for Coming to the College*	% of All	Fed.	NFWI	Open
to get away from domestic routine	18	23	14	17
to have an enjoyable break	60	71	46	58
to learn something completely new	73	77	74	70
to extend my knowledge/skills	81	82	85	80
to be with other WI members	53	65	59	42
to be in lovely surroundings	66	75	59	63
to enable me to do my job better	32	16	87	19
to get a qualification	9	3	27	5
to have expert tutors	80	82	79	80
to exchange ideas with others	67	71	83	57
because I won the bursary	16	5	9	26
to have some intensive study without distractions	40	33	42	44
to get a specialist course not available at home	52	45	61	53

*Percentages of respondents answering 'Important' or 'Extremely Important' to the question, 'Here are a number of reasons for coming to Denman. How important is each of them to you?' Respondents are grouped according to the kind of course that they were on: Fed. = Federation, NFWI = Training course, Open = Open programme.

From these results it is clear that members come on open courses at the college to 'extend their knowledge and skills' and to 'have expert tutors'. These reasons were rated as 'very important' by four fifths of the respondents. Almost as important was 'to learn something new'. 'To be in lovely surroundings', 'to have an enjoyable break', and 'to exchange ideas with others' were all rated as important by more than half the respondents. More than half the respondents also gave 'to get a specialist course not available at home' as a reason for coming.

So members come to the college on open courses primarily for educational reasons, with social reasons second and vocational reasons the lowest. The balance is different when we look at the responses for those who had been on NFWI training courses. For them social reasons are the lowest and vocational reasons second, which is not surprising as members have come on these courses to be trained to carry out some rôle in the organisation.

Why do members not come to the college?

If most of those who have never been to the college show an interest in it, why do they not attend? At some times in the past there could have been problems in getting a place on the course of one's choice, but this is no longer the case. It would seem that it is more a question of members finding time to go in a busy life, or getting away from domestic or other responsibilities. About half of the respondents cited reasons of this kind.

Cost is also quite important; one fifth of the respondents mentioned the cost, either of travel or of the course itself or both. Here are two examples:

> I would love to stay at Denman College, but as a pensioner the cost of just three nights, travel and extra for course is too much. I can have a five day coach tour for less.

> The cost is very high if you have a young family.

When comparing the members who go to the college with those that have not been, the questionnaire results do reveal some differences. Those who don't go are likely to have left school earlier and to have fewer or no academic qualifications. One might expect this to be reflected in lack of interest in the college, but it is not. Members who were in full-time education to age 18 and beyond are just as likely to say that they are not interested as those who left school at 14 or 15.

They also differ in their participation in other WI educational activities. Most strikingly, among those who had been to Denman, almost two thirds had also been to WI day schools. In the other group, little more than a third had done this.

Difficulty in travel may be important. Although the college is situated in the heart of England, travelling to it is not easy for members who live at a distance and possibly in a quite remote rural area. When the college first opened there was a branch railway to Abingdon; now the nearest station is either Oxford or Didcot, both about eight miles, and an expensive taxi ride away. The nearest bus station is in Oxford.

The perceived problem of travelling to the college can discourage potential students. Analysis of the questionnaire showed that the majority of those who came on open courses travelled alone, three quarters travelling by car. It was surprising that so few shared a car; when a member has been accepted on a course she is given a postcard to complete to send to her Federation's Denman Representative indicating either if she can offer a lift or would like one. From this figure it would seem that the scheme to offer lifts is not much used.

Perhaps this also explains why inability to drive is a significant factor in keeping potential students away; non-drivers are less likely to go to Denman. As might be expected, those who live far away from the college are more likely to say that their reason for not going is that it is too far to travel, but they are also more likely to say that they don't want to go alone. Maybe the car-sharing scheme needs to be more actively promoted to encourage more members who say they don't wish to travel alone to get to the college.

One of the reasons for the success of the Federation visits is that the Federation can book coaches, or arrange car sharing, and members can be transported door to door. Almost all of those on Federation visits travelled with the Federation.

In recent years the college has negotiated a reduced coach fare scheme with National Express. Members coming on a course can apply for a £16 voucher which will cover their travel to Oxford on a National Express coach from anywhere in the country. The college taxi picks up students from the bus (and railway) station. In 1995/6, 274 students applied for vouchers from the college (4% of students).

In a further attempt to help those who live in distant Federations with their travel costs, the Denman Travel Fund was set up in memory of National Chairman Agnes Salter who died in office in 1988. The income from the fund is divided between all Federations (on a sliding scale depending on distance from Marcham and the size of the Federation). The fund continues to grow and the interest is distributed every two years. In 1997 £10,039 was distributed.

Why do students choose a particular course?

When asked to explain why they chose a particular course, over half of the students who were on open programme courses indicated that they had chosen their course because it was an interest they already had; of these a third said it was an existing interest or hobby, and nearly a fifth specified that they wanted to extend their knowledge or skill for a particular purpose. One member wrote:

> Although trained as a caterer, detailed chocolate work was not included, so I wanted to gain further knowledge.

9% replied that they had chosen the course for the particular tutor, either because they had been on a course with that tutor before or they had heard from others that the tutor was good. Three quarters of the responses showed that members made their choice primarily for educational reasons.

Those who come on Federation courses have much less choice. There are usually only five courses on offer, so there were comments such as, "it was the only one on the Federation weekend which appealed to me."

Those on training courses did not usually choose their courses, as such students are typically sent by their Federation. Some (11%) sounded slightly unwilling when they wrote comments like "had to do it," many of these being VCOs coming to refresher courses.

How satisfied were the students with their experience at the college?

The majority of students are highly satisfied with their visit to Denman. The questionnaire invited respondents to rate different aspects of the college, from tuition to accommodation. The students had come to the college to get expert tutors, and they were not disappointed, more than 90% gave high ratings to the tuition. They also rated equally highly the teaching facilities, the information provided during the course and the welcome they received. More than 80% were equally satisfied with all other aspects of their experience with the exception of the shop. Even the shop was rated 'below average' by only 5% of the students. One Federation Denman Representative summed this up when she wrote, "As Denman rep. I am in a position to say that the complaints from our members are very few and far between. It is a super place to learn."

More detailed analysis shows that there is only a very small difference between the responses from those on the Federation visits, training courses and open courses. Those on the training courses are the most critical. They are the people who are most likely to have been several times before, and they were the ones who answered the earlier question about why they came as "had to" or "was sent"!

Students who had graded any aspect of their experience as unsatisfactory were asked to explain what was wrong. The largest number of complaints (22) was about having accommodation in 'Croft', a building which has since been demolished. 16 people complained about food, six of them saying, "Food not as good as usual"! Ten people felt that they had not been given adequate information before they came. Insufficiently clear instructions on what they had to bring with them for the course was the main complaint.

In July 1997 a team from the Adult Residential Colleges Association (ARCA) carried out an independent review of the college. Similar questions were asked of the students who were attending three particular courses. These were asked to classify various aspects of their experience as 'very good', 'good', 'adequate' or 'poor'. 'General atmosphere' received the highest rating, with 96% classifying it as very good. 82% considered both the tuition and the residential accommodation as 'very good'. The lowest rating was for pre-course information; 23% considered it only 'adequate'. This is an area that the Management Committee realises they must improve, but they can take heart from the fact that 100% of these students said that the course was very good value for money. [7]

What do students gain from a Denman course?

Most obviously, of course, they learn something, whether it be a new craft or skill, an introduction to a new area of knowledge or a deeper understanding of something that they are already interested in. But they gain other, less obvious things as well.

In order to try to discover something about these things, the students who filled in the questionnaires were asked to describe "anything else that you have gained from your stay." About a third of those who chose to do this wrote of the pleasures of learning. One student wrote, "I don't think I've ever stopped learning since I joined the WI and Denman has enhanced that knowledge." Another student wrote of the satisfaction she had from "knowing you have improved even though not in an earth-shattering way." The encouragement to learn was appreciated by a student who wrote, "At Denman the word FAILURE does not exist. Everyone learns something; maybe not always immediately obvious."

Almost equally important, was the fellowship or companionship that students experienced. Many reported that they stayed in touch after they left the college, sometimes by continuing to share what they have learned (an interesting example is described on p 111) but more often just as friends. Some respondents noted that they still wrote to or visited friends they had made at Denman years before.

One member tells a moving story about keeping in touch with someone she met on a course:

> We would exchange cards … I had this year a most touching note to say her husband had committed suicide and "Do you remember, you said to me once – be yourself. You gave me courage. You did not know me or what I was going through, but you saw deeper into me. I don't forget." [8]

She goes on to say that she had no idea that she had any qualities of "knowingness", but on receiving this note she phoned up her friend and had a "wonderful conversation." They hope to meet again at Denman. This shows how a course may be short but strong bonds can form; there is even one member who tells of a romantic attachment. [9]

One student wrote that she had gained "Company of other like-minded women; time for myself and enthusiasm for a future course"; another, with a touch of wistfulness, wrote that she found "the all-female atmosphere wonderfully friendly and supportive, though sadly eroded in recent years as more and more men are allowed on courses."

One effect of a visit to Denman that would greatly have pleased the founders is that many women report an increase in confidence and self-esteem. "[Confidence that] my work is as good as others"; "I gained confidence and great pleasure in exploring my own capabilities"; "confidence in meeting and talking to new people from all over the country; also confidence in attempting new projects". One student wrote of help in "finding myself in middle age; often difficult for a woman once the children have gone," and another student said she had gained "confidence, self esteem, awareness, knowledge, and enthusiasm to build on knowledge already gained."

One other theme recurred, that of the WI 'family'. One member wrote of how much she had appreciated the "experience of mixing with WI members taking different courses and coming from all over the country – friendliness," and another described the "feeling of being part of a family of women from all areas and walks of life."

The pride of ownership is sensed, as one member explained, "The comradeship of belonging to the owning organisation gives the students and the college something that is unique." The opportunity to share ideas when "meeting members from other Federations" and, as one member who had been at the college for the first time put it, "an opportunity to talk and make friends with members of other WIs, and a sense of belonging to a bigger family."

Since 1993 a small number of open courses have offered an opportunity for the students to gain some form of accreditation (see Chapter 14). The questionnaire replies show that 7% of those on open courses obtained Open College Network (OCN) credits. Other awards included WI certificates, which were mostly gained by those on NFWI courses (16%) and included judges, trainers and demonstrators, as well as VCOs. Qualifications from outside bodies included: Sports Leaders Award, and Croquet Association Teacher's Award. The 2% on open courses who received certificates were either gaining Home Economics Certificates, the RSA Advanced Spoken English Certificate, or membership of the Institute of Advanced Motorists.

What do students do afterwards?

Students at short-stay colleges (or indeed taking any adult education course) disappear at the end of the course and the college rarely knows what, if anything, the students do subsequently.

The questionnaire replies show that the majority of the students who come on Denman courses follow them up afterwards in some way, formally or informally, and that the effect is felt not only in the WI but also in the wider community. Over half of Denman students shared their experience with their fellow WI members, usually by giving a short talk at a WI meeting, or by displaying what they had made. In many WIs this is expected of a member who has had a bursary. A few members reported that they had tutored or given a demonstration to other WI members.

16% of members shared what they had learned not only with their WI but also with the wider community. A member who had taken a course in church flower arranging reported that she "went on the flower-arranging rota at my church." Others shared what they had learned with members of a local club; an art club, a bridge club, and a University of the Third Age study group were all mentioned. A member who had been on a drama course "put on several plays in the village and entered the Festival."

As a result of a WI member attending 'The Historic Churches of Oxfordshire' a monument has been restored in a village church in Chiddingly, East Sussex:

At one lecture we met Professor Brian Kemp, an authority on church monuments. I spoke to him about our Jefferay Monument, which he told me he had once visited. He said it was an important memorial in much need of repair and that it was one of only two of the early 17th Century in England where two of the figures were upright. [10]

Subsequently, when the church was offered some money, this member wrote to Professor Kemp and with his encouragement and advice she took on the task of co-ordinating the restoration and the accompanying fund raising. The project was completed in March 1997.

The analysis of the questionnaire showed that a quarter of the students built on what they had learned by continuing to work at home. Some students reported reading more about the subject, others practised what they had learned. This varied from one student who said she "tried harder with my writing" and another who "carried on with my new craft at home" to someone who had been on the Advanced Driving course and who claimed that she used what she had learned every day when she drove her car.

Many students reported visiting places, near and far, that they had heard about on their course, sometimes taking their families and friends as well; comments included, "lots of travelling to see paintings", "went to more Shakespeare plays", "visited Florence".

Several students reported joining a local club or association, so that they could continue with their new interest. Several mentioned art clubs, and one member said that her Denman courses led to her getting "Membership of the Society of Limners".

5% of students reported booking for some other course to continue learning. Some were going to come on another course at Denman (sometimes a 'stage 2'), others went on courses locally, including ones run by the WEA or the Open University. One member took private music lessons, and another took lessons with a freelance photographer.

For a few members their experience started them on a path that led to further and higher education:

I hadn't done much history, then I attended a course about William the Conqueror at Denman and got enthusiastic. I am now working on an access course at the local university on 'Relating Past to Present'. [11]

From that first magical visit [to Denman] doing local history, called 'Discovering your Neighbourhood', I knew I had so much information about my community of North Kilworth in Leicestershire, where I have always lived and my family for 4- 5 centuries before me – that I ought to write it down … so I decided to take 'O' level English language… [12]

This member then went on to take 'O' level English Literature and O level Maths and after successfully completing these took British Social History. She has written the history of her own WI.

Eirian Roberts of Clwyd-Denbigh left school at 15, as she was needed at home on the farm. After a life of bringing up a family, and caring for elderly relatives when the children had left home, she wondered what to do. She had been to Denman, on two of the Wales courses, one on 'The Mabinogion' and one on 'Welsh Mythology and the History of Wales' which had fired her interest, so when she saw an advertisement for an external degree course at Aberystwyth University she enrolled, and after seven years of hard studying she has now got her Honours BA degree in Welsh. She is the NFWI Adult Learner of the Year for 1997, receiving her award at the NIACE-Cymru Celebration in May. [13]

It is not the intention that the majority of courses at Denman College should lead to income generating activities, but for a small number of members (6% of questionaire respondents) this has been the result. Some sell the products they have made or grown at WI Markets. Other members sell craft items or paintings:

> Going to Denman College has enabled me to learn skills to pass on to others and I have sold a lot of what I have made. It has given me a push. I'm extremely grateful to the WI and the College. [14]

Learning a craft or a skill and then becoming a tutor, speaker or demonstrator to WIs, at Denman, as part of LEA adult education services, or elsewhere, has provided numerous WI members with jobs. Three of them explain:

> I have a lot to thank Denman College for; as well as attending numerous courses on crafts, cookery, gardening, I also attended courses on public speaking, judging, demonstrating and teaching and, after all the wonderful tuition, help and guidance I received over the years, I eventually became a county judge, a tutor in adult education working for the Local Education Authority as a lecturer and demonstrator and it became my full time job. [15]

> I attended a 'Welsh Week' at Denman and chose 'Paper Sculpture' although I had no idea of what it entailed... I made use of this craft in many ways for a long time afterward... I visited almost every WI in Caernarfonshire as well as many in neighbouring federations and other organisations, giving demonstrations and classes... [16]

> I owe my career to this place [Denman]! I was involved in co-ordinating 'The Complete You' when Miriam Stoppard came with TV. I felt that I could do as good a job as the person who came to do the colour co-ordination then, so I got myself trained and have been doing it ever since, at Denman, in the Federations and to outside organisations, even to Marks and Spencers. [17]

The 'income generation' is not always for personal gain; it can be raising money for charity. Sheila Gray, a retired police sergeant from Slough, raises money for the Royal National Lifeboat Institute as a result of coming to Denman on a 'Middle Eastern Dancing' course. She says, "when I retired I felt I've got the time – I'm going to do something with it. I've always wanted to do belly dancing." Sheila is now an expert on the history and origin of the dance and on making the costumes. She raises substantial funds by giving performances for groups and societies, and has even been back to Denman to teach when the tutor who had been booked fell ill at the last minute. [18]

Some members have even claimed that Denman has 'changed their life':

'Denman College changed my life. I have tried many things but flowers are what I'm good at. I am now a demonstrator, tutor and judge.' [19]

In 1968, after hearing a talk on the radio about corn dollies, I booked up for a weekend at Denman… the Chairman of our Handicrafts committee asked me to provide one for a Golden Jubilee display at a local show. After this I was invited onto the speakers panel and went out all over the county and beyond doing talks, demonstrations, classes, exhibitions, shows, judging competitions, even lending out corn dollies for shop window displays. In 1976 I had a corn dolly accepted for the Tomorrow's Heirlooms exhibition at the Commonwealth Institute. My local museum asked me to make a set for their permanent collection. I have met so many people and learned so much from them, all because of what was intended to be a leisurely weekend break at Denman College. [20]

My visit to Denman was to prove quite a turning point in my life… I had been in a car accident and had given up my office job and was searching for more stimulation in my life… Thanks to a bursary I enjoyed a course for press officers… I became press officer for my institute and in addition for many years the village correspondent for the local newspapers. I now find that I have more leisure time and, encouraged by that memorable few days at Denman, am capable of writing for a wider readership. [21]

Conclusion

The founders' vision was that by coming to Denman a member might widen her horizons, and be led on to something she might not even have considered learning. In this chapter we have show that this vision has truly been realised. Let more of the members speak for themselves: [22]

Denman College is certainly the jewel in the crown and something every member should treasure and support.

Denman College is marvellous – we should promote it more.

Some Denman myths need to be exploded. It IS much easier to get into courses now. It IS more reasonable than other similar college courses. It DOES cater for all types of women. Standard of accommodation IS improving all round. I am convinced that appropriate courses and better marketing would bring in younger women.

I attended a travel course at Denman in 1965; I joined the Berkshire travel committee which led to me arranging 65 Federation holidays; in 1997 a tour of Canada – it certainly widened my horizons.

CHAPTER THIRTEEN

"... Focus for the Educational Work of the Organisation ..."

VISION OF THE FOUNDERS
That the College would provide a focus for, and give a framework to,
the educational work of the organisation.

Introduction

As a short-stay residential adult education college intimately associated with a national membership organisation, Denman is probably unique. [1] When the college was founded there were no models for how such an association might work and it is probably fair to say that the history of the relationship between the college and the National Federation presents a series of attempts to find such a model. None of them has been entirely satisfactory and it may be of some interest to examine them, in order to illustrate the problems inherent in such a relationship.

This chapter falls into three sections. The first considers the various management structures used during the life of the college, the second section reviews the staffing of the college, and the final section considers financial questions.

Section 1 – Management

Charitable Status

In 1947 Denman College was set up as a trust. It was at the same time registered with the Ministry of Education under section 87 of the Education Act 1944 as an educational establishment. In 1963, as required by the Charities Act of 1960, the college was (re)registered as a separate charity with the Ministry of Education. At the same time NFWI was registered with the Charity Commission. In 1974, under section 1 of the Education Act 1973, responsibility for educational charities including "voluntary establishments of further education" was transferred from the Department of Education and Science to the Charity Commission. [2]

The college is now registered as a charity with the charitable objects of providing "a college, residential or otherwise, for the education of members of the Women's Institutes in accordance with the objects of the body corporate called the National Federation of Women's Institutes of England and Wales, the Channel Islands and the Isle of Man."

Trustees

When NFWI was an unincorporated body, separate trustees for the college were never appointed. It was assumed that the NFWI Trustees would also assume trusteeship of the college, although the formal appointment of the trustees never referred to their responsibility for the college. "This is implicit. The Charity Commission has never questioned this." [3]

After the incorporation of NFWI in 1990, the National Executive Committee of NFWI became the corporate Trustees of the Denman (College) Trust. The land and buildings are held in trust on behalf of the WI members. The management of the college is delegated to the Denman Management Committee and the Principal, as laid out in a Scheme of Delegation.

The rôle of the college in the educational work of the organisation.

The founder's vision was that the college would "provide a focus for and give a framework to the educational work of the organisation." Throughout the 50 years there have been tensions and uncertainties about exactly how the rôles of NFWI and Denman College interrelate.

Before the college was set up Lady Albermarle, the National Chairman, had suggested that there should be a Board of Governors, which would include some professional educationalists. However, this was not adopted, although the suggestion of a Board of Governors was to be raised again at intervals over the coming years. Lady Albermarle could see clearly that there might be confusions. At the conference held in December 1947, when all the subcommittee members came together to discuss how the college was to be used, Lady Albermarle took the chair and introduced the discussions by saying:

> We need to clarify our picture of the place of the college in the movement. There are two approaches:
>
> 1. As an educational experiment founded on the WI organisation and providing simple liberal education for the countrywoman and giving new realisation of the dignity of her calling as a home builder.
>
> 2. As an extension of our work and a training ground for leaders and teachers and technicians through whom the influence of the college would be spread. [4]

In fact they chose to do both. Having dismissed the suggestion for a Governing Body, the Executive Committee decided to divide the running of the college between two committees. The story of the management of the college over the 50 years is one of regular changes, where the focus of the decision making swings one way and then the other. **Figure 13.1** attempts to summarise the different ways in which the college has been managed over those years.

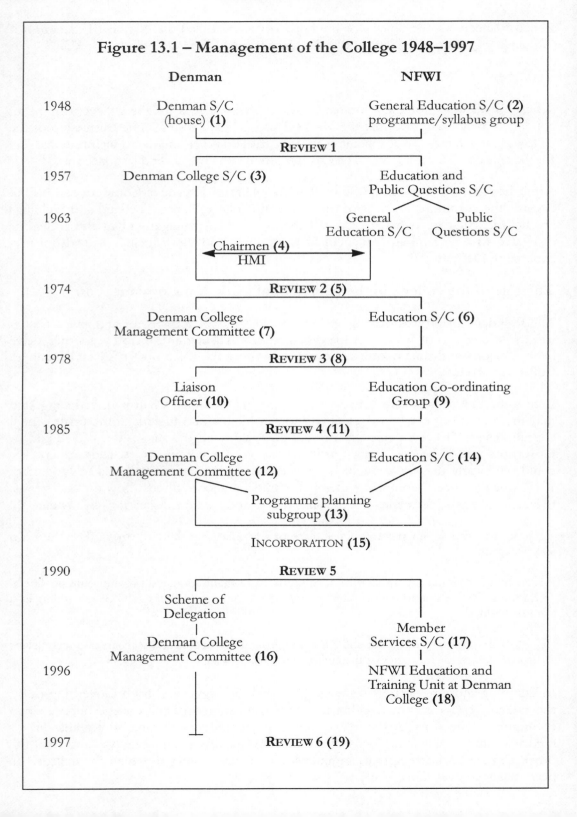

Figure 13.1 – Management of the College 1948–1997

Notes to Figure 13.1 – Management of the College
(All quotations are from the Annual Reports (AnnReps) for the appropriate year)

(1) Denman College S/C was chaired by Lady Brunner and looked after the fabric.

(2) The General Education S/C had new terms of reference, "to plan the Denman College syllabus in relation to the other educational services provided by headquarters." It appointed a 'syllabus' group whose name was later changed to 'programme'.

(3) After Review I a newly appointed Denman College S/C took on responsibility for both fabric and the programme.

(4) There was liaison between the General Education and Denman S/Cs. The Chairmen attended each other's meetings and the HMI appointed to NFWI by the Ministry of Education served on both. The Denman College Subcommittee was large: the four National Officers, 14 members from Federations (appointed by NFWI), three members of the National Executive committee, and two co-opted members.

(5) In 1974, Review II of NFWI committee structure, the work of the General Education S/C and the educational work of Denman College were allocated to one Education S/C **(6).** On this were "represented various educational interests of the movement." Membership included the HMI and representatives from several other educational organisations, eg NIACE, the BBC. The Denman College Management Committee **(7)** now only dealt with "matters concerning the house, estate and staff."

(8) Review III followed the report of a working party 'On the Future Education Policy' which decided that "As the work of the whole movement is educational in the broadest sense, it was felt that the rôle of the NFWI Education Subcommittee should be to act as a co-ordinating and stimulating body, not working in isolation."

(9) The Education Co-ordinating Group, chaired by the National Chairman, was set up for all S/C chairmen to discuss and co-ordinate their educational work where outside experts could advise. The remit was "to co-ordinate and rationalise the services offered by the NFWI to the counties and to plan the Denman College programme in conjunction with the Warden and Director of Studies."

The Denman College S/C was disbanded and one Executive Committee member was appointed as a Liaison Officer **(10)** to work with the Principal. There was no body with particular concern for the fabric.

(11) Following the 'crisis' and the decision to 'Save Denman' a new Management Committee **(12)** was set up with greater delegated powers and a remit "to ensure that the [NFWI Education] policy and training were implemented at the college as well as overseeing and monitoring every aspect of running a successful, profitable and secure adult education establishment." This committee included a number of experts who could advise on buildings, estate, finance and education who were full voting members. There was a Programme Planning sub-group **(13)** which included all the national S/C chairmen which met once a year to discuss and advise on future programmes.

(14) The NFWI Education S/C's brief was to "determine the educational policy of the whole movement and co-ordinate the content and conduct of all training carried out nationally". This committee also had outside experts. A full time education and training officer was appointed. However at this time the Chairman of the Education S/C did not sit on the Denman Management Committee (unlike **(3)** and **(4)**)

(15) NFWI became incorporated and set up the Denman Trust. The Denman Management Committee **(16)** continued as before, but now was responsible to the Trustees. The reorganisation of NFWI structure and committees led to a period when the education brief was less clear. The Member Services S/C **(17)** dealt with training. In 1996 the NFWI Education and Training Unit **(18)** was set up, located in a house in the college grounds.

(19) Yet another review of Denman College is commissioned by NFWI.

There had been a well-established General Education Subcommittee, on which a variety of outside 'experts' sat, for many years. This committee was reformed, still including 'outside experts', and given new terms of reference that included planning the college programme, in a way integrated with the other educational work.

The *ad hoc* committee which had originally been set up to find a house was disbanded as its job was done, but was immediately resurrected, with Elizabeth Brunner remaining in the chair, to oversee the house and estate. At first it was called the Denman College Subcommittee, though the name was subsequently changed to 'House'. This committee was made up of WI members only and also included Dora Tomkinson from the original committee.

The frequency with which the organisation has reviewed how it should govern the college is indicative of the difficulty of getting the right balance between the general educational policy of NFWI and the specific way in which this is implemented at the college. As is the case for most voluntary organisations and charities, those who carry the ultimate responsibility are the 'volunteers'. Whoever the membership choose to elect to the National Executive Committee bear this legal responsibility. It is unlikely that many of these women will have had past experience in governing a college and the experience and advice of experts is very important, but for much of the time the 'experts' were on the Education Subcommittee meeting in London and not on the 'House' Subcommittee meeting at Denman.

Review I – 1957

After nearly ten years the pattern of the college programme was formed, indeed had become almost too set, and for much of this time most of the energies of the Education Subcommittee had been given over its planning. Now the NFWI Executive Committee decided to alter the terms of reference of the Denman College Subcommittee so that the college would be administered by a single body. "This was not only a better arrangement from the administrative point of view, but gave the new committee far more scope to plan future policy." [5] The terms of reference of this new committee were:

1. To advise on the administration of Denman College.
2. To advise on the education programme of the college in full co-operation with NFWI subcommittees.
3. To have authority to delegate a full measure of responsibility to the Warden.
4. To supervise the finances of the college.
5. To submit periodical budgets and reports to Office and Finance, and to advise the Executive Committee on the fees to be charged to students, and on the expenses of administration.
6. To advise on the appointment and work of the college staff.
7. To advise, in co-operation with the Berkshire County Council, on the use of Home Acres in connection with the college courses. [6]

On this committee were Lady Brunner, Charlotte Bawden, Margaret Rotherham and Sylvia Gray from the old House Subcommittee and two newcomers, Lady Angelsey and Dr Enid Browne. Two members were co-opted and became unofficial 'advisers' on the educational work, Marjorie Fisher, an author and critic, and Mrs Ing, an Oxford don. The responsibility for the educational programme was now much more in the hands of the college committee.

Review II – 1960

In this year Marjorie Moller became Warden, after a difficult period with acting Wardens (pp 188–189). She had considerable experience of management as Headmistress of a large girls' school and she was not happy with the system. The following extract from the minutes of the College Subcommittee describe the shortcomings which she found and what was done about them:

> It was first suggested that the committee should be divided to deal with different aspects of the college management, but there was another plea for less committee 'interference' and for more responsibility to be given to the Warden.
>
> Miss Moller, invited to put forward her view, explained that the initial establishment of the college, by people with little experience of the organisation and needs of a residential college had focused attention on the quite lovely equipment of the rooms but had fogged any view of the real educational work of the college. She felt that the plan of the organisation needed overhaul now that the college was enjoying a period of stability.
>
> ... there was a need for help and advice from professional and qualified women, experts in various branches of education, to help the Warden, to keep a check on educational policy, to provide wide information on the trends in adult education and to give advice from experience of residential communities.
>
> Temporarily Miss Moller asked that there could be appointment of up to three to the sub-committee with special knowledge and gifts until the whole question of reorganisation could be considered ... members felt that the College Committee was ... on a somewhat different footing from other subcommittees and it was finally agreed that the Denman College committee should be empowered to appoint three experienced educationalists to serve on the committee until the end of the present year. [7]

The 'whole question of reorganisation' was considered, and in the end it did not affect the Denman Subcommittee very much. It continued with responsibility for both fabric and programme and the HMI appointed by the Ministry of Education was the only 'outside' member. By contrast the National Education Subcommittee included the same HMI and representatives of the National Institute of Adult Education (NIAE) and the BBC.

The Ministry of Education chose to appoint an HMI to the organisation because they gave an annual grant for the 'liberal education for women'. As part of this grant was used at Denman it was appropriate that the HMI should serve on both the national and the Denman committees. The various HMIs attended most of the meetings of both the Education Subcommittee and the Denman College Subcommittee and took an active part in their proceedings. Brenda George, the HMI in 1973, wrote to Sylvia Gray (National Chairman at the time):

... about Denman College courses. While recognising the values of the college to the movement, Mrs George felt that perhaps it was not moving forward in the new methods of learning and not making the contribution it could in educating the membership for community service. If a research project could be undertaken it might be of great value to the organisation and to the education of women generally... [8]

At the following meeting:

... Mrs George was disappointed that there was no evidence that we were prepared to take any of her suggestions further .... she particularly hoped to see some project recording the work of Denman College and thought it would be possible to find money to finance it ... some doubt was expressed as to who would be interested in such a report were it to be written. Mrs George felt not nearly enough was known about the college within the movement and in the general education field ... inconclusive discussion... [9]

Review III – 1974

A full review of the educational work of the WI was undertaken at a time when the whole organisation was reacting to the changes in local government boundaries. Some completely new Federations were formed and many WIs were moved from one Federation to a neighbouring one. The main reason for going through this painful process was that many Federations still received grants from their Local Authorities to help with classes; it would help to ensure that this continued if the boundaries equated. By the time the Unitary Authority boundaries were being drawn up in the 1990s this was no longer the case; very few Federations continued to receive any grants from their Local Authorities.

The 1974 review changed the balance again between the London committees and Denman College, bringing the responsibility for the Denman programme back to the NFWI Education Subcommittee. In effect the college staff drew up the programme and presented it to the NFWI Education Subcommittee for approval. The Denman College Committee reverted to being just a house committee once more.

The Russell Report, which reviewed non-vocational adult education and recommended ways of setting up a system of education 'continuing through life', was published in 1973. This review stimulated NFWI to produce its own consultative document on the education policy of the National Federation. County Federation representatives came to a conference held at Denman in 1977 to discuss the policy paper and also to hear "Sir Lionel Russell give an outstanding address on 'The Future of Adult Education'." [10] An NFWI working party 'On the Future Education Policy' was set up – comprising the four National Officers, the Chairman of the Denman Subcommittee, a Federation Chairman, and Arthur Stock, the Director of NIACE – which consulted widely, receiving responses from 49 out of the then 63 Federations. They visited other organisations working in the field of adult education and a variety of adult education colleges.

The College Subcommittee gave its views:

Lady Brunner thought that the committee was in danger of becoming too inward looking and that ideas from persons outside would widen the field and broaden our horizons. It was handicapping for the committee to be drawn only from executive members. Mrs Shallard would like executive to consider having a Board of Governors... the Warden felt that there was a risk that contact with the Education Committee would get less... [11]

The result of all this consultation and discussion was a full report, [12] which made a number of recommendations (only some of which were subsequently followed). The most significant of these was the formation of an 'Educational Forum' (later renamed the Co-ordinating Group) where all the subcommittee chairmen could discuss and co-ordinate their educational work, supported by various advisers.

The other recommendations included:

... to appoint an Adult Education Officer in the near future, based at Denman College and working at headquarters, at Denman College and in the Counties... The ultimate aim would be a system of paid part-time Regional Liaison Officers... [13]

This recommendation was not implemented at the time because of financial constraints. NFWI applied to the Department of Education and Science for extra funds but they were not successful.

When considering the rôle of Denman, the Working Party decided:

The College is very much part of the total NFWI and is increasingly becoming a *communications centre* for the whole of the movement. Co-operation between the college and the other parts of the movement is of vital importance. It is this that makes it different from many other residential colleges and its function in this area could probably be expanded. [14]

They went on to make various suggestions as to how the national subcommittees could use Denman to publicise the work they were doing and the things that they had to offer to WIs. A new category of courses was suggested ('C' courses), which would attempt to improve communication. Such courses might be conferences of Federation officers, study conferences, or workshops. "They must be true Conferences, i.e. there must be conferring and interaction." [15] The 'C' category was never used but this type of conference did become more common.

The report also discussed the planning of the Denman programme which was felt to be:

... geared too closely to the financial situation, i.e. to the need to fill the beds and to keep the fees as low as possible. The balance is so fine that it is not always possible for the college to do what it might like to have done educationally... While the college must continue to play its part in maintaining the practical skills, especially those in which instruction is not available locally, it must also provide opportunities for members to learn about contemporary issues. [16]

As a result of this review, the Education Co-ordinating Group was set up:

... signifying yet another logical step forward in the process of integrating and inter-relating all aspects of the work. This group considers all the plans of work of all subcommittees, plans the Denman College programme and keeps a watching eye on all educational developments inside and outside the movement. [17]

Now Denman College was not to have any committee specially to look after its concerns. The committee was replaced by a Liaison Officer, a member of the National Executive Committee, who worked with the Principal and served on the Education Co-ordinating Group.

What happened from 1980 onwards, however, was that the Education Co-ordinating Group spent much of its time looking outwards and 'keeping a watching eye on educational developments outside' and probably not enough time considering the requirements of Denman College:

Recognition of the unique rôle of the NFWI in the provision of adult and continuing education in rural areas was confirmed in October 1980 by the appointment by the Secretary of State of Anne Ballard, the General Secretary, to the Advisory Council for Adult Continuing Education (ACACE). The council was asked to give particular attention to distance learning and the use of volunteers.

The organisation continued to press for closer co-operation with Local Education Authorities and other institutions so that the existing partnership between the voluntary and statutory sectors in adult education would become both more significant and more beneficial to the millions of potential consumers and also provide a fulfilling and creative answer to the likely increase in non-work hours in the future. [18]

Since the college had no committee of its own at this time, much responsibility fell on the Liaison Officer, Kate Foss. Herself a teacher, she had knowledge of and interest in education, though she says now that her main job was to watch the finances. She and the Principal, Hilda Jones, worked easily together. As Kate said:

Denman was part of her [Hilda's] soul ... hours didn't matter. [19]

Hilda herself, looking back on this time, reflects:

... we had a Liaison Officer and for a few years at the end of the 70s it worked fairly well. But with hindsight, it would have been better for the college if the Denman College management team wasn't abandoned during the 1980s. Helen [Anderson] and I always fought to have a Governing Body to secure its viability, so that they had a body with the well-being of the college in view, rather than just being a sub-committee of National Executive. That was mooted at one time but never got off the ground... [20]

Hilda worked at the college from 1961 to 1981 and in those 20 years saw a variety of ways of managing. She thinks that it was always less satisfactory when the running of the college was shared between 'House' and 'Education' subcommittees, as she explained here:

There was more division; it was better when the two came together. It is very important to have a committee which is concerned with the college and looking at things from the college's point of view; making the college the first priority and not the rest of the WI, which is what the NFWI Executive Committee have to do. To the National Executive member Denman is just another subcommittee, but the college is *big* and a *college;* it is not like another subcommittee. [21]

The Education Co-ordinating Group was encouraged to look to the wider educational world partly through the contact with the outside members of the committee, including Dick Smethurst, Konrad Elsdon, Arthur Stock and Neil Barnes of the BBC, all well known and respected in the adult education world.

One of the results was that, for the first time, the organisation linked its own training with that of an outside body:

Training of tutors will be in line with the proposals of the Advisory Council for the Supply and Training of Teachers. [22]

In 1983 NFWI became the first voluntary organisation to put on a programme training tutors of adults which was validated by a Regional Advisory Council. This started the pattern, followed ever since, of linking tutor training to external qualifications. Now the training is linked to National Vocational Qualifications (NVQs) in Training and Development and accredited by City and Guilds.

In 1982 a special conference on 'Work and Leisure in the 1980s', organised by the Education Co-ordinating Group was held at Denman College and attended by representatives of Local Education Authorities, other women's organisations and relevant national institutions as well as WI members:

Sir Keith Joseph, Secretary of State for Education and Science and Mr Geoffrey Holland, Director of the Manpower Services Commission, were the two main speakers. Discussion on the rôle of adult educators in an adverse economic climate and on ways they might respond to the needs of the unemployed, emphasised the partnership between statutory and voluntary providers and the needs for action at local level. [23]

These activities were organised by the Education Co-ordinating Group, whilst Denman College was being run by the experienced Hilda Jones. As long as Hilda remained the Principal all was well, but once she retired in April 1981 a succession of new staff were appointed (described in more detail in the next section) who needed more support than a Liaison Officer alone could supply. The Liaison Officer rôle was dropped, and the Education Subcommittee took on the full responsibility:

In its co-ordinating rôle, the Education Group looks two ways: to co-operating with other agencies in the education field and to integrating the NFWI educational work done at national and local level with that provided by Denman College… [24]

In retrospect it would seem that, by looking two ways, the Education Group were not able to give sufficient attention to Denman. By 1983:

[the] staffing of Denman College presented a particular problem and it was with regret that the Executive Committee received the resignation of both Principal and Deputy Principal during the year, especially as members were very much aware that the college required a period of stable administration. It was for this reason that when interviews for a new Principal were held in the summer no appointment was made in the belief that a wider field of well-qualified candidates was required before a final choice could be made. The committee was also aware that after 35 years of gradual and successful development at the college, certain changes now required to be phased in slowly, both to incorporate into the programme current educational and management practice and to meet the needs of present day staff who were no longer willing to work the long hours without adequate time off, which earlier employees had been willing to accept . [25]

Time for another review.

Review IV – 1985

During the last ten years or more, the organisation's work and policy in education has been administered in a number of different ways. In the last few years an Education Co-ordinating Group has brought together and examined the educational work carried out by the subcommittees, relating it to the Denman College Programme. During [1985] it became increasingly clear that present arrangements were still not entirely satisfactory and talks began about how better to co-ordinate and plan the NFWI's educational work, and, in particular, how to integrate it with the course programme and policy in operation at Denman College. [26]

This time a much smaller working party was used to carry out the review. It consisted of Jean Varnam, National Vice Chairman; Suzanne May, National Treasurer; Elizabeth Reddrop, National Executive member, and a tutor at Denman; Anne Stamper, National Executive member, Chair of Environment and Public Affairs and also serving on NIACE Executive Committee; Wendy Thorogood, Principal of Denman; Anne Ballard, NFWI General Secretary; Richard Smethurst, Oxford University Department of External Studies. The decision to 'Save Denman' (p 94) was being made at the same time, and everyone felt that it was important to get the management structure right. The minutes of the working party record the views of Richard Smethurst:

[He] … felt that Denman had in the past been 'isolated' and it was agreed that Denman should be integrated into an educational policy for the whole movement … he suggested that the NFWI should first clarify its educational remit and then consider which aspects of this remit were best carried out through courses at Denman. Denman courses should not be 'one-offs' but linked to 'outreach' activities in the Federations. [27]

As a result of the working party recommendations, a Denman College Management Committee was set up. Agnes Salter, the National Chairman, took the chair of this new committee. The membership was: the National Officers, two National Executive Committee members, two members elected by the National Council, John Baker of

Brockenhurst College, Brian Hoare of Eton and David Kinnersley of Mansfield College, Oxford. This was the first time that outside 'experts' had been included as full voting members of a Denman Management Committee, with the intention that they should be able to cover not only education but provide experience of maintaining the fabric of the college. Having the National Chairman in the chair emphasised the status of the new Management Committee, after what came to be seen as a period of relative isolation for the college.

The Education Subcommittee and the Denman College Management Committee worked in parallel during these years. The 1985 review had also stressed, as in 1978, the need for a National Training Officer. This time one was indeed appointed, but the post was based in London, working to the Education Subcommittee, not at Denman as had been suggested previously. Dorothea Hall, the newly appointed training officer, helped the organisation to begin to analyse its training needs and a modular training scheme was planned to meet those needs; its full implementation was still some time in the future.

Having a training officer also gave fresh impetus to the educational work of the organisation and Denman was used to start some new initiatives. In 1986 an 'Open Door Education Workshop' led to setting up a network of Federation Voluntary Education Co-ordinators (VECs) to stimulate more educational activities in their WIs. In the years since, VECs have built up good links with both WIs and local colleges, and now they are administering the Travelling Tutor programme in Federations.

Another training weekend, this time organised and funded jointly by the BBC and IBA was held in 1988. Representatives from Federations explored ways of using broadcasting as a stimulus to discussion in their WIs. Many returned home to set up viewing and discussion groups based on radio and TV programmes. Using broadcasting as a stimulus to discussion and study had been something that Grace Hadow supported back in the 1930s; she would have approved.

Meanwhile the Education Subcommittee was keeping a watching brief on what was going on in the outside education world, and in 1988 The Education Reform Bill became the main focus of work. There were three areas of this Bill which were of particular concern to the WI: the position of Home Economics in relation to the National Curriculum; the use of school premises by community groups; and the need to safeguard adult education. The Chairman of the Education Subcommittee (the author) spoke to this brief at the First Standing Conference on Education. There was a titter round the hall when I announced that I was speaking on behalf of the WI, a common response from those who just see the WI as a butt for jokes. I did subsequently receive warm applause and many people told me that if 'even the WI' were opposing this bill the Government might begin to think again.

NFWI representatives subsequently held meetings with Baroness Hooper, the Minister responsible for the adult sector, and Angela Rumbold MP, the Minister for Education, to press the case further.

Review V – 1991

When the NFWI changed its legal status and became incorporated as a company limited by guarantee, the Denman Trust was set up, and a new management structure was required. Although the possibility of having separate Trustees for Denman College, and appointing a governing body were considered, the chosen option was to have the NFWI Executive Committee working corporately as Trustees, and delegating the management of the college to a Management Committee through a Scheme of Delegation. The new management committee's composition was very similar to that of the existing management committee, which was working effectively.

After incorporation the national subcommittees were reorganised. There was no longer a national subcommittee with 'Education' as its remit; a new Member Services Committee became responsible for much of the training, but the relationship of the national subcommittees to the Denman programme was less clear. Although all the national subcommittee chairmen were invited to attend the Denman Programme Planning Subgroup, few of them did so and the links between the subcommittees and Denman became looser.

Once more the NFWI became involved in a national education debate. The Government White Paper, *Education and Training for the 21st Century,* was published in the early summer of 1991, with only a short consultation time. The intention to classify any adult education courses which were not leading to vocational qualifications as 'leisure courses' which would therefore be liable for VAT was a serious threat. Many adult education establishments were taking their traditional academic summer break, but the WI, with its well tested methods of lobbying, was able to swing into action quickly and took a leading rôle in persuading the government to reconsider its proposals. The rest of the adult education world was grateful:

> The rôle played by the WI in persuading the Government to alter its hard line on liberal adult education between the publication of the White Papers and the drafting of the Further and Higher Education Bill is something of a 'cause celebre' in adult education circles. [28]

After three years it was clear that the new NFWI committee structure " … did not work as well as we planned". [29] In the changes, four of the NFWI departments were relocated to Denman. These were departments which covered Home Economics, Sport the Arts and Training, all areas of work which used Denman facilities frequently. By moving to Denman it was hoped that their work could become better integrated with the work of the college and the Federations. A new National Training Officer was appointed, based at Denman as had been first suggested in 1978. In 1997 a new post of Head of Education and Training was created, to head this NFWI Unit at Denman.

As a way of making both WI members and the outside adult education world more aware of the rôle that Denman College played in women's liberal adult education, a series of Sir Richard Livingstone lectures was planned. The inaugural lecture was given by Richard Smethurst in 1993, in the Oxford Examination Schools.

Review VI ..

In 1997 the NFWI Executive Committee has commissioned yet another review, which will look at the management of the college and its relationship with the NFWI. The Education Policy of NFWI derives from the Objects in the Memorandum and Articles of Association – a 'user friendly' version of this is shown in the top box on the next page. In the lower box is the Denman College Mission Statement.

In the middle box is an NFWI 'Education Policy and Action Plan' produced in 1992. Mike Boice of Sussex University used the WI as a case study for research into adult education in rural areas (his findings were published in *Out of Sight, Out of Mind? Barriers to Participation in Rural Education*). Of this 'Policy and Action Plan', he commented that this "appears to have been produced with more than half an eye on the current political educational agenda and seems to reflect the struggle that all liberal adult education is having presently to justify itself in the face of crude vocationalism." He is right, this document was intended for use when approaching potential funders. Perhaps after the new review the relationship between the two will attain the creative balance that has been sought throughout the 50 years.

This has been a complicated story of changing management structures, reflecting the shifting emphasis on the rôle of 'education' within the organisation. This section should not close without stressing that, however the college is managed, and whatever committee structure is currently 'in vogue', the students at the college experience a warm and happy atmosphere. One college tutor summed this up by commenting that everything is "so warm and wonderful at the 'coalface', actually in the courses, even if things are fraught and divided on the management side…" [31]

SECTION 2 – THE STAFFING OF DENMAN COLLEGE

What kind of people do you need as Principal and staff of a short stay college?

Ross Waller (founder of the first short stay college), explained what he wanted of his staff:

> Ideally the staff of residential colleges ought to be the best and best educated people in the teaching profession. They need before everything else to like people and believe in them, to be themselves … in simple and unaffected sincerity. Their friendly accessibility needs to be combined with first rate intellectual gifts of great range. [32]

It is not clear what qualifications, if any, are required of the Principal, or Warden, of a short stay college. It is not clear from what background to recruit; the candidate requires a knowledge of adult education, but also managerial skills and the ability to run a residential establishment, with all the pressures that entails.

In 1969, in a submission to the Russell Committee, the criteria for a college to be defined as a short-stay residential adult education college (and thus belong to Adult Residential Colleges Association) was described:

THE PURPOSE OF THE WI

To provide a democratically controlled educational and social organisation for women, providing an opportunity of working and learning together to improve the quality of life in the community, particularly in rural areas, and to enable them to develop their own skills and talents.

Synopsis of purpose used in 1992 NFWI Annual Report

NFWI EDUCATION POLICY AND ACTION PLAN FOR THE 21st CENTURY

- Education is high profile.
- Education planning, provision and assessment is becoming regionally based.
- Our classes and courses are being organised in simple units of work and reflect modern trends.
- We are offering nationally recognised certificates for members who wish to take them.
- Our members expect and will receive good educational advice and guidance.
- Educational provision is one important method of recruiting new members.
- Educational provision throughout the WI is based on quality.
- WI members take pride in their education.
- We plan and learn together.

DENMAN COLLEGE MISSION STATEMENT

We are committed as an integral part of the Women's Institutes Organisation to provide residential learning opportunities in a friendly setting which enables individuals to achieve their personal, educational and employment goals.

With the NFWI Executive Committee and the County and Island Federations we will help to develop the WI organisation to increase the effectiveness of individual WIs, and to stimulate the demand for education by all WI members. In doing so we will work towards achieving the educational objectives of the WI organisation and aim to act as an education learning and resource centre for the organisation.

We will collaborate with other agencies in the national and international community to enable us to be responsive to the needs of WI members now and in the future.

Endorsed by the Denman College Management Committee in 1997

A Warden should have academic status, or its equivalent, or have sufficient experience in the field of adult education to enable him or her to undertake work of high academic standard… The college must have a standard of work which satisfies the Association and which includes in its programme non-vocational courses planned by the Warden… Residential establishments such as staff training centres, halls of residence, conference houses or any other establishment in which the Warden is not in control of the programme of work, or is not engaged in non-vocational adult education, are excluded from membership. [33]

What kind of a person do you want as the Warden/Principal of the short stay college that belongs to a women's organisation? The movement has been trying to answer the question for the past 50 years. Sometimes they have found successful solutions, sometimes not. Some of the Principals have been successful, some have been much cherished, some have been both, some have been neither.

The first person to hold the post was **Elizabeth (Betty) Christmas** who described herself as "a little girl from the country who made good." [34] When she left school she worked in the village post office, then learned shorthand and typing and became a WI employee. She worked first for Buckinghamshire Federation, eventually becoming the County Secretary. In 1939 she was appointed 'General Organiser' to the National Federation, being particularly concerned with the formation of WIs. Cicely McCall, who was on the staff at the same time, remembers her as the youngest of the NFWI Organisers, who was everyone's favourite, with a "delicious sense of humour." [35]

Betty Christmas was a popular choice as Warden. She was only 37, but had been the General Organiser for eight years, during which time she had travelled widely, including the visit to Canada in 1945 (p 82). Already known and loved, her charm and welcoming smile made her a success from the start. She may not have had the academic status suggested by Ross Waller, but she did have the warmth and sincerity and 'friendly accessibility', and those were essential qualities for the first Warden who would be welcoming members who were very nervous indeed about coming to this 'college'.

Her salary was £200 per annum. This was considerably less than that paid to Wardens of other short stay colleges at that time (and about half that of a school teacher). Walter Drews, in his doctrinal thesis on *British short-term residential colleges*, comments that "these salaries and expectations of the staff reflect the enthusiasm and voluntary spirit of the Women's Institute movement of the time." [36] Is he just being charitable? Perhaps the low salary reflects the unrealistic expectations of the WI.

Betty was the 'hostess' at the college, a rôle that was vital when so many of the WI members who came were venturing away from home on their own for the first time. Lady Brunner believes that Betty wore herself out because all the members wanted to confide in her, and share their problems. She may equally have been worn out because the college ran with so few staff. When it opened there was a college secretary (Christina Beckton), a Warden's secretary (Barbara Lilley), a housekeeper (Miss Messer who had worked previously at Radbrook College), a cook (Mrs Parker) and two Swedish girls who had come to learn English. They were assisted by various domestic staff recruited from the village.

By the end of 1949, when the college could take up to 50 students and thus run two or three courses at a time, Betty and Christina Beckton had been working 14-hour days. At this point she was given an additional staff member, Edith Leathart, who was appointed resident tutor. Edith had replaced Cicely McCall in 1945 as Education Organiser at NFWI. Staff from the London office have been appointed to posts at Denman from time to time over the years. It has not always been a success because a job at a residential college is very different to a general office job.

In 1950, after only two years as Warden, Betty became ill and after some months she was operated on for cancer. She returned to work quite soon, having apparently made a good recovery. Shortly after the fifth birthday of the college in 1953, however, she became ill again, and by early 1954 was spending much of her time in bed at Christmas Cottage.

> It was a difficult and distressing time for the staff. Loyal and devoted, they gave her all possible help, going back and forth to her bedside, so that she was kept in touch with all that was going on, yet spared the small day-to-day problems and protected from too many visitors. They and the committee knew that Denman was her life-line and all were agreed that so long as she was able to control the College and plan its future there would be no question of anyone else taking over. [37]

Cicely McCall remembers:

> One of the staff told me that although Betty insisted on having the files kept under her bed, she was no longer capable of going through the applications. I used to visit her from time to time and it was heart-rending to see her, surrounded by worshipping staff and a few carefully selected WI members, and quite incapable of administering anything. [38]

In the Spring of 1955, Betty heard that she was to get an OBE. She planned an outing for the staff to celebrate, but sadly she was too ill to join them. Soon afterwards she resigned and went at first to stay with Edith Leathart (who by this time had left the college) and then later to a nursing home in Beaconsfield. She died of cancer in November 1956.

The College struggled on. Christina Beckton, helped by Barbara Lilley, had been looking after the residential side from the beginning but knew little of education. She had been called College Secretary, but was now officially up-graded to Bursar, with general responsibility for running the household and estate. Planning the courses and booking the tutors were left to Delphine Dickson, who had been appointed Tutor in 1953. The NFWI asked Christina and Delphine to run the College in double harness until a new Warden was appointed.

For more than two years (1955–1957) Denman had no official Warden. The Bursar and the Tutor carried on as acting Wardens:

> … but the lack of one person in overall control to co-ordinate the work of the College and plan ahead, inevitably brought a general running down. In retrospect it may seem odd that so long a time was allowed to elapse before the appointment of a new Warden; the difficulty was that, to those who had known and worked with Betty Christmas, she was irreplaceable. [39]

This provides an example of how sentiment can prove a barrier to the effectiveness of running a voluntary organisation. The organisation was also inexperienced at managing and running a college, and decisions were being made in London where some of those involved had little detailed knowledge of what was happening at the college.

Cicely McCall became Warden in 1957. In appointing her the NFWI Executive Committee was again turning to someone they knew, who had been at the Radbrook conference and who had been involved in drawing up the initial plans for the college. Cicely only left NFWI because she was required to, as she was standing as a (Labour) candidate in the 1945 election:

> NFWI thought that adoption as a candidate would be incompatible with my work, and when the general election day was announced, they terminated my appointment in 1945. [40] [NFWI do not now take this view. A member of staff who had been adopted as Parliamentary candidate in the 1997 election was given leave. She was not successful and returned to her post. AS]

She was not elected, and found a new job as a psychiatric social worker. When she was invited by Lady Dyer, NFWI Chairman, to become the Warden of Denman she hesitated, as she had a pensionable job at the hospital, but:

> I had helped to give birth to Denman College and I knew that after Betty's illness they were in trouble … [41]

So, at the age of 57, she sold her house and moved to the college:

> It struck me at once that it was hopelessly uneconomic of the college to close every weekend, for some two months during the summer and for a fortnight at Christmas and Easter… While WI members raised large sums for the college they were not allowed to visit it except during two weeks in August when the place was empty. [42]

Day visits were introduced so that members could come and see their college, and 11,000 members came in the first year:

> It seemed to me that my task was to get the college going again after its time of retreat from reality during Betty's illness… I initiated three courses which were at the time considered completely revolutionary: a weekend course for husbands and wives; a three day course for mothers and babies; and a family weekend. [43]

The finances were also in a very precarious state because the college had been under-used for so long. In order to raise funds, and to encourage members to come to visit, there was a huge Flower Festival, opened by Constance Spry. 4,500 people attended over the two days and it made a profit of £700.

Christina Becton, Barbara Lilley and Delphine Dickson, who had been keeping the place going since Betty died, were still in post. There were problems; Cicely was considered to have moved too fast, as she recognised herself:

When I took up my appointment as Warden, some of the staff did not find it easy to adjust to the quickened pace of life after having been used to so much free time. With hindsight I think I tried to change too much too quickly. [44]

The Annual Report for 1958 included the rather brief note:

The committee also regrets the termination of Miss McCall's appointment as Warden of Denman College and wishes to express its thanks for the new ideas and enterprising experiments which she introduced into the college programme.

She must have begun to have concerns when:

In an abrupt and troubling unfair dismissal on the part of our NFWI employers, our tutor Delphine was replaced by a younger Oxford graduate... [45]

Christina Beckton went on prolonged sick leave, returned on half-time duties and then on doctor's advice retired. "She had never disguised her opposition to any change from the routine of 'Dear Betty'." [46] Lady Dyer, the National Chairman of the time personally came to Denman to deliver a letter terminating Cicely's employment:

I was dumbfounded and asked why. She said there was a staff crisis, that my administration was hopeless and Executive had decided I must go... I was, she wrote, "a square peg in a round hole". Yet I had halved the college deficit in a year and doubled the intake of students. [47]

It seems that she was sacked largely on allegations made by the two Bursars – past and present. There was obviously a considerable amount of support for Cicely, many members wrote letters of protest at her treatment, "Miss Duff registered her deep disapproval of the way in which Miss McCall had been dismissed" [48] and resigned from the Denman subcommittee.

In January 1959 the college was again without a Warden, but the staff who remained found that they could not cope. Geraldine Wirgman, the tutor who had replaced Delphine, had already indicated that she intended to leave, the new Bursar had insufficient experience and resigned a few months later, and Barbara Lilley was close to retirement.

For the first time NFWI advertised for a Warden (at a salary of £1,000 p.a.). There were over 60 applicants for the post, of whom seven were interviewed in London and three invited to a second interview at Denman but no appointment was made, which shows how difficult it is to find the right person for the job. So once more the organisation looked to some of its past staff to 'hold the fort'.

From January to Easter 1959 **Lesley Ferguson** was acting Warden. She was in her 60s and retired from being a part time General Organiser for NFWI. She lived near Marcham with her two daughters, and agreed to do the job "until Maundy Thursday." As she had no academic qualifications she was paid at the lower rate of £900 p.a. [49] She found the job was too much for her, and declined to continue in the post after April.

Until then the Bursar had undertaken the accounts as well as managing the household. Miss Gray (who was National Treasurer at the time) received a letter from the Auditor expressing the view that it was not possible to do both jobs. The existing Bursar resigned and a new one was advertised for at a salary of £600–800 p.a. but did not take up her post until September.

The staffing of the college seemed in such disarray that closing the college was discussed. During the Easter holiday, however, NFWI received a letter from Marjorie Moller, a local Headmistress, who was about to retire. She had heard from a friend that the college was seeking a Warden and asked for details. Frances Farrer, the NFWI General Secretary, invited her to meet the committee, and they offered the post to her even though she could not start work until September.

In order to cover the months until then **Jan Bateson**, a past Chairman of the Denman Subcommittee, agreed to be Acting Warden. She was married to a tutor at Corpus Christi College, Oxford, and they lived not far away at Brill. She took over as 'temporary part time Warden' though there was not much 'part time' about it! She did return home at night, but otherwise was at the college full time. As the posts of Bursar and Tutor were both vacant, she involved her husband and daughter as well on occasions; indeed her husband helped her to complete the planning of the following year's programme.

Lady Angelsey, Chairman of the College Subcommittee at the time, was also involved in programme planning. She wrote to Jan Bateson, "Music 'B' Conductors has only asked for 28 beds … what about trying a course for car owners? " They did, and it was over-subscribed. She continued:

> I imagine that had you known what all this would involve you might not have touched D[enman] C[ollege] with a barge pole – but thank goodness you did; we are grateful; and I more grateful than anyone.
> Yours, Shirley [50]

In September Mrs Bateson handed over to **Marjorie Moller**.

Marjorie was aged 60. She had just retired after being Headmistress of Headington School for Girls in Oxford for 25 years. She had been a science teacher before becoming a Head and had never had any contact with the WI, or with adult education. She came to the college at a low point. "The lack of one person in overall control to co-ordinate the work of the college and plan ahead, inevitably brought about a general running down." [51] This was somewhat of an understatement, as shown by the figures in **Figure 13.3** (p 197).

It did not take her long to assess the situation and report to the committee:

> The new Warden, Miss Moller, spoke of the heavy strain upon the administrative staff, and the long hours they had to work and said that there was urgent need of help. It was said in discussion that the staff of the college always worked under considerable strain, and it was agreed that the Warden should bring definite plans and proposals for increased help to the January meeting. [52]

This she did. She proposed that there should be an additional full time member of staff, who should be residential and share in the residential duties, preferably a graduate, and with a salary of £700–800 pa. The NFWI decided to ask for an independent assessment and invited a Mr White (Clerical consultant) to go to Denman College to "advise on the administrative side, although it was obvious that he would have to take in the domestic picture." He visited the college and recommended the structure shown in **Figure 13.2**. [54]

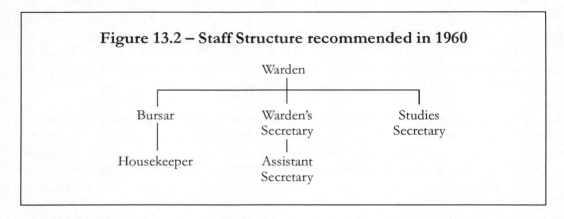

Figure 13.2 – Staff Structure recommended in 1960

Warden

Bursar   Warden's Secretary   Studies Secretary

Housekeeper   Assistant Secretary

This plan was implemented, but extra money for equipping offices was not available. The Warden came to committee to ask for about £140 for this purpose and the money was provided by an anonymous gift from a member of the committee, a striking example of the difference between a voluntary organisation and a statutory one.

The post of Studies Secretary was offered in May to Miss McWilliam (who had been Acting Bursar). She accepted but resigned in October. The committee heard that she "had said that she was unable to continue under the strain which working at the college imposed upon the staff." The Warden also "spoke of the serious overstrain of work at the college upon members of the administrative staff, including herself." [55]

The post of Studies Secretary was advertised again and Hilda Jones was appointed. On 2nd January 1961 she began her long association with the college.

> [Miss Moller] treated me like her 'headgirl' at first … neither of us had any adult education background. Things were in a mess, I was handed files and told to get on with it and run courses as before. The programme was not very exciting, craft and practical courses and country housewives and 'B' courses. Members came not so much to learn but because it was their own cosy college. [56]

The committee also agreed that there should be further part-time help. As the financial situation was so difficult they decided to apply to the Ministry of Education for a direct grant to the college, rather than having to share the grant with NFWI. This request was not accepted. [57] "It was clear that a direct grant to the college would not be considered by the Ministry. Any increase in grant if given would be to the Federation." However, two further resident staff were taken on and were given rooms which had been used for students. This meant that two of the larger rooms in the main house had to revert to 'dormitories' with four beds rather than three, a situation which continued for a long time. [58]

Elizabeth Harris, who was Chairman of the Denman subcommittee at this time, remembers Miss Moller as an excellent manager, who brought a professionalism that was badly needed, although she also remembers some grumbles at first because she "didn't know the WI." On the education side her knowledge of people in academic and teaching circles, and her own high standards, had considerable influence on the enrichment of the programme. "When ideas for adventurous courses came up at committee meetings she was always ready to support them, although it must be said that such courses did not always catch on right away." [59]

Marjorie Moller was an educationalist, and she kept in touch with the education world; she represented NFWI on the National Institute of Adult Education (NIAE). At this time a new way of encouraging members to come to the college was introduced. Federations were invited to book for their members to take over the college for a few days and the Federation then recruited people, and arranged for all to travel together, which encouraged the more timid to come. The 'Mothers and Babies' courses gradually disappeared and the family weeks also finished. However a new course was introduced for 'Mothers and Daughters', though daughters had to be 15 to 20 years old. Dealing with young children had caused too many problems.

Marjorie Moller retired in June 1964, at the age of 65, leaving the college in much better heart. During her time as Warden the number of students attending had risen by nearly 60%. Elizabeth Harris wrote in *Home and Country*:

> By the retirement of Miss Moller Denman loses an outstanding Warden. She brought to the college wide experience and a great organising ability, and it must be a source of pride to her that the college has an assured place in the education world. [60]

When her replacement was being sought, it was noted that the salary being offered was low in comparison with that of Wardens' salaries generally (according to figures supplied by NIAE). Did this still reflect the 'voluntary spirit'? However the new Warden, **Ann Dolphin**, was appointed in time for a month's 'take over'.

Aged 39, and a graduate of St Hilda's College, Oxford, and the London School of Economics, Ann Dolphin had been a social worker, then travelled round the world working at various jobs. Her last job before getting the Denman post was as catering organiser of Guildford Cathedral. She was already known to Lady Anglesey (who became National Chairman in 1966), as they had been at school together.

She came to a college with a much more stable staff. The Bursar, Dorothy Collett had been in post for five years and Hilda Jones had now become Director of Studies and had taken responsibility for the programme. She began to introduce courses which were more varied and exciting, which aimed to widen horizons and provide things which members could not get in their own Counties.

Ann Dolphin concentrated more on marketing than had been done before. She spent much of her time promoting the college in the Federations so that members could feel confident about applying to come; she could reassure them that the college was a friendly place and for all members.

She resigned after four years, in 1967, 'because of family obligations'. Helen Anderson took over in October.

After reading music and modern history at Oxford, **Helen Anderson** became a professional singer, singing for six seasons in the chorus at Glyndebourne. Following this she had been part-time music adviser to the Townswomen's Guilds, so that when she came to Denman she had already had experience of working for a women's organisation, and had indeed met the WI already as she had adjudicated at county music festivals. Her musical talents were used often on Thursday evenings for the joint sessions when she entertained the students.

When she took over as Warden the plans for the new Teaching Centre were already completed and it became her job to liaise with the architect and see the building through. She recalls how tiny the hexagons looked in the foundations of Brunner House, she even lay down on the site to prove that it was possible to get a bed in the space. [61] The visit of the Queen Mother to open the buildings was the highlight of her ten-year stay at the college.

Helen also tried to open up the college to people from the village, some of whom felt that they were rather excluded. Local people were invited in to visit the house and grounds and, once the new buildings were opened, both Marcham WI and the Parish Council held their meetings there.

Throughout Helen's time as Warden, Hilda Jones continued as Director of Studies. These were very stable times and the college was almost always full. It was in this period indeed that the 'myth' that you can never get on a course at Denman first appeared.

When Helen retired in 1977, **Hilda Jones** was invited to become Warden in her place.

Hilda accepted the job, but wished to continue to be the person who developed the programme, so the rôles of Warden and Director of Studies became amalgamated and Hilda became the first Principal. A graduate of London University with a degree in English she had served in the WRNS for 15 years as an Accountant Officer, and had played both squash and tennis for the WRNS. After leaving the services she had worked for six years at Barnett Hill House, the British Red Cross Society's College in Surrey, before her appointment to the Denman Staff in 1961.

Here was someone already utterly devoted to the college and familiar with WI members and their needs:

What Denman College can do is unique – for women residential education is so important, our members are coming back into education often after a long gap, the relearning process benefits vast numbers of people in retirement as well. [62]

During her tenure of the post the College Subcommittee was disbanded; this was the time when there was a Liaison Officer who reported directly to the National Executive Committee. In retrospect Hilda feels that the management of the college would best have been done by a governing body that met at the college, and could relate finance to the educational programme.

Hilda's long and valuable service to the college and to women's adult education was recognised both inside and outside the WI. In 1978 she was awarded a special medal of the Adelidie Restore Society of Italy, and in 1983 she received an honorary degree from the Open University. When she retired in 1981 the college entered another period of unsettlement and crisis.

Her immediate successor was **Marjorie Wright** who had a doctorate in Geography and had lectured at Goldsmiths College in London and McGill University in Canada. She had also worked as a District Inspector in the Inner London Education Authority, so that her previous experience had been in higher education and in urban settings.

She was the first (and only) Principal not to live on site. She was married with a ten-year-old daughter, and the family bought a house in The Farthings (the name of the housing estate built in the old walled garden). A gateway (which has now been bricked up again) was made from her garden into the college grounds. Quite soon both sides decided that this was not the right appointment and she left after about six months.

There was an embarrassment about advertising the post again so soon, and in a way familiar from the past NFWI looked to internal resources. Anne Ballard, the General Secretary, suggested **Wendella Smith**, the NFWI Press officer. She had no education experience or academic qualifications, but another NFWI employee from the London Headquarters, Michael Seymour (who was a B Mus. and an ARCM and also had a Certificate in Education), was appointed as Deputy Principal, a newly-created post, to give the 'education bit'.

Wendella decided very rapidly that this was not the job for her and resigned, and Michael Seymour left soon after.

Left with a college to run and no one to run it NFWI was back to 'crisis management' and took once again the route of finding someone the WI knew already. **John Ellen** had been employed for three years at NFWI to manage the Town and Country Project. This was a project to encourage WIs to make links with similar groups in urban areas. Although he had a services background, he did have some educational experience. He became Acting Principal and kept things going whilst a fresh recruitment process started, and Michael Seymour was re-engaged to compile, and administer the production of, a new-style course programme to be inserted in

Home and Country. The National Executive Committee was anxious to get things right this time, and the selection procedure developed was described in the Annual Report as:

the most in-depth and sophisticated interview procedure ever undertaken. [63]

The outcome of these deliberations was the appointment, in 1984, of **Wendy Thorogood** as the new Principal. She had previously been a matron at Eton, and so she came with experience of managing a residential establishment, and she drew on quite a number of her Eton contacts to advise on the fabric. It was also on her recommendation that the college catering was put out to contract. The whole of her stay at the college was dominated by the crisis over the condition of the fabric of the college which is described in Chapter 12. Wendy held a certificate in education, and in addition a new Deputy with adult education experience was appointed, Janet Garner, who had previously worked for the WEA, and who was to have particular responsibility for the programme. Unfortunately, after only a few months, she was diagnosed as having breast cancer and resigned. Six months later she was replaced by a new Deputy, Bernard Batchelor, who also had previous adult education experience.

Very soon after he arrived, and after only two years as Principal, Wendy Thorogood resigned "for family reasons." The newly appointed Deputy was left holding the fort while the post of Principal was advertised again.

The successful candidate was **Pauline Brown,** who had been Headmistress of an army boarding school in Germany. She came with experience of managing a residential establishment but did not have a great deal of knowledge of adult education. Bernard Batchelor, who continued as deputy Principal, was able to compensate for this, though he resigned at the end of the year.

The crisis about the future of the college continued. Not surprisingly staff morale was low. The Principal's report to a management committee not long after she had taken up her post reflects the problems of the time:

Principal's Report, or Reflections on the Stench of Opprobrium
Reports always late; figures never produced on time; senior staff never available; gardens overgrown; teaching resources inadequate and non functional; letters rarely answered on time; course tutors double booked; filing system inadequate; kitchen under pressure; staff morale surprisingly low. Standing in the National Federation lovable to many and exasperating to many.

I have now had longer to assimilate the atmosphere, the life and the activities of the college... From the manner in which I have been received and the reiterated demand from tutors and course attenders that they hoped I would stay, (this without even knowing what I am like) I have begun to realise something of the effect that the turbulence of senior staff has had on the life of this college... I have to ask for a period of stability against which change and development may take place steadily.

Everybody who is employed here has to be prepared to have overlapping responsibilities across a number of functions. The strain on the whole staff is considerable and they are all busy. [64]

Things did improve — the organisation raised the million pounds needed to 'Save Denman' by 1988, the repairs and refurbishment went ahead, staff were not made redundant. A Denman College Management Committee was set up, chaired by the National Chairman, Agnes Salter, who was a great support to Pauline. A period of stability was returning.

During the rapid changes of Principal from 1981, essential continuity was provided by David Austin, the Bursar who held the post for 17 years, retiring in 1992. The rôle of the Bursar is an important one in a college where the job involves not only looking after the finances but also the fabric and the estate. David Austin dealt with all the work that followed the crisis of 1984 and of the subsequent instability.

Then ill health struck again, Agnes Salter died of cancer in January 1989, and later in the year Pauline Brown developed breast cancer. She went into hospital, and resigned in August. Unlike Betty Christmas she did not wish to leave the college uncertain about the future. The vacancy was advertised internally, and the Deputy Principal applied and was appointed.

Graham Jones had been appointed Deputy Principal in 1987 as successor to Bernard Batchelor. The first male Principal, he formally took up the rôle on 1st October 1989. The Annual Report commented:

This is the first time the WI Adult Education College has had a male Principal, which caused a few raised eyebrows. However Mr Jones is well qualified for the job, already experienced in Denman procedures and well known to members, we wish him well. [65]

He came with a considerable experience of education administration, having been a Local Authority education officer. His contacts in the adult education world were numerous, and he was able to draw on these to the advantage of the college. During his years as Principal he has encouraged the Management Committee to develop a long term-plan for the development of the college. One ex-Chairman of the Management Committee said of him:

Graham has given people a better grasp of their own college. [66]

The college, repairs and renovations done, had won renewed confidence from the members, leading to a steady increase in the numbers attending. This has been made possible as the college has gradually worked towards continuous opening, offering an even wider range of courses. Graham, the first Principal since Marjorie Moller to have a science background, has actively sought to find ways of supporting new initiatives in science and technology. Some of these are described further in Chapter 14.

Graham has also been able to build up contacts with other local educational organisations like Abingdon and Oxford FE Colleges and Oxford Brooks University, and to tap new sources of funding. The Training and Enterprise Council funded a project offering the RSA Advanced Diploma in the Organisation of Community Groups, working jointly with the Oxfordshire Rural Community Council (which had been started by Grace Hadow in the 1930s!). At the end of the project Kathy Tiernan, who had been the project co-ordinator, joined the college staff as Director of Studies. She went on both to develop further the traditional contacts with Abingdon College and forge new ones with the Open College Federation.

With continuous opening, the staffing has had to increase and a team of senior staff take the weekend duties on a rota basis. The pressures of running a short-stay college are considerable when it is continuously open, has over 6,000 students in the year, five courses running at a time, and with two and sometimes three change-overs of students in a week.

Summary

This review of the Wardens and Principals shows how difficult it is to get the right person for the job. It is probably an impossible job, very demanding, with too many sources of potential interference, and yet very isolated.

Figure 13.3 (p 197) shows how the college has developed over the years. It also shows how a period of stability is important for the college. The rapid changes in 1953–59 and again from 1981–89 really affected the college; it seems amazing that it came out of it all so well.

The staff of the college has increased as the number of students has increased:

In 1949: with 1,579 students in the year:

Warden, College Secretary, Warden's Secretary, Housekeeper, Cook, two Swedish girls and a gardener, all resident. Also three staff to maintain fabric and grounds, and various domestic staff recruited from the village.

In 1994: with 6,294 students in the year:

Principal, Deputy Principal, Bursar, (all resident) Director of Studies, College Administrator, Programme Planner, Project Development Worker, (Rural Development Commission funded post for three years) supported by 17 education and administrative staff (some of whom were employed part time), seven estate staff, and 28 domestic, catering and bar staff, many of whom are part time. [67] The catering staff were employed by the contract caterers. A number of the domestic and catering staff have worked at the college for many years. Mable Luker, as the longest serving staff member, was invited to lay the foundation stone of one of the new cottages in 1993.

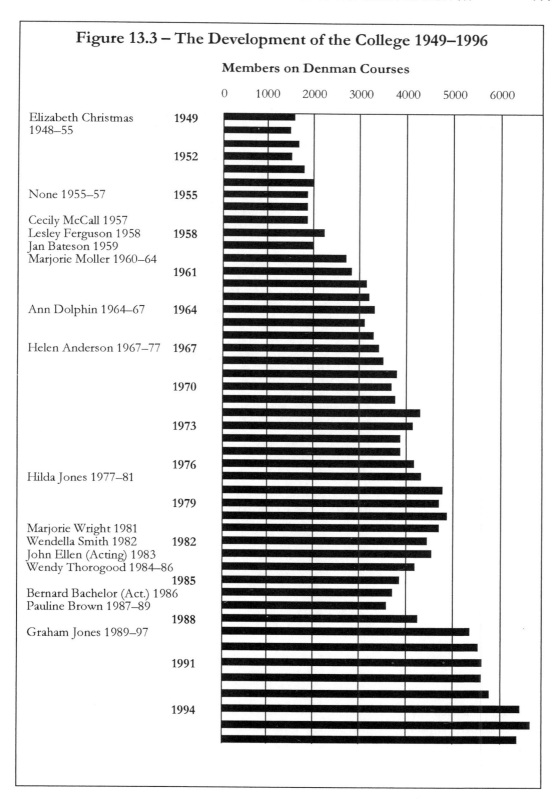

Figure 13.3 – The Development of the College 1949–1996

Members on Denman Courses

SECTION 3 – FINANCE

Lady Brunner, in her speech at the AGM proposing the setting up of the college, had warned:

> … WIs in supporting the idea of a college of their own, must expect to have some financial responsibility in the raising of funds, whether for purchase of premises or endowment. By careful planning it should be possible to keep student fees reasonably low, and in some cases Local Education Authorities and County Federations might give bursaries. [68]

Her warning was justified. Throughout its existence the college has required support from members. It has come in a variety of ways: through direct appeals; through subsidy from the NFWI (much of whose money comes from the members via their subscriptions); from the fees paid by the members who come to the college, and in some minor way through trading.

Money from outside sources has not been easy to find; NFWI is not a charity that readily attracts support. Some of the outside funding has come from Government grants, either from the Department of Education or from the Rural Development Commission. Denman College has, over the years, been the recipient of corporate sponsorship, both in money and in kind; it has also been generously treated by various bequests and donations from private individuals.

The story of the finance of the college is marked out by crises and appeals.

The first appeal

The first challenge was to raise the money to buy the college. The target set was £60,000, which was to match the amount promised by the Carnegie United Kingdom Trust (£20,000) and to raise extra to set up an Endowment Fund that would create sufficient income to cover the maintenance and development costs of the college. Raising this money took longer than anticipated, as was explained in Chapter 7. This meant that there was very little money from investment income in the early days, and NFWI had to transfer money from the general funds. In the first few years as much money came from sale of produce from the market garden as from investments. However, as we have seen, the profitability of the market garden did not continue.

The greatest proportion of the income of the college has always come from the fees of the students. However, for many years the fees were kept below the level that would cover costs in the hope that any member of the organisation would be able to come. The salaries and fees paid to staff and tutors, too, have never been high, often lower than those paid in other adult education colleges. On the other hand, the upkeep and repair of the buildings and estate has often cost more than was anticipated. The original amount raised for the Endowment Fund was not enough to meet these costs.

Money for capital developments has for the most part come from sale of land or from appeals to members, supplemented by some generous gifts from sponsors or private benefactors. See **Table 13.1**.

Table 13.1 - How the College has Paid for Buildings		
Year	**Project**	**Source of Funding**
1945	Purchase of Marcham Park	Carnegie Trust £20,000 Appeal to members £60,000
1950	Home Acres conversion to teaching rooms for Rural Domestic Economy Centre	Funded jointly with Berkshire CC
1953	Croft	Anonymous donation
1957	Dining room	Funds raised in memory of Lady Denman
1970	Teaching centre	Appeal to members plus anonymous donation of £30,000
1978	Home Economics Centre	Sale of Market Garden, £128,500 and members £28,000 'birthday present'
1993	Beech and Willow cottages	Donations to 'Buy a Brick' plus revenue surplus
1997	Maple and Oak cottages	Donations to 'Buy a Brick' plus revenue surplus

In its early years, the college was not used as fully as it might have been, because the staffing levels were low and the use of additional income to recruit additional staff was not considered. The college did not develop as rapidly as might have been possible because of Betty Christmas's illness. This meant that the income from fees was not high, but the expenses of upkeep were, and the college ran at a loss. After the death of Betty Christmas the college went through a period of uncertainty, and the losses were even greater.

By 1955 the 'deficiency grant' from Headquarters funds was £2,632, and there was considerable concern lest it should become even greater. In 1956 a conference of the General Education Subcommittee with other subcommittee chairmen was called to discuss these concerns. Lady Albermarle (who was National Chairman at the time) tried to put things into perspective:

Denman College was running at a smaller loss per student on the educational expenses than any other adult education college, and our tuition fee was not lower. The alternatives were, therefore, either to ask the students to pay more than they would at other colleges, or to lower the standard of what we provided. [69] [The other colleges with which Lady Albermarle was comparing Denman – the other ARCA colleges – were for the most part run by LEAs and many of their costs for upkeep, maintenance, etc., were covered by the LEA and not a charge directly on the college budget and thus the student fee. AS]

The Treasurer "thought that it would do no harm to raise the tuition fees, thus making the people who were benefiting from the college pay for it." Lady Brunner reminded the meeting that the original resolution had welcomed the clause in the 1944 Act regarding grants and had not envisaged that the college would be self-supporting, and she felt that further grants should be sought.

These discussions highlight what has been an on-going debate for the whole of the life of the college – should the students pay the full cost or should there be a subsidy? For the first ten years of the college the proportion of the costs borne by the students remained fairly constant at about 60%. [70]

The conference went on to consider what proportion of the Ministry of Education grant should go to Denman; at that time two fifths of the £1,000 grant went to the college, and it was suggested that more of the education grant should be allocated to the college, and that the NFWI should approach the Ministry of Education "or other public body for further grants in view of the pioneering work that is still being undertaken at the college in very difficult times." [71]

In order to raise some extra income, Sylvia Gray, the National Treasurer, suggested that the college should take outside bookings in slack periods. In 1959 the college facilities were used by the Young Farmers, and the Rural Domestic Economy Department of Oxfordshire County Council. From time to time other organisations hired the College, either for day use of for residential courses, but only at times when it was difficult to fill courses with WI members, the second half of December and the whole of January, for example. It was only let to 'kindred' organisations; these included the Townswomen's Guilds and the Red Cross.

The second appeal

The hoped-for grants were not forthcoming, and so in 1959 the National Executive Committee decided that there should be an appeal to members for further money in order to increase the size of the Endowment Fund to produce a regular income for the college:

Miss Gray (Treasurer) reminded members that unless it was known that there was money coming in from the Appeal, the budget would again show a heavy deficit and there would be a further drain on reserves. After a full discussion it was agreed that the Appeal should be launched at the AGM under the heading of 'Denman College & the Future'. [72]

This Appeal raised £39,243 from 6,590 WIs. It also had the effect, as appeals often have had, of raising the profile of the college. It is almost as if members think, "We've raised this money, now let's go and see how it has been spent!", so more students came. The College was now being managed well by the new Warden, Marjorie Moller, and the finances began to look healthier.

WIs had given bursaries to members to attend conferences and training long before Denman College was opened; it naturally became a recognised practice for a WI to budget each year for a bursary for members to attend the college. How that bursary was allocated varied. Sometimes it was given to a member who the WI felt to be especially deserving (see, for example, Joyce Cormack and her twins on p 106) or in recognition for service to the WI, to a President for example. In other cases, and increasingly in more recent years, any members who would like to be considered enter a draw.

In 1964, when the Ministry of Education sent letters to all the Local Education Authorities making reference to supporting short-stay colleges, Miss Moller, the Warden, sent a letter to all Federation Secretaries enclosing a questionnaire to find out how many Federations did get support. 51 Federations returned the questionnaire which showed that 23 of them received block grants, ranging from £50 to £1,000, and about half said that they used at least part of these grants to pay for Denman Bursaries. 19 replied that their LEAs gave or were willing to give bursaries, mostly for 'B' courses. The assistance ranged from 59% to full cost. So at that time at least some members were coming to the college supported by their Local Authority.

With the Endowment Fund now larger the college was not requiring so much support from the NFWI General Fund as **Figure 13.4** shows. Occasionally the college has been generously treated, as happened in 1962 when an anonymous donation of £10,000 allowed a benefaction fund to be set up to support the educational work of the college. Much of the improvement to the fabric was made possible by gifts from very generous friends over the years. The New Croft, for example, was paid for by an anonymous donor, and in 1970, when the Teaching Centre and Brunner buildings were opened by the Queen Mother, it was reported that:

> The buildings, following a familiar pattern, exceeded the budget, but Sir Felix and Lady Brunner made up the balance 'in order that the standards should not fall'. [73]

In the 1970s, with the new Teaching Centre and a full college, things were going well, but there were still financial problems because costs were rising fast and the college fees were having to be increased to keep up with inflation (and they were, **Figure 13.5**, p 204). The increase in fees concerned many people who thought that some WI members might be prevented from coming.

In 1971 there was a full debate at Consultative Council on the financing of the College. Pat Jacob, the National Treasurer, introduced the session:

During the last ten years the proportion of the Denman College income provided by the NFWI General Fund has been 6% to 9% … expenditure had risen on average of 8.8% for each five-year period since 1956… In order to meet this the fees to students had to be increased more in 1971 (45p a night) than in the previous four years (30p a night). [74]

She went on to ask if Council felt that more members were now being 'priced out' of Denman? Did they feel that more money should be allocated to Denman out of the General Fund? She asked, "Should there be another Appeal?" and ended her presentation by saying:

Denman is part of NFWI. It belongs to every member. Every member is responsible for its upkeep. 3,500 members come to the college per annum. This does not reflect the value of Denman College to the Movement. Every member returning to her WI from the college enriches her Institute. The college trains teachers, demonstrators, VCOs, VCMOs, WI Officers, Produce Guild Leaders. *It enriches us all.*

At the end of the discussion, "An expression of opinion was taken from the Council and it was agreed that more of the college costs should be met from the NFWI General Fund." [75]

Through the 1970s the college ran reasonably smoothly on a mixture of sources of income. **Figure 13.4** shows the investment income as a percentage of the total income, and it also indicates the percentage of the total income which came from grants from the Ministry/Department of Education, and from NFWI General Fund. It can be seen that, as the investment income varied, the deficiency grant from NFWI fluctuated to compensate. In real terms the value of the grant from the Department of Education gradually diminished, although this grant had never contributed more than 10% to the college income.

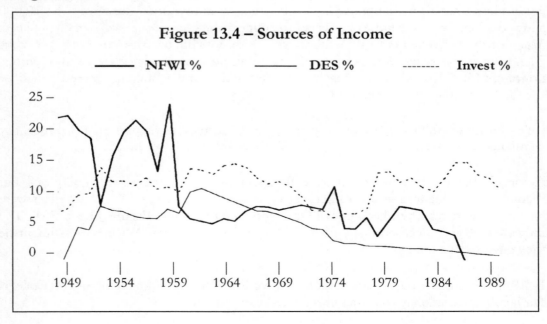

Figure 13.4 – Sources of Income

During the 1970s plenty of maintenance work was done, though in the light of subsequent events one might suggest that the fabric of the building was probably not being looked after carefully enough. One potentially expensive job emerged in 1980 when the very long stone boundary walls started to need attention. After initial concern about how all this work would be paid for, the college was lucky once more. Quite 'out of the blue', Mr Duffield, whose family had owned Marcham Park in the past, asked if he could buy the 77 acres of land surrounding the college. He offered to pay a price per acre far above the market value, and also agreed to repair the boundary wall and look after the woodland. The college accepted this offer with delight, especially as they were given permission for students to continue to walk round the nature trail, but were themselves saved the worry of maintaining the woodland.

In 1978, when the Home Economics Centre was built it was funded out of the sale of land, and from donations. Funding buildings from the sale of land, however, is a bit like living off selling the family silver. It is not ideal, and the college really required a sounder financial base.

Crisis and appeal

The most serious crisis came in 1984, as already described in Chapter 8. The decision to 'Save Denman' was taken after conferring with the Federations. The Appeal was set for £1 million, so that the Endowment Fund could be increased to a level that would bring in a realistic income to be spent on maintenance and development, and to allow the college to be self supporting. The £1 million was raised in two years – a triumph.

The investment income was at its greatest after the success of the £1 million appeal in 1984. The decision by the Executive Committee of the time to set a target of £1 million, rather than the lower figure required to pay for the repairs, showed determination to put the college on a sound financial basis, so that money would no longer be required from the NFWI General Fund, and that is what has happened. Calor Gas donated £50,000 to the Denman Appeal, but the donations from other outside sources were fewer than hoped for.

Since 1986 the college has been supported by those members who attend it and pay fees, plus the income from the investments bought with money raised by the whole membership. This has meant that the fees have had to increase. Agreeing the level of fee has always been a matter of balancing financial necessity against that highly subjective figure, 'what the members will stand'.

The Department for Education and Employment continues to give a grant to NFWI, but it is no longer a block grant for 'liberal adult education'. Now NFWI has to apply to the Department for grants to support specific areas of work that equate with the Government's own objectives. In recent years these have been for training courses, for example tutor training and rural adult educational guidance.

In the last few years the college has offered some courses which lead to qualifications which are eligible for support by money from the Further Education Funding Council. As an Adult Education College, Denman is unable to access these funds directly and so a franchise agreement has been drawn up with Abingdon College; they apply for the funds which are then passed on to Denman. This means that the college can offer these particular courses more cheaply than would otherwise be the case.

As **Figure 13.5** shows, the fees that members have paid in the 1990s have increased in real terms, which was bound to happen when the subsidy was withdrawn from NFWI's General Fund. On the other hand more members now come on bursaries. In 1995 one in three members attending the college came supported by some kind of bursary and seven out of ten of these bursaries covered at least half the cost of the course. [76]

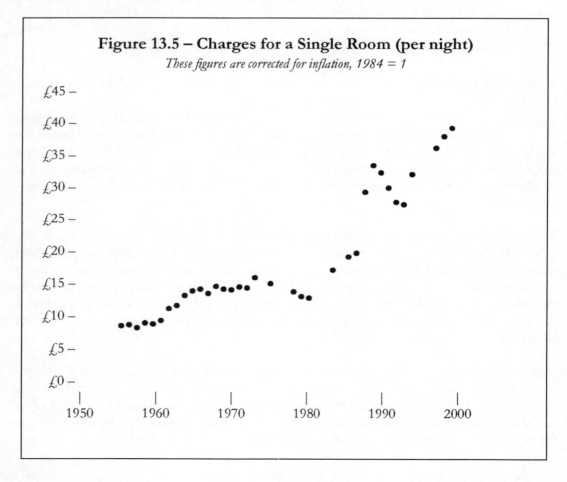

Figure 13.5 – Charges for a Single Room (per night)
These figures are corrected for inflation, 1984 = 1

The intention of the current Management Committee is that the staffing costs should be kept below 50% of the course fees and expenses (in 1996 they were 48%). The Management Committee also aim to spend in any one year only the income earned during the previous year.

The VAT battle

In 1991 the college had to register for VAT for the first time. This has to be paid on such income as bar takings and sales of souvenirs, and on those events which are purely social. But when the Government White Paper, 'Education and Training for the 21st Century', and subsequently the Further and Higher Education Bill were published, also in 1991, it appeared that changes were being introduced which would have some very serious consequences for the college. As we have seen earlier in this chapter, NFWI took a leading role in persuading the government to reconsider its proposals. If the government had introduced VAT for adult education courses, Denman students would have had to pay £9 extra a night. This is an area where NFWI and the college will have to remain vigilant, as short-stay residential colleges do seem to be viewed by VAT inspectors, who do not understand liberal adult education, as fair prey.

Today's student

The questionnaire (**Appendix 2**) distributed in 1996 included questions about the cost of coming on a course.

80% of those who had been on open courses said that the fees were about what they had expected, while 14% said that they were higher and 1% that they were lower. There were some comments that Denman was one of the few places where there is no 'single supplement'. (Although there have been times in the past where those in a single room had to pay extra, this is not the case at the time of writing.)

Many members found the extra cost of travel was as significant as the fees. Of those who replied to the questionnaire who had not been to the college, only 12% gave money as the main reason for not going, though 20% gave 'I have never won the bursary' as the main reason. It seems therefore that at present at least the fees are 'what the member will stand for'.

Since the withdrawal of the NFWI subsidy, WIs have been encouraged to increase the value of their bursaries to a realistic figure which really covers the cost of course and travel. In recent years it has been suggested that it might be better to offer a bursary every other year and to make it large enough to cover the full cost.

The questionnaire confirms the importance of bursaries. 75% of all those who had been on open courses had received a bursary at some time, and of those 53% had a bursary for their first visit to the college.

More than three quarters of the respondents indicated that their WI gave a bursary, though the amount varied widely (**Figure 13.6**). It seems that very few of those who come on a bursary have all their costs covered. In 1996, £120 would cover the fees for a weekend course.

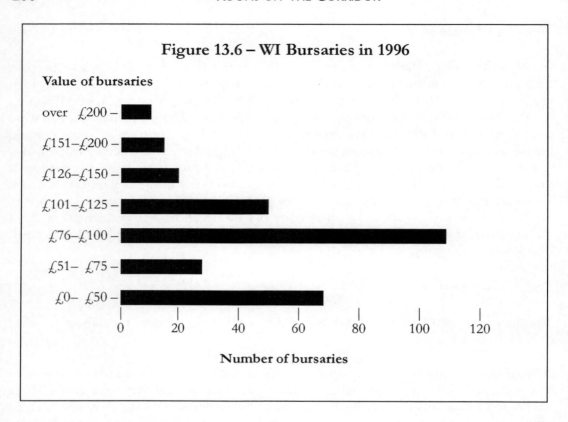

Figure 13.6 – WI Bursaries in 1996

There are also a number of special bursaries awarded both within Federations and nationally. Some are for particular courses, like the one sponsored by Stork Margarine for 'A Beginners Guide to Cookery'. Others are for members with particular needs; for example the Isabella Jane Bursary for a member with a young family, or the MWM Bursary:

> given by a member in memory of her mother is available to a member who has heavy home nursing responsibilities. It is intended to cover fees, travelling expenses and the cost of replacement nursing help throughout the duration of the course. It is available for a four-night or shorter course if wished. [77]

Conclusion

The vision of the founders was that the college would provide a focus for, and give a framework to, the educational work of the organisation. The conclusion has to be that this vision has only been partially met. As this chapter has shown, the relationship between the college, the National Federation and the county Federations has never been entirely clear, and the emphasis has changed over the years.

Before the college opened Lady Albermarle said that there was a need to clarify the place of the college in the movement. She suggested two approaches, that based on the

Snapshot of the College Finances in 1996

There were 6,200 enrolments on some 500 courses.
1,181 members (19%) were on courses specially arranged with Federations.
536 members (9%) were on NFWI training courses.

Income	£	Expenditure	£
Student fees	998,207	Education	425,364
Grants	88,278	Administration	256,666
Trading	14,892	Household	360,393
Day visits	9,331	Buildings & grounds	25,885
Other income	10,586		
Donations	3,143		
Total	1,169,437	Total	1,209,998

	£
VAT	4,708
Operating deficit before investment income	35,853
Investment income	56,820
Transfer to accumulated reserve	20,967
The market value of the investments was:	1,379,130

liberal adult education of the individual WI member, and the other as a place providing "an extension of our work and a training ground for leaders and teachers and technicians through whom the influence of the college would be spread." [78] In the early years it tried to do both, but after a while the provision of courses for the individual came to dominate the work of the college.

In 1958 the Denman College Subcommittee wondered how it could have a closer tie up with Federation's educational programmes and decided to ask those Counties with long term plans to contact the college. This never happened. Was this because the Counties did not have any long term plans, or because they could not imagine how Denman might help? The charitable objective of the college is to provide "a college, residential or otherwise, for the education of members of the Women's Institutes in accordance with the objects of the body corporate called the National Federation of Women's Institutes of England and Wales, the Channel Islands and the Isle of Man."

Just what is meant by "or otherwise"? Does this mean, as perhaps is just beginning to happen, that some of the work begun at Denman can spread out into the Federations? Travelling Tutors are now starting to take courses (with Open College Accreditation developed at Denman) out into the Federations. Some Federations are planning ways in which they might build on what they have done at Federation courses at Denman. 'Cascade' conferences are stimulating new ideas and increasingly support is being given to those who return to implement the new ideas.

The college is a resource to be used to serve the organisation. It serves the NFWI as a training centre and a place to explore ideas. It serves the Federations by offering them a place where they can bring their members to extend their learning and possibly link in with what they are doing, or might continue to do in the Federation. It serves the WIs and individual members by providing a college of liberal adult education where they can learn in a friendly and 'safe' environment. The college does all these things, and has to try to keep the balance. This has been a challenge for 50 years; it will continue to seek to 'get it right'.

This chapter has told of some of the struggles and difficulties 'behind the scenes', but finally let the students speak for themselves: [79]

Runs extremely well. Is this because it is women?

I think the original concept of Denman was marvellous, and the way it has progressed over the years is to be praised.

I attended meetings when Denman College was considered. I heartily approved and think that it has lived up to its early promise.

There should be some effort made to reduce costs of, say, a particular course or series of courses for those who cannot afford to attend, perhaps a self-catering room for a few weekend courses.

Taster courses if possible; small discount for students returning for another course within, say, two years. As well as the contribution to adult education which has been great, include the joys of companionship and friendliness, which has been a part of the comfort for many students, particularly the normally lonely and shy person.

I do think that Denman is the jewel in the WI's crown, and the people who had the original idea and carried it through had enormous vision.

Denman College is certainly the jewel in the crown and something every member should treasure and support.

Denman College is marvellous and we should promote it more.

CHAPTER FOURTEEN

"... TAKE BACK FRESH INSPIRATION TO SHARE WITH OTHERS ..."

> **VISION OF THE FOUNDERS**
> That the College would provide a place to continue the learning begun in the local WI, and from which to take back fresh inspiration to share with others.

In the debate about founding a WI College one speaker said:

> ... it is not fair to ask the ordinary member to raise money for something from which she will on the whole receive no direct benefit. It will be for the few, whereas the money will be raised by the many. [1]

There have always been those who feel that the college is only for the benefit of the few who can go there, but this is to ignore the 'ripple' effect. When a member returns to her WI or her Federation she very often carries with her new ideas and 'fresh inspiration'. This is true for those attending open courses, it is even more true for those who come on one of the training courses whose intention is to 'cascade' information back to Federations and WIs.

This chapter considers five different examples of the ways in which the work of the college links with what happens at NFWI and in the WIs. Denman College is an important resource to be used in the educational work of the whole organisation; these examples illustrate some of the ways in which this happens.

Art

When reading accounts of the activities of the WIs in the 1920s and 30s, art receives hardly a mention; craft dominates. Grace Hadow had been anxious to bring "cultural subjects to those who were starved of them." [2] In order to do this she persuaded many of her Oxford associates, included artists, to go and speak to Oxfordshire WIs. It does not appear that this happened in many other Federations. Only slowly was art introduced into WI programmes, for the most part by talks on aspects of art appreciation.

Once the Second World War was over, an interest in 'cultural' subjects re-emerged with new vigour. Lady Albermarle, the National Chairman, was a member of the Arts Council and Lady Listowel, another member of the National Executive Committee, was a Governor of the Victoria and Albert Museum. In 1948 when the college opened, both pictures and embroideries were loaned by the V & A for display. This was all part of the plan to use the college to bring 'culture' to the members.

The college programme did not contain any practical art courses for the first three years, partly because there were no facilities, but also because art was not thought to be a subject that would interest members. However, by the autumn of 1952, when Home Acres with its craft room had opened, it became possible to run practical courses:

> Painting had always been the Cinderella of the arts amongst the institutes, and up to this time there had been no courses in oil painting. For some time the Education Subcommittee had hesitated to include any practical course in the graphic arts believing that there would be little or no demand. However their views had been changed after an art appreciation course during which the young woman art teacher had suddenly announced "Now I am going to make them draw!" and to everyone's surprise, including the students themselves, did just that... [3]

From then on, drawing and sketching courses began to appear in the programme and, later, painting in oils and watercolours was included, too. As has been so often the case the new initiative was sparked off and developed by particular enthusiasts. In this case there were two 'enthusiasts', Charlotte Bawden and 'Duffy' Rothenstein.

Charlotte Bawden was an authority on design in art and was married to fellow artist Edward Bawden. She was a member of the Denman House Subcommittee and later one of the Education Advisers. She played an important part in widening the college's horizons in the field of art and design, and helping to find good tutors and lecturers for courses on these subjects.

'Duffy' Rothenstein (later Ayres) painted the portrait of Betty Christmas which hangs at the college. It was painted in the last few months of Betty's life and an unsigned letter to the artist dated 24th November 1955 [4] thanks her for the picture and goes on to say, "what real pleasure you have given Miss Christmas. She has loved the sittings, and the Matron says they have done her a great deal of good." Duffy became a regular tutor at the college, often heard her students saying how little opportunity they had of getting to exhibitions at home, and discovered how they would welcome the chance to see the work of contemporary artists. As a result Charlotte and Duffy started to arrange exhibitions of work by contemporary artists at the college. Amongst the first to exhibit, in 1953, were Michael Rothenstein and Edward Bawden.

Recognising that this interest in art and artists was something to be developed, and in order to help Federations to expand their 'Speakers Panels', the NFWI Education Subcommittee organised a 'B' course at Denman on 'English Landscape Painting' in 1955. This course was for members who would be prepared to go onto their Federation Speakers' Panel and be available to give talks in the WIs.

Another way of responding to the growing interest in art was tried in 1956:

A highly successful one-day school on Modern Painting was held at the Tate Gallery, London, in October. From a total of 165 applicants from 24 counties, 31 students were selected mainly from the more distant counties. The school was honoured by the presence of Sir John Rothenstein CBE who welcomed the students and spoke of the history and purpose of the Gallery. The Chairman of the course was Mrs Edward Bawden and excellent lectures on Contemporary Continental and British painting were given by Miss Mary Chamot, Assistant Keeper at the Tate. [5]

This school was repeated in the following year and was "heavily over-applied for." In 1958 there was again "an overwhelming application," so this time two schools were held. Miss Chamot was the lecturer at the first school, and at the second was Mr Lawrence Bradbury. This was the first contact with the WI for Lawrence Bradbury who subsequently became a tutor at Denman and has continued to come regularly ever since.

The growing interest in art among the members encouraged the NFWI Executive Committee to hold a National Art Exhibition in 1963. There had already been many craft exhibitions and it was natural to adopt the same pattern; Federations held their own Exhibitions, or collected entries together in some other way, in order to select the pictures for the National Exhibition.

This whole process took three years. After a small *ad hoc* committee had drawn up a schedule, a conference was held to discuss the details with 125 members representing 59 Counties. The schedule was then circulated to all WIs.

But this was not just to be an exhibition. The WI has always used exhibitions and shows as a means of teaching and improving standards, and this was to be the case now:

> ... a very generous offer of grant-aid for art courses and classes run by the County Federations has been received from the Carnegie United Kingdom Trustees, and the Counties have been informed that they can apply to the trustees for grants of up to £75 a year up to the time of the art exhibition in 1963. [6]

These classes had to be taken by an "artist/teacher of repute." In 1960 the Carnegie Trust gave grants totalling £3,660 to 52 of the Federations to help with art classes. In order to encourage beginners, a new leaflet called "Preparing to Paint in Oils" was published by NFWI. To help those in the Federations who would be planning the preliminary stages of the Art Exhibition, there was a 'B' course at Denman College where they were given advice by professional artists.

The National Art Exhibition, called 'Painting for Pleasure', was finally held at the Galleries of the Federation of British Artists in London from 20th April – 3rd May 1963 and was opened at a private view by John Betjeman. Every county and island Federation was represented and 440 paintings, drawings, prints and sculptures were shown, ranging from first paintings to the work of professional artists. Just over 5,000 people attended in the 12 days that the exhibition was open.

Following the London show 80 pictures were selected to go 'on tour' to five venues in 1963 and five more in 1964. The tour was arranged by the Art Exhibitions Bureau, and allowed a far larger number of WI members to see at least some of the pictures. There does not seem to be any record of how many people saw this travelling show, but the interest in art continued and was aided by further initiatives:

> Negotiations have been carried out with the Carnegie United Kingdom Trust which have resulted in WI art groups being accepted as eligible to join in its scheme for grant-aided classes organised by groups of art clubs. We feel sure that this will make a real contribution towards keeping up the enthusiasm for art in the WIs which has been stimulated by the national and county exhibitions. [7]

After the Exhibition, the General Education Subcommittee sent a questionnaire round to the Federations asking about their art activities. In the light of the responses they made plans to help spread interest in art among WI members.

Their first venture was 'Programmes by Post'. These programmes consisted of a long-playing record of a talk, lasting half an hour, and a set of slides to illustrate it, along with the text of the talk and other relevant information. The first of these was 'Going to the Pictures' by the senior art master at Bedford School. It was sold to Federations for four guineas and was then hired out to individual WIs. This was particularly useful if a WI was let down by a speaker at the last minute. 46 copies were sold in the first year.

Day schools in London galleries continued in the years 1964–1972 and extended to other galleries, including the Courtauld Galleries, the Royal Academy, and the Victoria and Albert Museum. At Denman the art courses increased in number and variety while Federations began to organise their own exhibitions. In 1971 for example the author was involved in organising such an exhibition in East Sussex, also called 'Painting for Pleasure'. It was very successful. 614 pictures were submitted from 217 members and the LEA County Art Adviser helped to select the 224 pictures shown. Over 1,000 people visited the exhibition and 30 pictures were sold. [8] Similar exhibitions were organised in other Federations, and are still being organised. Some WIs have their own art groups, other WI members have joined local art clubs and classes, spurred on by what they have learned. The effect of the initiatives first started at Denman spread far.

The college is still providing tuition and inspiration to those interested in art; practical art courses now take up a similar proportion of the programme to social studies, history and public affairs. They offer tuition in a wide range of techniques. Some of the art courses at the college, 'Botanical Illustration' for example, have Open College Network accreditation (see p 218). Charlotte Bawden and Professor Edward Bawden are remembered at the college in the Bawden Workshop in the Teaching Centre. Thousands of WI members have had their lives enriched through art appreciation or by learning to draw and paint. Some have gone on to become professional artists.

The first Denman Workshop

In 1973 NFWI sent the following letter to all Federation Secretaries:

> Denman College would very much like to ask Counties to join in an experiment. We think that if it proved successful it could affect one of the most important activities of County Executive Committees – programme planning in the Institutes...

> The college has unique opportunities to be the channel between the NFWI and all those sources of information which are available in this country and abroad on subjects of major interest to WIs. These opportunities are not being fully shared. We think that a dynamic way of sharing them could be to have a 'Workshop' Conference at the college in which Counties take part.

> The aims of the 'Workshop' Conference would be to open up a project for exploration and action, to provide a power-house from which shared ideas, information and methods could be generated through the Counties to the Institutes. A successful 'Workshop' depends, of course, on co-operation before, during and after! [9]

The letter then announced that the theme of this first Workshop would be 'European Architectural Heritage Year, 1975' and explained how the Workshop would provide a new way of using the facilities of the college:

> The present over-riding service the college gives is to individual members. If the workshop idea proved to be successful the college could also serve the WIs as a whole – on rather the same principle as 'B' courses are intended to do. Moreover, the feedback after a workshop would be all-important because Counties would develop their own programme and, from their experience, could suggest further services or activities to be provided at national or inter-County levels, or by the college. [10]

In 1973 'European Years' were a novelty, and taken seriously. This particular 'Year' was under the Presidency of HRH The Duke of Edinburgh, and Sylvia Gray, the NFWI National Chairman at the time, was appointed to the Council. The objects of the year were:

> to awaken the interest of the European peoples in their common architectural heritage; to protect and enhance buildings and areas of architectural or historic interest; to conserve the character of old towns and villages; and to assure for ancient buildings a living rôle in contemporary society. [11]

32 Federations were represented at the Workshop, where they learned more about the Government plans to set up Conservation Areas, and how they could find out more about the plans in their own areas. They received information about grants available for tree planting and housing improvement; they heard about 'Operation Eyesore' and about money which was available for tourism projects. The delegates returned to their Federations with plenty of suggestions as to what they might do next, including organising 'Treasures Surveys' in conjunction with Local Authorities, devising guided walks of villages, and drawing local maps to show points of special interest for visitors.

The author's own Federation in East Sussex became very active and organised a 'Countryside Resources Survey' in conjunction with the County Council Planning Department. The local survey organisers attended a briefing conference and received instructions and a questionnaire and a large scale map of their allocated 'area'. In completing the questionnaires and filling in the maps, all the WI members involved learned a lot more about their villages. The author recalls thinking, at the time, that this was just something being done in East Sussex, not knowing anything about the Workshop that had been held at Denman. The 'ordinary' member does not necessarily appreciate how what goes on at Denman is of relevance to her.

Subsequently many East Sussex WIs wrote illustrated booklets of Village Walks. In the usual WI way, a Federation competition was held. The assistant County Planning Officer agreed to judge the booklets and the County Council Planning Department agreed to publish the winning one. In the event they were so impressed by the standard of the guides that they published five of them, which went on sale to the public through Tourist Information Centres and other outlets, incidentally bringing in a steady income to the successful WIs for a number of years.

The first Denman Workshop was deemed a success and others followed. In 1975 there was one on 'Voluntary Work'; in 1976 the subject was 'Visual and Other Aids'. The name 'Workshop' became more widely used, but the principle of using Denman College as a venue for promoting new ideas to representatives of Federations continues to this day.

Home economics

The teaching of Home Economics, as we have seen from the first part of this book, has been central to the work of the WI since it began. When Denman College opened, cookery, gardening, and household management were all part of the 'Country Housewives' courses. The training that had been going on in the past for tutors, demonstrators, and Produce Guild Leaders, now took place at Denman.

The college was not able to teach practical cookery very effectively when it first opened, as there was only a small demonstration kitchen in the main house and anything 'messy', like cutting up a pig (p 120), had to be done in the garage.

Although students indicated that they would like to do more practical work, this was not possible until proper facilities were available. To convert the RAF huts in the grounds required a lot of money, but by a happy chance Berkshire County Council were looking for a site for a new Rural Domestic Economy School and Doris Cumming , their RDE Instructress, suggested that they might combine with the WI and convert the huts. NFWI leased two and a half acres of land and two of the huts to the County Council and contributed half the cost of converting these into a Demonstration Centre, to be renamed Home Acres.

Many counties had Rural Domestic Economy departments as part of their adult education service. This was a direct result of the work of Lady Denman who, in 1925, had chaired a committee set up by the Ministry of Agriculture and Board of Education to consider the "practical education of women for rural life". The resulting Denman Report was published in 1928.

There was a delay in starting the conversion, and in the meantime The Croft had opened, so the college could now accommodate up to 50 students. The old demonstration kitchen in the house now had to be used to provide more dining space and there was nowhere to give cookery demonstrations. This was when the Kent Federation's caravan came into its own – in 1948 this caravan had been given to the college, which at first thought that it might be used as extra accommodation, but then found that it was fitted up as a canteen. Now it was used until Home Acres was ready. Home Acres life is recalled by someone who worked there:

> [It was] arranged in the shape of an 'H' with the front door in the centre of the corridor which connected the two wings. The left hand side contained a flat used by Miss Cumming and her sister, office, preparation kitchen, lecture and demonstration room and storeroom. The right hand side was used by Denman College mostly for craft subjects… Part of the grounds (away from Denman College) were used for growing a few vegetables and flowers, we took great pride in producing an annual border. We also fenced off a small 'field' and kept poultry, geese and goats… Most of our time was spent preparing and giving demonstrations to Berkshire WIs. We also gave demonstrations to Denman College students and supervised their practical work in such subjects as Wine Making, Fruit Preservation, Trussing Poultry. [12]

When Home Acres opened, Doris Cumming wrote an article for *Home and Country*:

> Many Berkshire women now look forward to taking part in an interesting experiment in rural education… new kitchens, gardens, livestock paddock and handicraft rooms will be very useful and will extend in an interesting way the scope of the work both of the Berkshire Education Authority's rural domestic economy service and of Denman College…

> The countrywoman can learn to select, grow and multiply her rabbits, use their meat, and eventually provide members of her family with warm gloves…

> The development of garden and allotment in close co-operation with the kitchen is an interesting feature, and it is probably the first time that an Education Authority has provided such complete arrangements for this type of instruction. [13]

At this time the Market Garden was operating from the walled garden just through the wall from Home Acres. Elisabeth Harvey, who worked as an assistant to Doris Cumming remembers that one of her jobs was to "go and buy fresh fruit and vegetables from the market garden … it had wonderfully rich soil and the blackcurrants were like grapes." [14]

The happy association of Denman with Home Acres lasted until 1967 when Berkshire County Council moved their Rural Home Economy centre to Abingdon, to the new Further Education College. NFWI had then to equip a kitchen themselves in Home Acres.

Three years later, when the Teaching Centre was built, Home Acres was demolished. In the new building there was a small preparation kitchen and two 'mobile' electric cookers that could be used for demonstrations, but it did not contain a kitchen suitable for practical classes, so students on such courses had to be taken to the Further Education College in Abingdon. This makeshift arrangement ended in 1979 when the Home Economics Centre was opened.

Now that there was a fully equipped practice and demonstration kitchen, the number and variety of courses offered was vastly increased so that members could take new concepts and practices back to their Federations. Speciality courses could be provided and new ventures supported. In 1980 Kellogs sponsored the first of a series of Nutrition Conferences. These were similar to the Denman Workshops described in the previous section; Federations nominated representatives to come who were then expected to go back and 'cascade' the information they had gained.

Federations could book the Home Economics Centre for demonstration days, and ten did so in the first year. The NFWI Home Economics Adviser had been closely involved in the planning of the new centre, and was used as a tutor in many of the courses. At this time the NFWI Home Economics certificates were being piloted for the first time, and Denman was a focus of much of this activity.

Accreditation

In the 1920s the Handicraft Guild was awarding certificates to WI members who took the 'Proficiency tests' (p 46). These were seen as an essential part of maintaining standards and gave a progression route for those who wished to become instructors, demonstrators or judges. Later, in 1939, when the Produce Guild was set up, it offered similar accreditation. It concentrated on the preservation and canning of surplus food as part of the war effort, and when equipment for canning was donated to NFWI by American and Canadian women (p 82) members had to be trained to use it. Perhaps NFWI was ahead it its time by offering a 'Certificate in Competence to Can' long before National Vocational Qualifications (NVQs) and other 'competence based qualifications' were introduced. The tests which formed the basis for these awards were arranged in the Federations but the instructors, demonstrators, teachers, examiners and judges were nationally trained.

In 1956, when the total membership of the WI was 457,000, the Produce Guild had a membership of 58,138, and examiners visited Federations on 61 occasions spending 118 days in testing candidates in the various subjects. From a total entry of 501 for the full tests there were 408 passes, and for the preservation proficiency test 499 passes out of an entry of 590. The Handicraft Guild membership was 24,717, travelling tutors took 55 schools in 25 counties and there were 166 entries for craft tests and 83 passes. [15] To support all this work in the Federations, training courses were run at Denman for the tutors, examiners and Guild leaders.

The Guilds continued to flourish, but in 1973 they were abolished on the grounds that it was wrong for WI members to have to pay an 'extra' subscription in order to be able to take part in what should be activities open to all. A new subcommittee for Home

Economics and Specialised Crafts was set up which reflected the changing interests of members; by the 1970s there were far fewer WI members who fitted the traditional 'countrywoman' image. A new system of Home Economics certificates was introduced and Denman became important as a focus for the retraining of tutors and assessors. A network of Certificate Organisers was set up to help to stimulate interest in the new qualifications and to organise classes and tests. In 1980, 500 students obtained certificates.

In the 1980s some of the Denman courses were leading to a qualification provided by an external examination board. The students came on a course, went home and did more work, and then returned to Denman for more tuition. These were the first examples of linking two courses together in this way. Three courses run in 1987 that led to awards given by City and Guilds Examinations Board were 'Guest House and Small Establishment Management: Module 3: Customer Contact and Business Aspects', and 'Trees and Shrubs' and 'How to Design your Garden', which were two modules towards a City and Guilds Certificate in Amateur Gardening.

Receiving accreditation for the public speaking programme linked NFWI training with the RSA Examinations Board. 'Speaking with Confidence' courses had been offered for many years in various forms, but in the 1980s these courses were revised and in 1987 the RSA Certificate in Spoken English was awarded for the first time. This type of development is expensive and usually requires some outside funding, in this case a grant from the Carnegie United Kingdom Trust. In addition, City Literary Institute provided some trainers. The NFWI now trains the team of tutors and assessors and courses are offered both at Denman and in the Federations.

To get a certificate from one of the national awarding bodies provides an important recognition of skills to some members. There are members who start by taking a WI certificate because 'it's only a WI certificate' and it does not sound threatening. However when they emerge with the certificate and new confidence in their skills, they then start to ask, 'What is this certificate worth outside the WI? What can it lead on to? Will it give me exemption from part of any other qualification?' It is in order to provide this sort of progression for those members who want it that NFWI has worked towards linking its internal training to external certification:

> WI qualifications, satisfactory as they are, are not now sufficient for all members. Therefore, as a result of Education department initiatives, negotiations are now taking place with other validating bodies. The aim is to gain either exemption from part or all of a nationally recognised qualification for holders of WI certificates, or for WI training to move closer to, or to encompass, that required by other examining bodies. [16]

Negotiations, carried out by both NFWI staff and the Denman Director of Studies, have finally come to fruition in the late 1990s. In conjunction with City and Guilds, and funded by a grant from the Department of Education and Employment, the NFWI Home Economics certificates have been converted to competence-based form, and they can now act as stepping stones towards other City and Guilds awards. At the same time the NFWI trainers, assessors and demonstrators awards have been linked to the relevant units from the National Vocational Qualifications (NVQs) in Training and Development at Level 3, so that the long awaited progression routes are now getting into place.

In recent years some of the Denman College courses, especially craft courses have been accredited by the Open College Network (OCN). Now tutors who have taught these courses at Denman are travelling to other parts of the country as part of the Travelling Tutor scheme and are able to help WI members to get OCN credits. OCNs are available on 40 courses with nearly 300 students opting to apply.

In the 1990s further 'linked learning' opportunities have been developed to enable students to work towards outside qualifications. There are some courses which have been taught partly by two or three courses at the College, with study at home between. Whilst working at home the student is supported by open learning materials and phone contact with the tutor, who marks assignments and returns them by post. There are members who have obtained the RSA Advanced Diploma in the Organisation of Community Groups in this way, and the City and Guilds Basic Counselling Skills Certificate.

The 'New Horizons' programme was introduced in 1995, offering members an opportunity to study for some GCSEs and A levels. In the first year five out of the nine students attained an A grade. Members are prepared to travel considerable distances to be part of the unique and supportive group; one WI Associate – a recently introduced category of member who can join NFWI directly rather than any particular local WI – who lives in France has travelled by Eurostar to attend the six weekly day schools. A member who was successful in A level English Literature and Language wrote that she had "a feeling of personal achievement after 600 hours of study."

This area of work will never be large, and it is important that no member ever feels either compelled to take a qualification or put off coming on a course at Denman because of the system of accreditation. The system is in place for those who want it, to allow them to progress further if they wish. One such member wrote:

> I left [school] without taking O levels … there may be a time when I have to fend for myself, perhaps I ought to 'collect' some kind of paperwork in the things I like best… I had gained a great deal of enthusiasm for needlework at Denman – so I started to gather it together for a Certificate in Embroidery and then one in Soft Furnishing… It made me bring my whole life's history of sewing together – because I did start doing embroidery at the age of four. It made me look at exhibitions, visit museums, find out how dying of modern materials and yarns was achieved and seek out more Denman courses in the more off-beat avenues of Stumpwork and Blackwork. I actually disliked every day I went to school, but this way of learning – the Denman way – has been a delight. [17]

Science

An introduction to one of the discussion topics at a recent conference of the Adult Residential Colleges Association read:

'I am a man; nothing human is alien to me.' The Roman poet who wrote this is unusual. In fact most adults have seemingly vast areas of experience which are alien educationally. For example, we know that wild horses won't drag even good adult students to study some science subjects in residential weekends. Is this a problem we should address? If so how? [18]

Denman College has been facing similar questions for many years. The first science course appeared on the college programme (as an 'A/B' course) in 1956. It had the rather 'gentle' title of 'Science and Ordinary People' and the course description read:

In these days of rapid scientific developments it is important that ordinary people should become used to scientific ideas and their application to our everyday lives, and for parents to be able to keep pace with the interests of their children. Examples will be taken from electricity, simple chemistry, and the peaceful use of atomic energy for domestic heating and health. For county committee members and VCOs and others who are prepared to stimulate interest in the subject in their Counties, but not necessarily give talks themselves. [19]

So this course was not really for 'ordinary people,' and the lecturers were hardly 'ordinary' either; they included Sir Raymond Priestly on the peaceful uses of atomic energy, Dame Kathleen Lonsdale on chemistry and Sir George Allen on electricity. It was reported that "all had a real gift for explaining scientific developments in simple terms of everyday things." [20] As a result of this course the NFWI was made an honorary corporate member of the British Association for the Advancement of Science, and four WI members attended its next annual meeting in Sheffield. A second science course followed in 1957, though the lecturers were less august.

The driving force behind these science courses was Pat Jacob, who had a scientific training herself and was a member of the General Education Subcommittee, and who subsequently became National Chairman. She hoped to use these courses as a way of stimulating more interest in science throughout the WI. In 1958 she chaired four inter-county conferences, also called 'Science and Ordinary People' with different scientists as speakers at each. In spite of all her efforts there is not much evidence of further activity – it would seem that the WI was not yet ready for science.

The science story starts again in 1990 at a meeting of the Women's Working Group of the Royal Society of Arts. Jill Nelson of COPUS attended the meeting as part of a COPUS programme to target 'women'. COPUS – the Committee on the Public Understanding of Science – is a joint venture of the Royal Society, the British Association for the Advancement of Science and the Royal Institution. It was established in 1986 with the aim of raising the profile and level of public understanding of science activities in the UK. The author was also at this meeting as a representative of the NFWI, and afterwards asked Jill if COPUS would consider putting on a course for WI members at Denman. She subsequently visited the college, and found in Graham Jones, the Principal, who was himself a scientist, a ready collaborator and thus a COPUS course was planned for 1992.

This was a three day 'science event', filling the whole college and called 'Science, You and Everyday Life'. It was fully sponsored by COPUS and 60 Federation representatives attended, the majority of whom had no previous qualifications in or knowledge of science. The intention was to show how science and mathematics could be relevant, accessible and, most importantly, fun. There was also an expectation that the WI representatives would promote science activities in their own WIs and Federations.

Many of those who attended this 'science event' did feel motivated enough to go back to their Federations and share something of what they had learned. In 1993 there was a second Science Awareness course, this time with OCN credits at level 3 from London Open College Federation on offer – the first to be offered at the College.

In 1994 a further science event was run. This time participants from just four regions were invited so that there would be room for each to bring a member of the Executive Committee from their Federation. Although there is no formal division of the country into 'regions', Federations are grouped informally into six regional groups or 'areas'. This event was an attempt to get support for activities 'back home' where there was much apathy to be countered. These were the pioneer 'Science Co-ordinators' who went back to set up science awareness programmes in their Federations. In 1995 further COPUS support enabled them to implement some of their plans.

The programmes varied. Some invited local scientists to speak at conferences, others organised visits. Some of the science co-ordinators themselves gave talks and demonstrations to WIs, many with unusual titles: 'The Scientific Approach to Spring Cleaning', 'Pink Elephants over the Rainbow', and 'Mad Music' which used all sorts of household equipment to make a variety of sounds.

This time it would seem that the WI was ready for science. Building on the success of this pilot, the scheme was extended to the whole country. In the spring of 1996, the first edition of a WI Science Newsletter was published. In the opening article Professor Lewis Wolpert, Chairman of COPUS, wrote:

> I am personally delighted at the speed and enthusiasm with which the WI have embraced science and engineering... The cascade effect of the courses at Denman College has been quite amazing! The 60 COPUS/WI members went back to their Institutes to organise science days, talks and visits thus enthusing more and more WI members, to the extent that COPUS and Denman College are now setting up a network of Area Science Co-ordinators, plus deputies, in each of the six areas...

> Don't forget that in 1994 COPUS commissioned a formal evaluation of its schemes and projects and that the initiative with the WI came out as being the most successful of all the many different projects COPUS is involved with. [21]

In September 1996 the WI Science Co-ordinators Network was formally launched at the British Association Annual Festival of Science held at Birmingham University. COPUS have also provided a grant for a Scientist in Residence at Denman. Mary Harris, a mathematician, worked with the textile courses 'Hand knitting', 'Cushions, Curtains and Blinds' and 'Patchwork'. In her report she wrote:

As anticipated by the Planning Group the main mathematical activity was concerned with geometry of the rectangle and triangle, with parallel lines and with accurate measurement. I have noted the high level of problem solving activity. There was a lot of work on symmetry and the development of patterns, though it was not called that … mathematics was deeply embedded in the activity, an integral part of the work, only becoming something daunting when removed from the context of the work. This is a major problem in mathematics education, not just at Denman. [22]

In due course this activity led to the setting up of the WI Mathematics Network, which held its inaugural meeting in January 1997. The first news letter appeared in the following May.

A satisfactory confirmation of the way in which an idea can develop and 'cascade' from a course at Denman to activities all over the country, was provided when the President reported to the members of the author's own WI, "As they are wanting us to do more about science, the committee thought we would arrange a visit to the Isaac Newton Telescope and science exhibition."

Has the founder's vision been fulfilled?

At the AGM just before she retired as Principal in 1981, Hilda Jones said:

My everyday dream is that the educational work we are doing at the college will not be in isolation – it will not benefit just the individual, though this is important, but will filter through to little and large institutes all over the country, and so play an important part in the work of the movement as a whole. [23]

The five case studies above illustrate that this dream, and the founder's vision, have, at least to some extent, been fulfilled.

PART 3

WHAT IS SPECIAL ABOUT DENMAN?

CHAPTER FIFTEEN

WHAT IS 'SPECIAL' ABOUT DENMAN COLLEGE?

How does Denman compare with other short-stay residential colleges?

Denman is one of approximately 30 short-stay colleges belonging to the Adult Residential Colleges Association (ARCA), most of which were set up in the immediate post-war period. Many of them were influenced by Sir Richard Livingstone and reflected his interest in the Scandinavian Folk High Schools – there is an account of a visit to a Swedish Folk High School in **Appendix 5**. Although Sir Richard was involved in the development of many of the colleges, Denman seems to have been a favourite. In 1953, speaking at the celebration of the college's fifth birthday, Sir Richard said:

> I may say I have always regarded Denman College as, in many ways, the most inspiring of all adult education colleges since the war. Since I retired I have travelled through the United States, Canada and Australia and I have always urged my audiences to come and see Denman College when they are in England and, on their return home, to 'go and do likewise.' [1]

Of the ARCA colleges Denman is the only one owned and run by a voluntary organisation; the others are run by Local Education Authorities or by Trusts. The majority are in big, historic houses, many surrounded by parkland and with an elegance not dissimilar to Denman.

> Livingstone and Waller used very similar vocabulary in arguing the virtues of residential adult eduction: 'graceful living', 'beautiful things', 'enjoyment', 'refreshment and light', 'fellowship', 'peace and inspiration', etc. – all in good and beautiful surroundings. But they did not have any sense of the social purpose, or belief in positive discrimination for the disadvantaged, that had inspired many of the long-term residential colleges. Their vision was of opportunities for cultural improvement available to everyone, regardless of their social or educational background. [2]

Walter Drews, a past Chairman of ARCA, and Principal of Wansfell College for 20 years, visited all the other short-stay colleges in the early 1990s as part of his doctoral research. He has also been a tutor at Denman for 20 years, and so he is well placed to compare them all. He considers that Denman is:

> … unique in Britain – it stands out in a class of its own; no other college has the practical facilities – for home economics and fine craft. [3]

Having the support of Federations to lavish care and attention on the furnishings certainly helps to make Denman unique. On Walter's first visit to Denman, Helen

Anderson, who was the Warden then, showed him round some bedrooms. At first he thought it was curious to show bedrooms to a potential tutor, but he was impressed by the care put into the choice of the soft furnishings, and found the way that the rooms reflected different parts of the country really interesting, and this gave him an insight into the nature of the college. [4] His PhD thesis provides an invaluable source of information about the short-stay colleges and allows us to see how Denman compares with the typical college. [5]

Denman students can be compared with those at other ARCA colleges because the latter are described in the Residential Colleges Research Project [6] which was carried out in 1989-90 by John Field, now Professor of Adult Education at University of Ulster, and then at Warwick University. The project involved six ARCA colleges but did not include Denman. This study showed that three quarters of the students at the colleges surveyed were female and over half were over 50 years old. This led John Field to conclude that:

> short-term residential colleges have become leaders in the field of Third Age Education … educationally it is a really exciting development. Older adults are massively under-represented in every other form of education provision. [7]

Equally we can claim that Denman is playing an important part in providing for this under-represented group, as very nearly all Denman students are women and almost three quarters of Denman students are over 55 years old.

The Warwick project showed that students who attend short-stay colleges also take part in other adult education classes, they show a leaning towards the arts, and display a firm sense of citizenship and sociability. About half of them left school at the minimum school leaving age and their income whilst at work was probably that of a skilled tradesman, secretary, administrator or even middle manager, but seldom above that rank. They attended their residential courses, not in order to train for a job but to learn for learning's sake.

Like the students in the Warwick survey, about half of Denman's students left school at the minimum leaving age and it is clear that very few of the respondents to the questionnaire were employed at a level above middle management. [8]

It seems that Denman students are similar in many respects to those students who go to other short-stay colleges. The differences are that they are all women (except for occasional male guests), that they belong to the WI, and that they have a slightly higher average age.

Denman's programme has a larger number of courses in a year than any of other short-stay college. The programme for Wansfell College in Essex, for 1997–98, for example, advertises 132 short courses, in addition to day schools and study tours. The 1997 programme for Urchfont Manor in Wiltshire, which lists courses from January to October, advertises 75 short courses, numerous day schools and some study tours and special events. In the Denman Jubilee programme, 1997–98, there are 335 short courses advertised in the open programme. In addition there are 24 Federation visits most of which will have between three and five courses arranged, as well as NFWI training courses, study tours, and a variety of special events and 'cascade' conferences.

Perhaps one of the main achievements of the short-stay colleges generally is bridging the gap between vocational and non-vocational adult education. [9] The Warden of Grantley Hall in Yorkshire summarised the main purpose of the colleges as being:

> … to provide general courses for all comers without qualification or restraint, to arrange special courses for particular groups such as teachers or supervisers in industry, and to give hospitality to other bodies seeking to hold courses or conferences of their own. [10]

This is true for most of the other short-stay colleges, but, as we have seen, Denman has only been let to outside bodies very occasionally in recent years. Because it is the college of a large national voluntary organisation it supports its range of activity itself, by running not only the open programme but also training programmes for NFWI and WI Country Markets, and the Federation programmes.

The open courses on offer at Denman, apart from the WI-oriented ones, look very similar to those on the programmes of some of the other colleges. [11] The Denman programme has a greater emphasis on craft, home economics, and personal development courses, but the 'cultural' courses are very similar.

Short-stay residential courses are criticised by some adult educators; for example, Derek Legge writes:

> Besides the difficult question of cost there are assertions that the courses are shallow and too short to allow for systematic study, that they lack coherence, and that despite the euphoria sometimes engendered, they fail to achieve any enduring worthwhile educational result. Against this, there is some subjective though substantial, evidence that residence makes a   significant impact on the development of interests and awareness, and that even a short absence from home and work can effect quite remarkable learning and attitude changes. There are no short cuts to learning and perhaps an enjoyable weekend makes it seem too easy, but a relaxed atmosphere helps to reduce emotional barriers to learning. This kind of relaxed, face-to-face, understanding atmosphere is what the colleges are supremely able to create and, with a full-time educational staff, they can claim to be more conducive to learning than most hotels or other hired premises. [12]

This 'relaxed' learning is especially notable at Denman. The 'safe' environment of being with fellow WI members is particularly important in encouraging less confident women to return to learning:

> Would the value of short-term residence be improved by devising consecutive series of courses, perhaps in the form of linked but spaced weekends or mid-week periods, a rather different kind of 'sandwich' course? If the short-term residential courses are only 'a hostel along the way, a temporary stopping-off place,' should not there be greater attempts to integrate them with surrounding non residential work? [13]

This extract was used as a basis for discussion at the ARCA Curriculum and Accreditation Study Course, Wedgewood Memorial College, December 1966, "Was the view expressed still pertinent?"

Denman is probably in a better position than many other short-stay colleges to attempt to bring about such integration. It is in the use of the college for training programmes that the work of the NFWI can best influence what happens in the Federations and WIs. This is well illustrated by the case studies in Chapter 14.

In recent years the introduction of accreditation, particularly working with the Open College Federation, has provided more courses in which the achievements of the students can be measured. Other short-stay colleges do also offer OCN accredited courses, and some offer a series of progressive courses leading to other outside qualifications, but Denman is unique in being able to offer, with the Federations, 'linked learning' opportunities (p 218).

Kathy Tiernan, Director of Studies at Denman, has worked with tutors to put together OCN submissions. To do this the aims, methods and outcomes of courses have to be clearly defined. Many tutors have welcomed the opportunity to work with Denman in this way, using it as a means of their own 'staff development', something which is usually difficult to offer in a short-stay college.

The Denman Management Committee is aware, however, that having too much emphasis on accreditation might lose the joy of learning for learning's sake, and they insist that there should be no pressure on any student to take OCN credits. There are those who claim that the short-stay colleges are the last bastions of liberal adult education and as such should be fiercely protected.

Almost half the tutors who completed the questionnaire indicated that they worked at other short-stay colleges, a total of 21 different ones were mentioned. Most said that Denman compared favourably with other short-stay colleges; many of them felt that there was something 'special' about Denman. The following extracts from their replies show how they express this:

[Compares] very well indeed … caring yet without fuss and ostentation.

… very favourably, these colleges are very different in character and course requirements, Denman has everything they have, plus a little extra.

The atmosphere of support, friendship, good fellowship and warmth is more pronounced at Denman than anywhere else. The community of staff, and therefore students, is uniquely warm and supportive at Denman.

It is unique, after nearly 50 years of rapid and constant social change, Denman continues to enjoy the support of NFWI and the majority of its students are enthusiastic and benefit from the residential experience.

… what the members bring to it – it feels 'owned'. It is for women, without being feminist.

I perceive the ethos of Denman, of making the students 'visit more' than the course they are taking, an added bonus: what is spoken of as 'the Denman Experience', this runs like a thread through everything.

Denman College is never still – always progressing and moving forward with vision *(from a tutor who has been coming to the college for ten years)*

first class leadership and vision at the top. [14]

Wardens and Principals

The Warden or Principal of a short-stay college has a very particular rôle to play, in addition to being involved with drawing up the programme. In an establishment that has constantly changing tutors and students coming in and out every week, the Principal provides the 'continuity' which cannot be offered in any other way. In many of the other short term colleges the Principal is also the host or hostess, at Denman the College Chairmen fill this rôle, but they are only there for a few days at a time. The continuity of the Principal is important, as has been demonstrated at Denman in the past. When the college has rapid changes of Principal, it can begin to lose its way.

Professional isolation is a problem for all Wardens of short-stay colleges. There are not many places where only a single institution of its kind exists in a county or region. This is especially true of Denman because it is independent of the LEA structure. It was in an attempt to relieve this isolation that the Standing Conference of Wardens was formed (changing its name in 1968 to the Association of Wardens/Principals of Short-Term Colleges of Residential Adult Education, and finally in 1992 to the less cumbersome Adult Residential College Association). Membership of the Standing Conference was limited to those colleges where the Warden was involved in the designing and promoting of a programme of liberal adult education which occupied the greater part of the academic year; this left out conference centres, staff training centres, and halls of residence. [15]

Denman Wardens were involved from the beginning, appreciating the opportunity to get together and exchange ideas; Denman hosted the conference for the first time in 1959, when there were 29 colleges with a total of 50,000 students attending in the year. In the mid 1990s approximately 100,000 students attend short-stay residential adult education in a year, 6% of these are at Denman College.

The advantages of short-stay residential adult education

To withdraw from the world in order to concentrate for a short period of time on one thing, is considered to have a special value by people as varied as leaders in industry who take their senior managers away to plan for the company's future and clergy who take their church members to retreat houses. The short-stay colleges incorporate the same advantages.

The college buildings are often old and attractive, many are in their own extensive grounds. The settings and the ambience of the college gives a relaxed and 'separate' feel away from normal pressures of life. They give the student a change in environment, and the opportunity to live for a few days in comfortable and 'civilised' surroundings. By getting away from the demands of everyday life students can dedicate themselves entirely to the task in hand – study, practice, reflection – Walter Drews calls this a 'cultural island'. [16]

The curriculum of many of the short-stay colleges centres around small groups where discussion-based courses can flourish, on literature, the arts, history, music, drama, current affairs; all subjects where there is an opportunity to share ideas. In those colleges where there are the facilities, practical arts and crafts are taught and creativity develops. All these courses gain added value from being taught in a residential setting where there is an opportunity to trade ideas across courses. There is also a hidden curriculum of increased self-confidence, through learning in such a supportive setting.

Staying in one place, away from home and work pressures and with no outside distractions, allows:

> concentration on learning, with education scheduled at all hours, and the whole person involved in the learning process without gaps for work and the family responsibility. [17]

This continuity aids concentration, and tutors comment that very little time is lost between sessions, time is not lost clearing and setting up the room where the course is held, and students can get straight back to work again each time they return after a break. A two to three day residential course can cover as much as a term's work done in an evening class.

Residential courses engender a sense of community, and friendships are easily made. Through constant association at meals, in sessions, or talking late into the night, individuals learn about themselves and others, and get support and encouragement from each other.

Sir Richard Livingstone wrote:

> Education is atmosphere as well as instruction; it is not an assemblage of piecemeal acquisitions and accomplishments, but the formation, largely unconscious, of an outlook and an attitude. [18]

The residential adult education college is the ideal place to create such an atmosphere.

> Within the range of adult education provision, the residential centre has a special role to play, offering the student an opportunity to study in a different, more detached ambience with time to concentrate on learning along with others in a supportive environment. [19]

These are some of the advantages of short-stay residential adult education which Denman shares with other short-stay colleges. When we compare Denman with the other colleges, however, we can see that, although there is a great deal that they have in common, in a number of significant ways Denman is different, and to some degree 'special'.

Seven Special Aspects of Denman

1. It is owned by a voluntary organisation

Being owned by the NFWI the college can reflect the needs and values of the parent organisation. The women who come to the college all belong to the WI and this gives it a 'family feel' and a special supportive atmosphere. This sense of 'ownership', and the welcome given both to members and tutors is obviously special.

Belonging to a national organisation means that the college can be used as a centre for training, and can be a 'hub' for the educational work of the whole WI. The courses can reflect what members want and provide a stimulus for new initiatives. Denman becomes the learning centre of the organisation, but that learning takes place throughout the country as well as at the college.

Members of voluntary organisations often do not appreciate how much they are learning through their membership. Keith Percy, in a project to investigate learning activity in voluntary organisations, came to the conclusion that:

> Generally, adults join voluntary organisations to do rather than to learn. However, *doing – and development in doing – seems to require learning activity, or even to be learning activity.* [20]

Konrad Elsdon has carried out extensive research into voluntary organisations, and in a six-year-long project he studied different kinds of voluntary organisations and asked:

> What is the formal *and* informal, educational *and* educative impact which voluntary organisations make on individuals, groups and communities? [21]

In a detailed study of Sibsey WI in Lincolnshire, he found for example that:

> in *all* instances joining the Institute was followed by (and usually considered responsible for) a great expansion and intensification of activity. This was seen by a high proportion especially as a preparation for, or even the source of involvement in, service to other organisations, or public service itself. [22]

These studies show that people who belong to voluntary organisations will acknowledge that they have learned through their activities, although few would describe it as education. It is 'education by stealth'.

In every WI this type of 'education by stealth' is taking place. Most women join their local WI in order to make friends and have enjoyable and interesting activities in company with other like-minded women. But in the process they may well start off along a learning path. Opportunities are offered, it might be a day school, or it might be winning a WI bursary to Denman, that can lead to things they never dreamt.

When the Denman programme is planned, the NFWI subcommittees are asked to suggest possible courses that relate to their interests and work, so that the college programme can reflect and support the wider educational work of the organisation. Any courses suggested can be included in the programme, but in the end there is no guarantee that a course will recruit sufficient numbers to be viable. The NFWI subcommittee may feel that the members ought to come to a course on some serious social concern of the day, but the individual member may prefer to spend her money on a course which will teach her some new skill to enhance her leisure hours.

For economic reasons the beds have to be filled. The college budget assumes that 60 of the 73 beds will be filled whenever the college is open. If a course has insufficient people enrolled (usually eight is the minimum number), it will be cancelled, sufficiently far ahead to allow another course to be slotted in its place. This will usually be a repeat of a course that has a waiting list. All adult education colleges know that not every course they advertise will recruit sufficiently well to be able to run. Denman's records show that the programme planners are usually 'getting it about right' as only 6% of courses have to be cancelled.

Cancelling 6% of the courses has been fairly constant over the years. In 1956–57, for example, the college records show that only five of the 89 open courses planned were cancelled (6%). [23] In 1995–96, 334 courses were advertised, of which 22 were cancelled (again 6%). [24] The most common reason for cancellation is low enrolment, although there are inevitable cancellations when a tutor is ill and no suitable replacement can be found.

Sometimes, for new courses, there needs to be some special marketing. The Management Committee has accepted that this is an area that requires improvement; in an organisation of a quarter of a million women there ought to be ten who are interested in a topic, however innovative it might seem, if only they can be reached.

The founders stressed that the college should be a comfortable place. To someone entering Denman for the first time, this is a striking feature. It is comfortable, warm, well lit, and kept this way because constant attention is given to repairs and renewals. The students who come expect high standards, they are the owners who appreciate that they will learn better if they are physically comfortable. Denman's team of voluntary 'College Chairmen' ensure that the students are relaxed and know who to ask if they need any help. In a similar way the tutors find the team of support staff provide for their needs and respond to their requests, giving information before and during courses. This caring environment brings out the best in tutors and students, and means that the maximum amount of learning can take place in the short time available.

2. It is managed by a voluntary organisation

The majority of the short-stay colleges are owned and run by Local Education Authorities, who are responsible for their repair and upkeep. They can also decide to close a college if the upkeep gets too expensive, or if for some other reason they no longer wish to support it. 17 short-stay colleges have closed since 1955. The LEA-owned colleges are governed by an adult education committee, or its equivalent. Wedgwood Memorial College in Staffordshire, for example, is governed by North Staffordshire Committee for Adult Education (Staffordshire LEA in association with Keele University, the WEA and other local education bodies). [25]

Denman College is owned and managed by a voluntary organisation, a situation which has both strengths and weaknesses. One strength is that the whole organisation owns the college; it could not be closed without the approval of the members who bought it. The successors of those members will rally round when required, as shown when a million pounds was raised to 'Save Denman' in 1984–86. Another strength is that the members provide a ready supply of volunteers who can be called on to act as guides, gardeners, hostesses, librarians, and in many other rôles. Finally the organisation which owns the college provides the students who come to it.

A disadvantage is that, in the case of Denman at least, the Trustees are elected and change quite often, and they may have very little experience of running a short-stay residential college. This leads to a lack of continuity and a succession of 'bosses'. Another potential disadvantage is that, if the voluntary organisation itself ceases to exist, then so will the college. Their lives are inextricably linked:

Denman adds value to membership, but Denman's 'health' depends on the WI's survival. [26]

There are, or have been, few other short-stay colleges owned and run by voluntary organisations so that it is quite difficult to make many generalisations. However, the experiences of An Grianon, run by the Irish Countrywomen's Association (ICA), and Kingsgate, owned and run by the YMCA, serve to illustrate some of the advantages and disadvantages of such a situation.

An Grianon Adult Education Centre is an attractive house, built about 1780, five miles from Drogheda on the east coast of the Republic of Ireland. It was purchased by the W K Kellog Foundation of America and entrusted to the ICA in 1954 for "the health, education and welfare of the people of Ireland." Although meant for all the people, 96% of the students are women. The programme of short courses is not dissimilar to Denman, with many craft courses "...keeping alive and fostering a love of traditional arts and crafts such as basketry, crochet, Carrickmacross and Limerick lace..." [27] There have been exchange visits with students on lace courses between the Denman and An Grianon.

The management of the two is similar and Walter Drews recalls that the Director of Education at An Grianan once complained to him that he felt he had 53,000 bosses, and that the job was impossible. [28] This exemplifies how working for a voluntary organisation, especially a membership organisation, is particularly challenging. In LEA colleges the students do not consider themselves the 'owners' in the same way, and although there may be student representation on a Board of Governors many of the other members will probably be educationalists.

In an LEA college the Principal is usually responsible to the Director of Education and is given freedom to run the college along agreed lines. Walter Drews recalls that as Principal of Wansfell he only had a meeting twice a year with his 'line manager'. [29] At Denman, as we have seen in Chapter 13, the management structures have changed frequently, the changes reflecting how the college was perceived in relation to the NFWI Executive Committee. Like the Director of An Grianan, Wardens and Principals must have felt at times that they had a multitude of 'bosses'.

There is another danger in voluntary organisations, that of internal conflict. This happened at Kingsgate:

> Internal conflict of ideology was the reason for the closure of Kingsgate, the YMCA college. Here two factions in the education department reached an impasse, each wanting their philosophy interpreted at their residential college. The reasons given for the demise of Kingsgate were many but finance and the lack of modern accommodation were high on the list. The total loss for Kingsgate at the time of its closure in 1974 was £2,000 per annum, a tiny figure set against the national expenditure of the education department of the YMCA. There were few if any empty beds at Kingsgate in its last year in operation, indeed it had never been short of students and there is no evidence to date that the enrolments at short-term residential colleges depend on hotel-type accommodation, it is the educational content and the companionship which rank well beyond en-suite bedrooms and silver service. [30]

Power in voluntary organisations rests with the members, and their constitutions require their governing bodies to be elected, but, as Charles Handy writes in *Understanding Voluntary Organisations*:

> … if democracy is to work at all then someone in the end has to be trusted to get on with the job. Democracy does not mean, cannot mean, that everyone runs everything. It means, literally, that power comes from the people but that power is then entrusted temporarily to someone else … the more trust you give someone the less you should or can control them. Democracy, if it is to work, means, paradoxically, giving away some power for a time. [31]

3. It is largely self financing

Although Denman College is quite well endowed, its investment income provides only about 5% of the total running costs, so the fees of the students have to cover the rest.

Comparing the results of our questionnaire with the Warwick survey (see p 224), [32] more Denman students thought that the fees were high and fewer thought they were low — 15% compared with 3%, and 1% compared with 10%. The fees at Denman do indeed fall into the upper half of the fee range of short-stay residential colleges, because the college receives no subsidy.

Although being independent might be seen as a financial disadvantage, it can have compensations. In 1973 there were 35 short-stay residential colleges. Most of these were LEA colleges which had been getting financial support from the local authority amounting, in some cases, to almost half their costs. However when the financial difficulties of the late 1970s hit, many of these LEAs told their Wardens that they had to increase their income and aim for financial sufficiency. Some were unable to do this and in due course the colleges were forced to close. Others increased their fees, while some adopted

> ... a more market oriented approach to managing the colleges. In some colleges, high educational standards were sacrificed at times for fiscal gain. With the retirement of wardens or principals, some were replaced by managers at a much reduced salary and with job specifications that reflected fiscal rather than educational objectives.

> Most colleges have survived by diversifying, but not always in the best interest of general liberal adult education. No new colleges opened after 1975 and 17 have closed since 1955. [33]

Diversification is possible in a number of different ways, but there can be problems. If the courses and activities being offered at a college start being more for 'leisure' rather than 'education', 'murder' weekends for example, then the college has to pay VAT and the slippery slope begins; education is eroded and a college stops being a 'college'. Study tours are one way of increasing funding that many colleges have used, but, for the reasons listed above, these should provide an extension of learning, and not be just a holiday. This has been the intention with the study tours organised by Denman College, all of which have been accompanied by one of the well-established Denman tutors.

As we have seen, many of the LEA residential colleges are used in the mid-week for in-service training courses, industry courses, management training days, and similar activities. These subsidise the weekend adult education courses. One of the ways to increase income is to develop this side of the work more, and at least one short-stay college has become a management centre (**Table 5.1**).

Brian Leighton, the Principal of Alston Hall (an ARCA college in Lancashire), wrote, "Frankly, liberal adult education is in a more threatened state than at any time this century," [34] and he goes on to outline how Government funding has been withdrawn and how colleges are having to find new ways of getting money. For some this has meant a change in nature, as more time is given to management training and less time for liberal adult education. He concludes:

> Demographic changes in society and politicisation of previously undervalued groups, particularly the increasing population of retired people, could lead to a voice for adult education, and residential work especially, which will have some influence... The commitment of individuals and the co-operative efforts of ARCA should ensure a future for the work provided that the clear sense of purpose in liberal adult education is not eroded, and leaders in the field become more adept at financial planning and management. [35]

Denman has been able to keep up its numbers in spite of rising fees and falling WI membership by opening all year round. Having the whole of the WI organisation to give it support gives Denman an advantage. Many WIs have always provided bursaries to enable members to come to the college. The average WI has fewer than 30 members, but according to the results of the questionnaire many are giving £120 bursaries (**Figure 12.2**). WIs are now being encouraged to give more generous bursaries every other year, to ensure that those who could not otherwise afford to come to the college will still be able to. This is important, as one tutor noted; compared with other short-stay colleges Denman has a:

> … Special quality of students, many come with encouragement of friends, or bursary, who would not normally attend adult education – 'safe' feel of college fosters an openness and group warmth/trust – residential aspect enables an in-depth experience, sometimes life changing. [36]

4. It is for women

Being the only short-stay residential college for women does make Denman unique. The recent NIACE survey results (p 160) [37] were explained in *The Learning Divide* by Naomi Sargant. They showed that significantly more women (41%) than men (31%) reported that they had not undertaken any learning since leaving full-time education.

Richard Smethurst in his Livingstone lecture explained why he felt that short-stay residential education was particularly relevant for women:

> Women have not enjoyed the same educational advantages as men, so the need for education later in life to correct deficiencies in initial education is even greater for them. Further, the multiplicity and complex intermingling of their rôles in adult life means that women need different kinds of adult education provision at different times. It is not possible or sensible to characterise some provision as vocational and other as non-vocational: the defining character- istics lie in the use made of the learning opportunity, not in the narrowly construed 'subject' of the course.

> Residential adult provision is particularly important for women, because the special characteristics of residence help to build confidence and self-esteem within an enjoyable experience, factors important in overcoming the primary barrier to successful learning. Residence can also help to resolve the crucial time management conflicts which adult women learners in particular face; whilst short residential bursts of activity boost the learning process without alienating women from the family and other relationships which they prize. [38]

Denman being the only short-stay college for women, there are those who feel that the policy of allowing women to bring male partners is wrong and that the college should remain for women only. Several tutors have commented to the author that the men are resented by some members who don't feel that they should be there. Two tutors explained why. Most wives were 'concerned' about their husbands and as a result did not relax or participate as well. [39] In courses that involve discussion there is a tendency for the men to dominate and the women to stay quiet (perhaps nothing has changed since Nugent Harris noticed the same thing (p 25).

So many members report that coming to Denman raises their self-confidence, that anything that might destroy it is to be deplored. An example given was of a recent course on miniature furniture where two women brought their husbands. These men already had skills and they were far better and 'showed up' the women and 'put them off' at this first time when they were starting something new. [40]

However, to put this into proportion in 1995/6 only 173 men came on courses at the college (3% of the total attendance).

Denman meets not only educational but also social needs of members. It is a place to which some women come for its therapeutic value when they are sad or lonely. One tutor who has been tutoring courses at the college regularly over the past 20 years estimates that this could be as many as 10–15% of all the students:

> Women who are bereaved say this is a warm place to be, the other students are very human and thoughtful and helpful to each other. [41]

Hilda Jones (Director of Studies and later Principal in the 1960s and 70s) sees how the college gives women confidence to return to learning:

> What Denman College can do is unique – for women, residential education is so important, our members are coming back into education often after a long gap; the relearning process benefits vast numbers of people in retirement as well. [42]

The 'special' thing about Denman providing, for most of the time, an environment of women with women learning together is noted not only by tutors and principals but also by students within and without the organisation. In a study of the WI movement from a feminist viewpoint, [43] Maggie Morgan (now Andrews) concluded that:

> I have argued that the Movement provided in the period up to 1960 a space where women could develop their potential away from the scrutiny of men, whether in a village institute meeting, the intrigue of County or National executive, the AGM or Denman College. What women learned could vary from: how to run a meeting or organise fund raising, to acting and directing in a play or elaborate craft work. But it all helped them to challenge the internalisation of their oppression. Such activities had the potential to allow women to work out, adopt or adhere to different, more female, value systems than those usually offered to them by society. Certainly reappraisals of the significance and value of housework, of skill and of the distinction between art and craft were all part of this…

Some aspects of the Movement are not perhaps as once they were perceived. Denman College, if not the spearhead of women's education that Cicely McCall had hoped, runs a wide range of courses from craft to computing. However for those who attend, it still offers radical potential. Betty Burton, feminist author of over seven books including *Women are Bloody Marvellous,* was a member of West Meon WI in Hampshire. It was at a Denman College course on 'The Place of the Thriller in Literature' that she gained the confidence to start writing. She realised, "not all authors are of the Somerset Maugham variety" and that it is possible for someone with her lack of formal education to write for a living. Thus NFWI goes on providing space for women to carve out their own road to feminism [44]

5. It provides for older women

The NIACE survey referred to above (p 234) [45] also showed that only one in four adults aged 55–64 and one in five aged 65+ are actively involved in learning; 19% of 65–74-year- olds in the population report current or recent participation in learning.

Of the respondents in the survey conducted for this book (**Appendix 2**), 26% of those who had been to the college were between 66 and 75 years old, and 74% were over 55. Denman College is providing learning opportunities for older women, who might hesitate to go to other colleges.

The importance of providing learning opportunities to older people is gaining recognition:

> In a changing world it is vital for there to be opportunities for adults to respond to and under-stand change; whilst in a world where life expectancies are lengthening adults need to continue their education to preserve their mental agility… [46]

In 1996 NIACE launched a initiative, 'Older and Bolder', in order to draw attention to the importance of learning for older people:

> Lifelong learning is the key to continued well-being. Medical evidence is beginning to grow that engagement in education can prevent the onset of dementia… recent research has shown … not only previous education but also continued mental activity may be important for elderly people. Adult education programmes and stimulating mental activity may help to improve coping skills and strategies for solving problems and in turn these may help offset the cognitive effects of normal aging and delay the clinical symptoms associated with Alzheimer's disease. [47]

The 'Older and Bolder' initiative is aimed at increasing the total opportunities for older people in education, particularly those who have participated least in the past. By providing the stimulus of learning, older people can be helped to stay fit and active. Money spent on lifelong learning may even save money on social service provision, there is a:

> … need to explore much more fully the notion that involvement in stimulating activities lessens current and future dependency and therefore reduces welfare costs. Within this debate there needs to be challenged the narrow definition of work and the fallacy that older people are NOT economically active. There needs to be promoted more, with evidence, the belief that older people are a valuable community and family resource and not a burden. [48]

NFWI and Denman College are playing their part.

6. It provides for women who left school early

Today there is an increasing interest in lifelong learning. The Widening Participation Committee of the Further Education Funding Council has recommended targeting those learners most in need of help because they have had least opportunities in the past. An RSA MORI State of the Nation Poll revealed that there is a hard core of the population for whom learning is not seen as an option. They include people over 55 … with few or no qualifications. [49]

Our survey (**Appendix 2**) showed that WI members who had left school at 14 or 15 were just as interested in attending a course as those who left school later. It would seem that the college is able to attract women who might not participate in other forms of adult eduction.

7. Most of the women who come to Denman live in rural or semi rural areas

Although the common view of the countryside is that it is a desirable place to live there has been evidence in a number of recent research projects and reports that this is not necessarily the case. Those living in rural areas can be deprived and isolated. The Archbishops' Commission on Rural Areas in 1990 found that there was an increase in the number of elderly people living in the countryside and yet a decrease in local facilities. Those who were better off and had a car could travel to find those facilities but:

> … although some women whose lives are based mainly upon the home, benefit from a caring community life, others without transport and jobs, and living in inaccessible areas, find life limiting and narrow. [50]

Because women who live in rural areas do not have such easy access to adult education provision the WI has a part to play in providing locally. The Federations can also help by running classes and conferences.

A team from Sussex University Centre for Continuing Education explored the experiences and issues in rural adult education in four case studies in Cornwall, Derbyshire, East Sussex and North Yorkshire. One researcher also looked at the needs of and issues relating to rural women. The North Yorkshire case study was carried out by Mike Boice who visited both of the WI Federations that cover that area and noted that:

> … the individual Institute member has access to a whole range of Federation generated events as well as to the programmes which make up the dozen meetings a year of the local group, to the WI certificates (in home economics, public speaking etc) and to Leadership training. Great encouragement is also given to members to use the facilities and programmes of Denman College – 14% of members of North Yorkshire East Federation went there last year. [51]

Susan McGrath, looking at the women's perspective , wrote of the WI:

> [There is a] dearth of 30 to 40 year old women coming into the organisation and onto the ladder of leadership. It is this age group which is now seeking paid employment… The current leadership and membership within many WI branches are well into retirement age with few coming along to participate in, or manage, future groups. For every branch that offers a day and an evening group to attract those women who are working outside the home, there is a branch which is facing closure due to falling numbers. When it works, however, the WI and its Denman College structure can offer personal growth and confidence within a supportive, women-centred framework. A recommendation in a recent

report on *Caring for Rural Carers*, compiled by the WI (1993), offered to provide a bursary (sic) to make it possible to attend a course at Denman College on a subject of interest.

The WI may therefore be the accepted face of feminism within the rural community as it is increasing the recognition of transferable skills, and just listen to what it's doing for Clarrie Grundy in 'The Archers'. [52]

WI member Monica Leonard surveyed the WIs in East Kent to discover how the members perceived the WI and compared this with the attitudes of feminist writers in their approach to WIs. Some of these writers, for example Maggie Morgan, consider that the WI presents the 'acceptable face of feminism'. Monica Leonard agrees:

It is clear that the Institutes, in common with other organisations, are going through a period of crisis, particularly financial. In some respects this can be seen as a crisis of identity as many of the original aims of the movement have been met, but there are still objectives to be achieved. What is perceived as the shrill, pugnacious attitude of the feminist 'lobby' does not appeal to the majority of WI members. Perhaps there is a mutual distrust of each other within the two groups, who while striving for the same ends cannot accept each others' methods.

Whilst the appeal of the Women's Institutes still holds good in many areas, there is a dearth of new members to renew and revitalise the old institutes. Headquarters has made many attempts to reinvigorate the organisation but their continuing location in London is seen by some to be too remote from the grass roots, the members in the institutes...

No doubt the Women's Institutes will survive into the next century, but in what form it is difficult to determine. There is a need for such an organisation to represent the opinions and wishes of that section of the community who are repulsed by the more overt feminist agenda and who see leadership as a force which pushes as well as pulls. [53]

Conclusion

The work that the WI has done over the years to introduce adult education to women in rural areas has been unsung, and very little mentioned in education circles, or in the literature; it tends to be 'put down'. This is, perhaps, because it is 'marginalised' on a number of counts: it is about women (and now mainly older women), it is voluntary, it is rural and it is 'low key – first step' learning.

This lack of recognition has been acknowledged occasionally. For example Martin Pugh wrote in *Women and the Women's Movement in Britain 1914–1959*:

In spite of its size the WI movement has not attracted the attention of students of women's history which it deserves. Stuck with the Jam and Jerusalem tag, it is easily passed over as a joke or a mild embarrassment but historians must rid themselves of contemporary assumptions. [54]

In the past the WI has had little attention from adult educators also, and has barely been touched on in the literature. In a recent publication, *A History of Modern British Adult Education*, [55] the WI gets two pages in a 400-page book. A chapter entitled 'Informal

Learning' contains a section on 'Voluntary Organisations as Adult Auxiliaries' in which the writer remarks, "The Women's Institutes may be recognised as a more important contributor to auxiliary adult education than in the 1930s…" [56]

In this book I have attempted to show that the WI should be recognised as an important contributor to women's education. I have tried to explain the rôle that the WI has played in the adult education of women, predominantly in rural areas, and to show how, in the early years, it helped to break down class barriers, while in its later years it has had an important part to play in the education of older women.

Denman College is one of the most successful of the short-stay residential colleges, and yet there are still many, even in adult education circles, who have never heard of it. It occupies an important place within the educational work of NFWI as a training centre, a conference centre and as a place where new ideas can be introduced and tried and then 'cascaded' throughout the country. In writing this book I have also discovered the varied life-enhancing effects that it has had for very many individual women over the last 50 years.

Susan Stockley who has been both Chairman of the Denman Management Committee and National Chairman writes:

> Above all else I want to see the college recognised in the education world. [57]

The measures of success are not just numbers, or qualifications, or enhanced economic activity, although all of these exist. The true and vital measure is the way in which liberal adult education improves women's lives.

Denman College was an appropriate place in which to site Kathleen Parbury's bust of Sir Richard Livingstone. When he opened the college 50 years ago he said, "This spirit, the spirit of imagination, of faith, of enterprise, of perseverance, of co-operation, has brought Denman College into being. That is a great tradition for those who come here to be inspired by and to maintain."

Those who have come over the 50 years have been inspired, and those who are here today are determined to maintain.

POSTLUDE

In July 1997, when this book was almost finished, I came to Denman as a student. It was a fine art theme week and there were six courses running in parallel, 'Art Appreciation', 'Silk Painting', 'Drawing for Beginners', 'Sculpture in Clay, Wood or Stone', 'Flower Painting' and 'Pen and Wash'. My choice was 'Pen and Wash'.

Why had I chosen this course? Although I have drawn and sketched as a hobby for most of my life and have used pen and ink as a medium, I have never mastered wash, and I wanted to learn how to do it properly. This three day intensive course was just what I wanted, and I had never seen a course on just pen and wash offered as a local adult education class near my home.

This time I drive to Denman on my own. Through the Federation Denman Representative, I had offered to give a lift to anyone from East Sussex, but on this occasion no one wanted one. I have a small plastic crate with me containing all that the tutor has asked us to bring — pens and ink, two lemons, a pepper (any colour!), embroidery wool and a small nail brush... Whatever for?

As I arrive at the college I am greeted first by the College Chairmen — one of whom is the Denman Representative from Hertfordshire and the other, doing the job for the first time, is the Federation Chairman from East Yorkshire.

I make my way to my room, in Willow, one of the more recent cottages. The familiar friendliness is already in evidence as members help each other to master the press button codes which open doors, and those who have been before show new people the way. "Where is your room? Oh yes, I know, I'll show you... " As I reach Willow I look to see how the two new buildings are getting on, and see for the first time the raised bed with seats at the centre of the new quadrangle.

I return to the main house to have a cup of tea; the talk is all about journeys. Someone has been brought by her teenage son. "He wouldn't get out of the car..." Another tells of her husband who, having delivered her, is off to have a short golfing holiday whilst she is doing her course. A young primary school teacher has just broken up, and is delighted the course is in her holiday. I meet Susan Stockley, a past National Chairman who is now giving her time to sorting out the NFWI archives. We take our cups of tea out into the sunshine and talk about the best way of housing the archive materials to keep them safe but still to allow access for study.

By 6 pm most people have arrived and settled in their rooms. People begin to gather for a pre-dinner drink in the bar, or, on this sunny afternoon, outside. Some are asking where the phones are in order to make calls home. There is still some anxiety about those left behind and how they will cope... Will husband remember daughter's music lesson? Will the family find the food left ready in the fridge? Will the dog be all right in kennels?

At 6.30 pm we all gather in the Livingstone room for the 'Welcome', and as my neighbour, who is visiting the college for the first time, admires the ceiling I remember its discovery in 1984. Graham Jones, the Principal, says, "Welcome to your college," reminding us that it is *our* college. The tutors introduce themselves and tell us where we are to go for the first session after dinner. This time three of them are tutoring at Denman for the first time; we need a constant supply of new and inspiring tutors.

This *is* a place to meet members from all over the country, I have dinner with members from Avon, Surrey, Lancashire and Northamptonshire, who appreciate a meal that they had not planned or cooked. Ones who live on their own say how lovely to have roast meat, others, who have chosen food from the salad bar, say they never get such a choice at home.

Then straight to our first session in the studio – we are all wondering what we will be doing, and why did we have to bring a nail brush? We come with varied experience, someone says she has never done anything of the sort before. Tutor Jane Brown, who teaches at Berkshire College and has tutored at Denman several times before, understands how tired people are this first evening, so gives us some simple pen and ink exercises – I struggle to draw a cork that looks like a cork and a golf ball that looks like a golf ball – encouraging comments from our tutor lift our spirits.

After an hour our tutor says we look tired, and there are indeed some white and weary faces round the room, and no wonder. One member with rheumatoid arthritis has travelled from Norfolk, using British Rail's assisted transport across London from Liverpool Street to Paddington for the first time. Several in the group are well into retirement and have travelled a long way today.

I return to the main house for a drink in the bar before going to bed and I sit with another member on her first visit to the college. She tells me that she works as an administrator at Leicester University and is having few days off to indulge herself before organising a hectic Summer School programme. I look up to the portrait of Grace Hadow above where we are sitting and think, yet again, that although she never knew the college she would have approved. It continues the work that she started.

No one is late to bed the first night.

Over breakfast comments like, "I never have a cooked breakfast at home…", "I came for a real break – no phone no children…", show that home is still in some minds, but already life back home is slipping into the background and the course, the tutor, the work begin to dominate conversation: "What are you going to be doing this morning?", "How did you get on last night?"

By 9.30 a.m. everyone, looking much fresher, is ready and eager to get going again with pen and ink, and now … the nailbrush – we draw a still life with half a lemon, a skein of embroidery wool and the brush. Time flies as the group enjoys its work with quiet concentration. By coffee time it is hard to break off, but the walk back from the teaching centre to the house stretches legs, and rests eyes after all that close work. Over coffee I talk to a group of members who are on the sculpture course. They are full of amaze-ment about the technique they have just learned, in clay modelling, for making eyelids "and the eyes just open!" they say in wonder.

By lunch time we have completed further exercises, the lemons, and red peppers are transferred to paper, in pen and ink and wash, and we are ready to take a short break. I have lunch at the same table as two volunteer gardeners – husband and wife who live nearby and give their services for one day a month. After lunch some go back to the studio early to finish their paintings, others go on the guided tour of the house, or return to their room for a short rest. I go for a walk, across the grass past the Agnes Salter border (I had been Vice Chairman when she was National Chairman and remember her with affection) and down Lime Tree walk, where the trees planted in memory of Mrs Watt, who brought the WI from Canada to Britain and died the year the college was opened, now meet overhead in graceful arches.

Later in my walk I come to the lake; here I find a member sitting on one of the 'wheel-barrow' seats reading a flower book. I sit beside her and she tells me that it is her first visit to the college. She is sharing a room – the first time she has done that with a stranger – she says it is not a problem, but she just feels the need for a little time to her-self away from other people. Here for less than a day but already she tells me that she loves the place – it feels so friendly and safe – "a place I can come to by myself – I wouldn't want to go away on my own." We discuss the lake and how sad it is that there are no swans at the moment, especially as the Denman logo is a swan. She tells me about a swan rescue centre that offers swans that have recovered from injury to suitable places and I make a note to mention this at the next Management Committee meeting.

At 3pm classes start again. Our course goes into the churchyard and people scatter about in the sunshine amongst the long grasses and gravestones. Our task is to draw in detail some small patch. When I return, my drawing completed, I stop to watch and talk to a member, in a sun hat and wearing protective goggles, who is working with chisel and hammer on a piece of stone, making it into a sculpture for her garden. "I've never done anything like this – but I'm really getting a feel for this piece of stone," she tells me. She goes on to say that she is on a limited income and that it took her about 18 months to save up to come but "if you really want to do something you will."

A break for 'Denman tea', lots of talk about how people don't have tea like this at home – but all the sandwiches, buttered tea loaf and cakes disappear. Then back to work again in the studio.

Later, over dinner, I talk to the others on my table; six on a table is just right for discus-sion over the meal. Those on the 'Art Appreciation' course are off to the Ashmolean and the Christchurch galleries tomorrow, and full of praise for their tutor. Later in the evening we have open studios – which gives us a chance to sample something of what the other courses are doing. I go to silk painting and hear Mary Day, the tutor, talking with enormous enthusiasm about her work, and admire the work in progress of her students.

Like most others I feel tired and ready for an early night again. This is really intensive. But by breakfast time we are all keen to get going again and over breakfast I hear from the 'learning to draw' people about the revelation of drawing the spaces between grasses. On the way over to the studio we stop to talk to Charlie the peacock who is moulting his tail feathers; members are on the look-out to find ones he has shed. Our tutor had told us that quill pens are good to draw with, but a peacock tail feather would be a bit unwieldy. Throughout the college the morning passes with members engrossed in drawing, painting, sculpting, one or two don't even bother to go for coffee.

After lunch I meet up with Tracey Strain and Rosemary Lynn, the staff members responsible for planning the programme. Up in their office they are working on putting together the programme for 1999 and we discuss some of the problems involved in juggling all the aspects of producing a balanced programme of liberal adult education to meet the needs of women in 1999. A tutor drops in to discuss a possible new course that she would like to offer, and I return to my pen and wash. I go out in the grounds to find inspiration, as WI members have been doing for the last 50 years, enjoying a 'big house of their own'. I settle down to draw the fountain and remember the story of the member whose oil painting of the lake blew off her easel, improving the final picture.

After tea I meet the Principal. He has just returned from attending a meeting of the National Executive Committee in London. They have been discussing the review of the college which is to be carried out later in the year; the latest in a line of reviews which have been carried out over the years, trying to make sure that the college is being run in the best way, and that the educational work of the organisation is integrated.

In the session before dinner we mount the work we have completed so far, and display it round the walls; 'Pen and Wash' is one of the 'open studios' tonight. I go to hear Dick Onians, the tutor on the sculpture course, talking about his own fascinating work and showing us slides. I talk to Dick; this is his first visit to the college he tells me that he has enjoyed it and hopes he will be asked back again – "everyone is so nice," he says.

This is the last night of our course and so we gather in the drawing room for the entertainment. Christine Whild, a member who lives very close to the college, comes in to play the piano for community singing; a number of members have offered 'party pieces', poems, two written by the member who reads them, light verse – nothing very demanding. A gentle companionable evening with friends. I think back to the description of the evening entertainments of the past, with Betty Christmas talking about Kathleen Ferrier and Margaret Deneke giving classical piano recitals. We are less serious now, but members take more part; it is relaxing and fun.

Breakfast, slightly breathless today as we have all been changing the sheets on our beds ready for the next students. As I try to make a good job of tucking in the corners of the sheets I remember the time when, as I climbed into bed on the first night of my stay, I found something that rustled. It was a note from the member who had made up the bed wishing me a happy time at Denman. Over breakfast I am asked why we allow men at the college. This member feels very strongly that this is a women's college and should be for women only. She explains that the course she is doing was not her first choice, she had been told that her first choice was full; now she is here she sees a husband and wife on that course "and he has my place!"

Our course ends; we are pleased with ourselves as we collect our work together and recognise how much we have progressed. We thank our tutor and tell her that to show our appreciation we have bought three 'bricks' for the 'Buy a Brick for Denman' fund — so that we can build for the future; she is pleased because she knows that one of the plans for the future, when we can afford it, is to build a new studio with better lighting.

It is lunch time again: this time my table companions discuss other courses, Denman Study tours, what is in the next year's Denman programme, what size the bursary is from their WI and how often they give it. This exchange leads to several people saying, "That's a good idea, I'll suggest that when I get back". One member tells me that her grandmother was on one of the first courses at the college, and knew the member who had donated the grand piano. Those who have been before talk about past experience, those who are here for the first time say, "I can't wait to come back." The talk moves to how can we make sure that all WI members know about the college, and encourage them to come … all these people are going back enthusiastic. Gradually talk changes to the impending journey home, and we begin the process of emerging from this special intense form of learning. Who was it said that you learn as much in a short residential course as in a term of evening classes? – they were right. I drive home seeing a pen and wash picture round every corner, planning what I will draw next. I have entered another room off the corridor.

Before I left the college I signed the visitor's book in my bedroom; I leafed through it to read what others had said. Let members have the last word in this book:

Lovely to be in our own bedroom and Willow is really bringing Denman into the 21st century.

'Public Speaking II' – terrific course, superb room – but then it is Denman.

Margaret Meritt's teaching is superb. It was a very enjoyable week.

Denman Reps and VEC conference, a thoroughly good 'talk in' on linked learning.

'Counselling skills'; first but not last visit. A rewarding course and a de luxe bedroom – thanks.

Course on 'Human Behaviour' very good; room very comfortable and luxury of loo and shower. First visit here I hope to come back.

'18th-Century Crafts'. My first visit to Denman – not the last. Was able to cope with physical problems easily thanks to private w.c. etc.

'Denman Fanfare'. Thank you for peaceful retreat after long happy days – an unforgettable experience.

Very interesting course, 'Behind the scenes at the BBC', met some characters, had such a laugh.

'Introduction to word processing, spreadsheets and the internet' was great.

First visit. I've enjoyed every minute and will be back. Going home full of enthusiasm to put all I've learned into practice.

APPENDIX I

LADY BRUNNER'S SPEECH PROPOSING RESOLUTION 5 AT THE ANNUAL GENERAL MEETING, 5TH JUNE 1945

That this meeting welcomes the suggestion of a Women's Institute College and notes with satisfaction the power to provide grants for such a purpose in Clause 100(1) (b) of the Education Act.

In eight minutes it is difficult to give an idea of all that we mean by a WI College. I must take for granted that everyone here has some knowledge of the Danish People's High Schools and the Swedish People's Colleges. *Home and Country*, like many periodicals, has published articles on both within the last year or two.

But I am afraid that quite a number of us here today may have been put off by the phrase 'adult education', and even by the somewhat formal and severe word 'college'. Let us be frank. There is something a bit intimidating about the former – and grim about the latter. Together they neither of them describe what we are after. They sound bleak, institutional, portentous. But when we are using these words – especially when we are thinking about our own WI College – I want you to imagine a place that will be homely and welcoming, where in the pleasantest possible surroundings, away from responsibilities and distractions of our usual lives, we can learn about useful practical crafts, and in addition where we can become better informed about the things going on in the world today, where we can learn more of our heritage, and consider and discuss our future.

At our college we want to be able to continue the work we have begun in our Institutes. We want to give our members opportunities for learning and thinking, in a less distracting atmosphere than the two and a half hours once a month into which, so optimistically, we crowd our manifold activities.

At a WI College of our own, we should be free to experiment along our own lines in the kind of courses we think would best suit our members needs. Besides this, there is an undoubted advantage in a group of people joining together for purposes of learning and study, who already have a common background and point of view. This does not by any means imply a narrow outlook or field of vision. Indeed, one of the advantages of a WI College seems to be that, including as we should women of all kinds and ages from the whole of England and Wales, we should have a richer and more diverse common background than would students at a local or regional college.

Subjects we would wish to include would be ones of general interest and which would create an active interest in citizenship – the future of the village and rural life – local government and education and housing – life in other countries as Lady Denman suggests – history and literature – as well as the more specialist ones of music, drama, handicrafts, agriculture, horticulture and the domestic arts. Besides these we should want to have occasional schools and conferences for the study of our own Institute affairs.

Courses would be short, to begin with anyway, perhaps only two or three days, some for as long as five days or a week according to the response and requirements of Institute members.

General opinion seems to be that accommodation for 40 to 50 students should be aimed at, housed in and around a traditional country house, with small holding and garden attached, and from which the College could be supplied with farm, garden and dairy produce. There would need to be ample facilities for dramatic and musical activities, such as a large barn which could be converted for the purpose if the house itself did not include a large enough room. The kitchen and service quarters should be planned with great care to afford examples of the best modern domestic equipment, managed with the maximum of efficiency. We would like to see in all bedrooms and living rooms examples of our handicrafts – cotton printing, patchwork, quilting, weaving, rug making.

With the utmost use of labour-saving planning and devices, and with domestic help to a certain extent of the students themselves, we believe that the costs for the students could be kept down. No Institute member would feel it unreasonable to carry out a rota of household jobs for an hour in the morning, with an occasional turn at washing up and laying meals. But comfortable beds, well-cooked plain food, plenty of hot water and central heating, combined with the goodwill engendered by the Institute spirit, will make short work of a lot of odd jobs.

So much for what we are to study, and the conditions under which we shall live at our college. Now for our students.

Are we right in anticipating that our members would want to attend such a college? How will they find the time and money? Will those attending be truly representative of our membership? For the last three years the National Federation has been holding at Radbrook, and has arranged to hold at Oxford this summer, residential courses on public questions and international subjects, which have obviously met a real demand. More students have always applied than there has been room for. So even now we know there is a demand for residential courses. But even if, to begin with, we could not fill our college all year round with our own students, it could be let to other organisations for adult education for a week or so occasionally.

If we succeed in making the college all we wish it to be, perhaps people will even come for holiday courses.

It is difficult to talk about finance, as we do not know what grants the Ministry of Education envisages in the clause we are welcoming. If the idea of a college gains support today, it will then be possible to approach the Ministry in order to find out to what extent they are prepared to help us. But WIs in supporting the idea of a college of their own, must expect to have some financial responsibility in the raising of funds, whether for purchase of premises or endowment. By careful planning it should be possible to keep student fees reasonably low, and in some cases Local Education Authorities and Country Federations might give bursaries.

One point that I would like to make, however, is that the Women's Institute movement helps its members to have hobbies that pay — by market stalls for produce and preserves, by teaching of handicrafts and the provision of handicraft shops — and many students might be able to finance their time at the college by their own efforts.

The time. At the moment we have all been very tied for six years; many of our most valuable members have always found that their circumstances of life made it impossible for them to leave home. But will the younger members find their circumstances quite so restrictive as their mothers' have been in the past? Won't their lives, spent away from home in the last six years, have given them a taste for going away occasionally? Won't they plan their lives, even when they are married, to allow of attendance at a short course in a subject that particularly interests them? (Perhaps their husbands will be doing something of the same kind?) And for unmarried women in jobs, won't public opinion encourage employers to release their employees temporarily to attend adult colleges, as is now done in the Scandinavian countries?

To sum up. A college centrally situated could become a much-needed home and focus for our movement. It would provide a means of attracting and interesting the incoming younger members, and it would open new vistas to our older ones. It must be able to welcome our most reluctant and diffident members; it must provide them with the sympathy and encouragement that their first approaches will undoubtedly need. It must provide fun and relaxation as well as instruction. It must not be a place where only our most forceful intellectuals vie with each other in solving the world's problems. What we teach must be related to the everyday practical things that make up our members' lives. In addition, there must be inspiration and a vision of wider horizons, so that life and the living of it becomes more important and worth while.

I beg to move.

Appendix 2

The Student Questionnaire

$\mathbf{A}$s a part of the introductory research for the writing of this book, surveys were conducted among students, tutors and past chairmen of the College Management Committee (or their equivalent) to generate a picture of the college as it is today. This appendix describes the student questionnaire.

There were in fact two questionnaires, one distributed to a sample of students who had attended the college, and one to a control group of students who had never been on a college course.

The questionnaires were developed in the light of discussions with WI members at Denman College, in the Federations and in my own WI, and a study of the findings of others who had done research on short-stay colleges. The two main examples are the 'Residential Colleges Research Project' [2] and the work of Walter Drews [3] on 'British Short-Term Residential Colleges for Adult Education 1945–1995'.

I also received some advice on questionnaire design from a professional market research executive and a recently retired computer manager (who also carried out some parts of the analysis).

The questionnaire for **students who had attended the college** (the 'students' questionnaire) contained 30 questions, covering factual details about when they came to the college and what courses they took, how they rated their experience at the college, what they did after they went home again to follow up what they had learned and a section about themselves, their previous learning experiences and their family and work commitments.

In many of the questions respondents were asked to rate their experiences on a five point scale. There were also opportunities to write in comments.

The questionnaire for **WI members who had never been on a Denman College course** (the 'no-goers' questionnaire) contained 17 questions. The greater part of these were identical with those in the final section of the 'student' questionnaire. There were also two questions about why the respondents had not been to the college.

Distribution

The questionnaires were distributed and collected by the Federation Denman College Representatives. Each of the 70 representatives was given ten copies of the 'students' questionnaire and five of the 'no-goers' questionnaire to distribute to appropriate WI members in their Federation. They received the questionnaires in early November 1996 and were asked return the completed forms by mid-December. In the event returns continued to arrive until the beginning of February 1997.

Response

Out of the 70 Federation Denman Representatives who were asked to circulate the questionnaires only three did not return any completed forms. From the remainder a total of 731 completed returns were received. This represents a 70% response, a very high value which must be due to the commitment of the Denman Representatives who distributed them, for which the author is most grateful.

'Student' questionnaire returns

493 of these questionnaires were returned, an 85% response. Of the respondents, 52% had been to the college within the last year and 25% within the last two years, so 77% of the responses are based on recent experience of the college. 40% of those who responded had been to the college more than three times and some of their comments were based on previous experience.

Of the 493 who had been to the college, 146 had been there on Federation visits, 98 on NFWI training courses and 219 on open courses.

The sample is not completely representative of all students as can be seen from **Table A2.1**

Table A2.1 – Comparison of Questionnaire Sample with all Students

Type of course	% respondents	% all college enrolments
Part of a Federation visit	30	20
NFWI training course	20	5
Open programme	44	75
Other*	6	

This includes students on:

Markets courses	*2%*	
sponsored conference	*2%*	
special event (eg day course)	*1%*	
country house weekend	*>1%*	
study tour	*> 1%*	

This reflects the way in which the questionnaires were distributed. Denman Representatives obviously found it easier to give the questionnaires to such people as Federation committee members who are more like to be attending an NFWI training course. Equally, if her Federation had recently made a Federation visit, the Representative would have been involved in arranging it and would have found those who had been on it an easy target for distributing the questionnaires. Where the analysis of the data has shown significant differences among the three classes, this has been indicated. In some cases only the returns from open course students have been included.

'No-goers' questionnaire returns

Of the 350 questionnaires distributed to those who had not been to the college, 238 were returned, a 68% response. This suggests that those with no experience of Denman had less interest in completing the form, or that the Denman Representatives found it more difficult to discover such people.

Full analysis

In a book of this sort it is not appropriate to include all the detailed analysis and findings of this research. They can be obtained in the full research report which is available, at a small cost, from Denman College. Copies are also lodged in the NIACE library in Leicester.

Denman College
Marcham
Abingdon
Oxfordshire
OX13 6NW

tel: 01865 393991
fax: 01896 391966

NIACE
21 De Montfort Street
Leicester
LE1 7GE

tel: 0116 204 4229
fax: 0116 285 4514

web site http://www.niace.org.uk

APPENDIX 3

THE TUTORS QUESTIONNAIRE

Questionnaires were distributed to all those who were tutors at Denman during a period of six weeks in January/February of 1997.

They were invited to grade, on a five-point scale, their responses to aspects of working at Denman, including support from the college, personal accommodation, teaching facilities, students, their interest and work, and remuneration. There were also opportunities to write in comments.

46 completed forms were returned. Of these seven (15%) were from people tutoring at the college for the first time, and nine (19%) from those who had been coming to the college for ten or more years. No record was kept of how many forms were distributed, but it was probably in the region of 60, representing a 76% return.

The author also held discussions with various tutors when they were working at the college during the autumn and spring of 1996/7. These are acknowledged in the end notes as appropriate.

Appendix 4

Chairmen of the College Management Committee

The author wrote to all those who could be contacted who had chaired the college Management Committee or its equivalent, inviting them either to complete a short, very open questionnaire or to talk on the telephone or to meet.

The questions were about how they saw the rôle of the college within the WI, what had been their main concerns about the college when they had been in office, in what ways they thought the college differed now, and what they would like to see for the future.

Ten people received letters of whom nine responded as detailed in **Table A4.1**

Table A4.1 – Contact with past Chairmen of the Management Committee		
	Date chaired committee	**Form of contact**
Lady Brunner	1948-51	interviewed by author (tape in archives)
Lady Anglesey	1958-60	informal discussion
Elizabeth Harris	1962-65	telephone discussion
Kate Foss (liaison)	1977-85	telephone discussion
Suzanne May (Vice-Chair)	1986-88	completed questionnaire
Jean Varnam	1988	completed questionnaire
Susan Stockley	1988-91	completed questionnaire
Elizabeth Southey	1991-94	completed questionnaire and informal discussion
Shirley Dunster	1994-97	informal discussion

APPENDIX 5

VISIT TO A SCANDINAVIAN FOLK HIGH SCHOOL IN 1988

The short-stay residential college movement, of which Denman forms part, was inspired by Sir Richard Livingstone and others (see Chapter 5 in particular) who had in their turn been influenced by the Scandinavian Folk High Schools. In 1988 Pauline Brown, who was then Principal of Denman, and the author, who was Chairman of the NFWI Education Subcommittee, went on a short study visit to Sweden. This was funded by a British Council Travel grant and grants from various other sources including NIACE. The author also received small grants from East Sussex County Council adult education staff development fund, and from Lewes Technical College INSET budget. We chose to go to Sweden to learn more about Swedish study circles as well as Folk High Schools, and to discover anything we could to help our work at NFWI and at Denman.

We visited Tollare Folkhogskola, at Saltsjo-Boo, a half-hour drive outside Stockholm, a Folk High School owned by the Temperance Association (the arrangements for this visit were made through the Folkbildingsforbundet, the Swedish Association of Adult Education Associations.) This is one of the 'popular education associations' – voluntary organisations – that founded Folk High Schools in Sweden. They provide adult education for those who have not had opportunities earlier in life, and do so whilst promoting their own aims and ideals. The first Folk High Schools were started by 'popular movements'. Now half are owned by county councils or 'municipalities'. Four of the 120 Folk High Schools are associated with the temperance movement. The aims of the temperance movement, started to fight the alcoholism rife in the Nineteenth Century, have now widened to include education and awareness of all substance abuse.

The main building of the school is a beautiful old house in a wooded valley overlooking the sea. Furnished more like a home than a college, we found it comfortable, friendly and relaxed, with an atmosphere not dissimilar to Denman. There were modern buildings in the grounds for residence, teaching and sports facilities.

About two thirds of the work of the High School is in teaching full-time courses, a general course, which lasts two years and can lead to university entrance, a two-year leadership course for youth workers, and a one-year media studies course. The other third of the work is in short courses, varying in length from two days to 15 weeks. About 250 of these short courses are organised each year, and many of them are commissioned by other bodies. 25% of the courses, however, must be planned and taught by the staff of Tollare, and all must include a core module about drug abuse.

Tollare has 18 full-time teachers, who, like all Folk High School teachers, are recruited from people who have already considerable experience of teaching. Their subsequent training acknowledges that they will be working with adults, and that there will be some degree of social work involved. Although the teachers' salaries are paid by the government, other costs of the school are met by the county and municipal councils and the rest by the founding Association:

> Needless to say, the Folk High Schools affiliated to the popular movements have been founded in order to propagate the ideas which these movement represent - to train leaders, improve knowledge and awareness possessed by members and perhaps to acquaint others with the view of man and society taken by the movement. [4]

We were struck by the open and democratic nature of the School. It was obvious that the staff held the Rektor, Lars Svedberg, in great esteem, and yet he was called by his first name and had coffee and meals with the staff and students together. This was something which the Folk High School movement had stressed from Christen Kold's day (p 57), that close contact between teachers and students, not just in class but at other times was an essential part of the process of learning together in a residential environment. We also heard that earlier in the term the school had been closed for a week so that all the staff, including the domestic staff, could spend the time together planning the future of the school.

We could recognise similarities with Denman, in the beautiful surroundings, and comfortably furnished house, the respect for the individual and the shared values. However there were considerable differences in funding, management, and curriculum, and in the reasons for students coming to the High School. In many ways it was less like Denman and more like one of the long-term residential colleges in Britain such as Fircroft, Hillcroft or Coleg Harlech. The majority of the students are seeking not only personal development but also access to other educational and training opportunities.

In 1947, when Elizabeth Brunner and Joan Yeo had visited Folk High Schools in Denmark (p 77), they had found them 'very bleak'. Tollare was certainly not bleak. We found that the visit gave us an opportunity to stand back from our work and it did help us to appreciate the value of the independence which NFWI and Denman College have. This may mean at times that there is a shortage of money, but it also allows development without the restrictions which often come with large amounts of finance from outside.

BIBLIOGRAPHY

The bibliography contains the books that have been referred to more than once in the Endnotes. After each, there are initials in brackets which show how they are referenced in the Endnotes.

Numerous other books are referred to in the Endnotes, where full details are given.

Andrews, Maggie, *The Acceptable Face of Feminism – The Women's Institute as a Social Movement*, Lawrence and Wishart, 1997 (MA)

Davies, Constance, *A Grain of Mustard Seed*, Gee and Son Ltd. (Denbigh), no date (CD)

Deneke, Helena, *Grace Hadow*, Oxford University Press, 1946 (HD)

Drews, Walter, *The British Short-Term Residential Colleges for Adult Education, 1945–1995*, D Phil thesis, University of Ulster, 1995 (WD)

Dudgeon, Piers, (ed.), *Village Voices*, WI Books, 1989 (PD)

Fieldhouse, Roger (ed.), *A History of Modern British Adult Education*, National Institute of Adult Continuing Education (England and Wales), 1996 (RF)

Goodenough, Simon, *Jam and Jerusalem*, Collins (Glasgow and London), 1977 (SG)

Home and Country, the monthly magazine of the WI movement published by the National Federation since 1918 (H&C)

Huxley, Gervas, *Lady Denman, GBE, 1884–1954*, Chatto and Windus London), 1961 (GH)

Jenkins, Inez, *The History of the Women's Institute Movement of England and Wales*, Oxford, 1953 (IJ) (Inez Jenkins was General Secretary of NFWI for 10 years from 1920)

Kaye, Barbara, *Live and Learn, The Story of Denman College 1948–1969*, NFWI, 1970 (BK)

Livingstone, R W, *The Future in Education*, Cambridge University Press, 1941 (RWL)

Lowerson, J, and Thomson, A, (ed.), *Out of Sight, Out of Mind? Barriers to Participation in Rural Adult Education*, 1994, Sussex University Centre for Continuing Education (JL)

McCall, Cicely, *Women's Institutes*, Collins ('Britain in Pictures' series), London, 1943 (CMcCWI)

McCall, Cicely, *Looking Back from the Nineties, an Autobiography*, Gliddon Books, Norwich, 1994 (CMcCLB)

MacDonald, Cheryl, *Adelaide Hoodless – Domestic Crusader*, Dundurn Press (London and Reading), 1986 (CMcD)

Robertson Scott, J W, *The Story of the Women's Institute Movement*, The Village Press, Idbury, Kingham, Oxon, 1925 (JWRS)

Sargant, Naomi, (ed.), *The Learning Divide – a study of participation in adult learning in the United Kingdom*, National Institute of Adult Continuing Education, 1997 (NS)

Smethurst, R, *Sesame and Lilies: Women and Adult Education*, Inaugural Sir Richard Livingstone Lecture, 1993 (given on the occasion of the fiftieth anniversary of his advocacy of an adult residential college for the NFWI – unpublished, copy in the Denman archives)(RS)
Speaking Out, A Public Affairs Handbook, NFWI, 1994 (SO)

Steward, Marjorie, *East Sussex Federation of Womens Institutes 1919–1979, A Short History*, East Sussex Federation of Womens Institutes (Lewes), 1979

Walker, Collins and M McIntyre Hood, *Fifty Years of Achievement*, Federated Women's Institutes of Ontario, 1948 (WCMH)

Walton, Marjorie, *A Quarter of a Century of Womens' Institutes in East Sussex*, East Sussex Federation of Women's Institutes, 1947 (MW) (Marjorie Walton was County Secretary of East Sussex Federation from 1929 to 1951)

Denman Archives

The college has never had a very satisfactory archive policy, and has certainly never had an archivist. What has survived might be described as a random selection of documents. A significant number of the early ones have been torn in half, as though they had been retrieved from a waste-paper basket. As a part of the research for this book the author has begun to catalogue some of this material. Catalogued material is referred to by a File letter and an item number in the references.

NFWI Archives

The archive material is currently housed at Denman College and is being reorganised and catalogued prior to being moved to a more permanent final home.

Minutes

The minutes of various committees and subcommittees have been one of the major sources for the founding and development of the college. The principle series are:

Minutes of the Denman *Ad Hoc* Subcommittee held at Denman.

Minutes of the Denman College Subcommittee held at Denman.

There are two separate sets of minutes for the College Subcommittee. Matters relating to staff conditions of employment were discussed in 'private sessions' when the staff were absent and the discussions were recorded in the 'private session minutes' in a separate book.

Minutes of the NFWI Executive Committee held at NFWI Headquarters.

Minutes of the NFWI Education Subcommittee held mainly at NFWI Headquarters.

Programme of Courses

The college publishes an annual (usually) programme listing the courses for the coming year. Copies of all of these are in the college archives. (Prog.)

Questionaires

As described in Appendices 2, 3 and 4, questionaires were completed by students, tutors and college chairmen. (Quest.)

Other Sources

Annual Reports of the National Federation of Women's Institutes (AnnReps). Copies of these are held at NFWI Headquarters.

Verbatim Reports of the Annual General Meetings of the National Federation of Women's Institutes (VerbReps). These are held at NFWI Headquarters.

Consultative Council Reports (CCR). The National Federation normally held two Consultative Councils per year, attended by representatives from every Federation. These are still held but are now called 'National Councils'. The reports are held in the NFWI archives, and more recent ones at NFWI Headquarters.

Interviews

During the preliminary work for the production of this book the author conducted interviews with Lady Brunner (Sept. 1996 – EBInt), Hilda Jones, a past Principal (June 1997 – HJInt), Graham Jones, Principal (Nov. 1996 – GJInt), and Walter Drews (Nov. 1996 – WDInt). The interview with Lady Brunner was tape recorded and the tapes are held in the Denman College archives. The notes of the interview with Hilda Jones are also in the archives.

There is also a tape in the archives, recorded on 9th October 1992, of reminiscences by Helen Anderson and Hilda Jones (HAHJTape).

Letters

The author appealed in *Home and Country* for reminiscences of Denman from WI members. The appeal included the following invitation:

> … I would especially like to hear from any member who has been to Denman and who can say that the 'experience changed my life'.

29 letters were received as a result and have been deposited in the Denman archives. They are referred to in the endnotes as Lett. There were also several telephone responses which are usually described in the endnotes as 'conversations'.

ENDNOTES

Introduction

1 Livingstone, RW, *Summary of Opening Speech by Sir Richard Livingstone*, Denman College Archives – file A item 5

2 Livingstone, RW, *Speech on the Occasion of Denman College's Fifth Birthday Party, September 22nd, 1953*, Denman College Archives

Chapter 1 – The WI starts in Canada

The material in this chapter derives mainly from *Fifty Years of Achievement* (WCMH) and *Adelaide Hoodless, Domestic Crusader* (CMcD). The latter quotes from the Hoodless Family Papers (HFP).

1 CMcD
2 quoted from a letter in (HFP), CMcD, p 15
3 CD, p 21
4 HFP, CMcD, p 45
5 HFP, CMcD, p 46
6 newspaper report HFP, CMcD, p 50
7 HFP, CMcD, p 72
8 Ruth Howes, *Adelaide Hoodless, Woman with a Vision,* Millett, Alberta, 1965, quoted by CMcD, p 75
9 JWRS, p 10
10 WCMH, p 7
11 CMcD, pp 76–77
12 SG, p 11
13 Mary Quayle Innis, (ed.), *The Clear Spirit – Twenty Canadian Women and Their Times,* University of Toronto Press, 1966 (quoted by CMcD, p 75)
14 From the Minutes of Stoney Creek WI, quoted in WCMH, pp 4–5
15 WCMH, p 7
16 WCMH, p 17
17 WCMH, p 18
18 WCMH, pp 21–22
19 WCMH, p 23

Chapter 2 – The WI comes to Wales and England

The principle sources for this chapter are *The History of the Women's Institute Movement of England and Wales* (IJ), *The Story of the Women's Institute Movement* (JWRS) and *A Grain of Mustard Seed* (CD).

1 IJ, p 1–2
2 quoted by RF, p 1
3 ibid
4 Board of Education Pamphlet No 25 (1912), quoted in JWRS
5 IJ, p 9
6 RS, p 22
7 JWRS, pp 2, 5
8 ibid
9 CD, p 56
10 CD, p 54
11 quoted by CD, p 58
12 from the first Minute book of Llanfairpwll WI, CD, p 88
13 CD, p 56
14 Annual Report of Llanfairpwll WI for 1915–16, quoted by CD, p 98
15 all from the Minute and Record books of Llanfairpwll WI, quoted in CD, pp 78 *et seq.*
16 CD, p 120
17 CD, p 115
18 CD, p 119
19 CD, p 202, an appendix entitled, *"The story of the first WI Market in Great Britain and the important part it played in the foundation of the Navy, Army and Airforce Institute known as NAAFI"*
20 IJ, p 16
21 IJ, p 14

Chapter 3 – Some Remarkable Women

The principle sources for this chapter are the biographies of Lady Denman (GH) and Grace Hadow (HD) and *The History of the Women's Institute Movement of England and Wales* (IJ).

1 JWRS, p 45
2 PD, p 26
3 GH, p 35

4　GH, p 65

5　GH, p 68

6　Bishop of Chichester's address at the memorial service to Lady Denman at Balcombe Parish Church, 9th June 1954, quoted in a commemorative leaflet produced for WIs at that time; in the Denman College archives

7　IJ, p 18

8　Watt, Mrs Alfred, and Lloyd, Ness, *The First Women's Institute School (Sussex 1918)*. The Executive Committee of the Sussex Federation of Women's Institutes. Some copies of this booklet are held in the archives of the East Sussex Federation

9　IJ, p 26

10　H&C, June 1919. There is a photograph of Mrs Watt on the front page, and an article written by her on 'A Women's Institute at Sandringham'

11　GH, p 71

12　JWRS, p 46

13　HD, p 45

14　Campbell, Margaret, *Pioneer Champion of Life in Rural England*, article about Grace Hadow in a 'Limited Edition' of the *Oxford Magazine*, date unknown but probably ca. 1988

15　SG, p 11

16　from the Women's Institute Constitution and rules before recent revision

17　HD, p 169

18　PD, p 99

19　PD, p 46

20　JWRS, p 96

21　IJ, p 66. Inez Jenkins had worked with her.

Chapter 4 – Education in the WI: 1919–39

Most of the material in this chapter is derived from articles published in *Home and Country* (H&C) between the wars.

1　Hadow, Grace, H&C, 1939

2　Hadow, Grace, *The Adult Education Movement and Rural Local Government*, probably unpublished, but reproduction *in extenso* in HD, p 103

3　ibid

4　Editor's Notes, H&C, December 1921

5　H&C, December 1921

6　H&C, March 1920

7　Minutes of the 6th Consultative Council, also H&C, December 1921

8　H&C, March 1920

9　PD, p 69

10　quoted by RF, p 5

11　H&C, March 1920

12　H&C, December 1921

13　H&C report on the first Consultative Council, 1919

14　H&C, January 1920

15　H&C, January 1920

16　H&C, 1920

17　Steward, Marjorie, 1979

18　quoted by IJ, p 93

19　H&C, December 1921

20　*Speaking Out*, p 72

21　H&C, report of the 1924 AGM

22　GH, p 86

23　IJ, p 112

24　H&C, September 1920

25　HD, p 176

26　Steward, Marjorie, p 4

27　Report of HM Inspectors on the *Educational Work of Women's Rural Institutes*, HMSO, 1926. There is a copy of this report in the Denman College Archives

28　H&C, 1921

29　Cecily McCall, 'Look Back from the Nineties', Gliddon Books, 1994

30　ibid

31　IJ, p 113

32　ibid

Chapter 5 – Interlude: a Look at Adult Education in Britain

The principle source for this chapter is *A History of Modern British Adult Education* (RF).

1　WD, p 25

2　RF, p 33

3　RF, pp 166, 168

4　Tawney, RH, *Design for Democracy*, The Manchester Guardian, 19th October 1956, quoted by RF, p 48

5　SO, p 72

6　Groombridge, Brian, *Broadcasting,* in RH, pp 354, 360

7   Grundtvig, NFS, Speech delivered in 1844, quoted in WD, p 13
8   WD, p 58
9   quoted by WD
10 Waller, Ross D, *Residential College, Origins of the Lamb Guildhouse and Holly Royde*, Manchester University Press, 1954, quoted by WD, p 90
11 ibid, WD, p 91
12 WD, p 94
13 WD, p 95
14 Waller, Ross D, *Learning to Live*, Arts & Educational Publishers Ltd, 1946, quoted by WD, p 101
15 Livingstone, RW, *The Future in Education*, Presidential Address to the Educational Science section of the British Association for the Advancement of Science, 1936, quoted by WD, pp 108, 109
16 Livingstone, RW, *Education for a World Adrift*, Cambridge University Press, 1943
17 RWL, p 64
18 ibid, p 65
19 ibid, p 62
20 ibid, pp 68–69
21 ibid, p 92
22 WD, p 247
23 *Educational Reconstruction*, Board of Education, cmd. 6458, 1943, p 22, para 87
24 Education Act 1944 7&8 Geo. VI, c31 section 41, quoted by WD, p 116
25 Table of the Short-Term Residential Colleges; part of a submission to the Warden's Conference, 1959, Denman Archives
26 Association of Wardens of Short-Term Residential Adult Education Colleges: *Submission to the Committee of Enquiry on Adult Education*, 1969

Chapter 6 – Planning for a Brave New World

1   MW, p 26
2   Hadow, Grace, *Women's Institutes and National Emergency*, H&C, 1939
3   H&C
4   MW, p 6
5   IJ, p 73
6   CMcMLB, p 78
7   CMcCWI, p 48
8   GH, p 171
9   NFWI Annual Report, 1942
10 EBInt
11 H&C, January 1943
12 CMcCLB, p 84
13 CMcCLB, p 84
14 NFWI Annual Report, 1943
15 EBInt
16 CMcCLB, p 84
17 Report in H&C, 1943
18 CMcCLB, p 90
19 Letter in H&C, December 1943
20 Letter from Lady Brunner to Pauline Brown, then the Principal of Denman College, dated Jan. 26th and no year but probably 1988. Denman College archives, File A, Item 53
21 NFWI Annual Report, 1945–46
22 ibid
23 ibid
24 ibid
25 ibid
26 ibid
27 ibid
28 ibid
29 ibid
30 verbatim report

Chapter 7 – Vision into Reality

The material in this chapter derives primarily from the writings of Sir Richard Livingstone, from conversations with Lady Brunner, and from various minutes books in the WI and Denman College archives.

1   NFWI Annual Report, 1945–46
2   Minutes of the WI College *Ad Hoc* Committee, 12th September, 1945, Denman College Archives
3   EBInt
4   Letter from Lady Brunner to Pauline Brown, then the Principal of the College, dated 26th January but no year – probably 1987 – College archives, File A 53
5   Lady Brunner's speech (Appendix 1)
6   EBInt
7   ibid
8   RWL, p 42

9   From the notes of Sir Richard Livingstone's address at the opening of Denman College, reproduced in full on pp 12–13

10   Esther Neville Smith, VerbReps, 1945

11   Sir Richard Livingstone, see note 9

12   Brunner, Elizabeth, *Speech at the 1945 AGM*, reproduced in full in Appendix 1

13   ibid

14   ibid

15   Sir Richard Livingstone, *Address at the Opening of the College* (see pp 12–13)

16   EBInt

17   Minutes of the meeting of the WI College *Ad Hoc* Committee, 12 Sept. 1945. The quotations in the two following paragraphs are from the same source

18   Minutes of the Denman College Subcommittee, 23 July 1947

19   EBInt

20   Lady Brunner, quoted by PD, p 119

21   EBInt

22   RWL, p 65

23   The details of the househunting are covered fully in BK

24   Minutes of the WI College *Ad Hoc* Committee, 12 Sept. 1945

25   VerbReps, 1946

26   AnnReps, 1945–46

27   Letter from Lady Albermarle to every WI secretary, July 1946, Denman College archives

28   Letter from Lady Albermarle to every WI secretary, March 1947, Denman College archives

29   ibid

30   Minutes of the WI College *Ad Hoc* Committee, 23 July, 1947

31   Lady Albermarle in letter to WIs, July 1947

32   Williams, Dorothy, *Madam President: Fellow Members,* Worcester Federation of Women's Institutes, 1980

33   EBInt

34   Minutes of the WI College *Ad Hoc* Committee, 23 July 1947

35   Minutes of the WI College *Ad Hoc* Committee, 10 Aug. 1948

36   Minutes of Denman College Subcommittee, 26 March 1947

37   idem, 26 March and 23 April, 1947

38   Minutes of the WI College *Ad Hoc* Committee, 12 Sept. 1945

39   WD, p 168

40   Minutes of the Denman College Subcommittee, 17 March 1947

41   WCMH, pp 62–63

42   WCMH, p 63

43   Minutes of the Denman College Subcommittee, 17 March 1948

44   Minutes of the Denman College Subcommittee, March 1947

45   Minutes of the Denman College Subcommittee, May 1947

46   Minutes of the Denman College Subcommittee, 23 July 1947

47   H&C, June 1948

48   see the Introduction, pp 12–13

Part 2 – Introduction

1   Pulford, A, 'Survey of Existing Members and Potential Members Opinions', Cheshire Federation of WIs, 1994. I have chosen to use this survey as more up to date than the first full survey, 'Survey of Attitudes to the Women's Institutes', commissioned by NFWI and carried out by Strathclyde University in 1980

Chapter 8 – "a Big House of their Own"

1   Miss Christmas to Miss Farrer, 11 Aug. 1948, Denman archives

2   Minutes of Denman College Subcommittee, 24 Nov. 1948

3   Vera Rolph, Surrey, Lett

4   Lady Angelesey, conversation with author

5   Minutes of Denman College Subcommittee, 26 Sept. 1948 and 23 Nov. 1948

6   CCR, Feb. 1949

7   EBInt

8   Quest.

9   Notes on Denman College, 1973, Denman archives. These were prepared in various versions for volunteer members taking guided tours of the house

10   Frances Farrer to Miss Lilley, 24 June 1949, Denman archives File B 6

11   HAHJTape

12 Miss Farrer to J Wilkie (Carnegie UK Trust), 10 Oct. 1947, NFWI archives
13 Minutes of Denman Subcommittee, 7 June 1949
14 Minutes of Denman Subcommittee, 14 March 1949
15 HAHJTape
16 Report in the *Evening News*, 3 May 1949
17 HJInt
18 Elsie Rippon, Briestfield WI, West Yorkshire, to Lyndsay Hacket Pain, Chairman of the 'Save Denman' Appeal, quoted in an appeal leaflet of 1987, Denman archives
19 Telephone interview with Mary Clarke, May 1997
20 Minutes of Denman Subcommittee, 24 Feb. 1959
21 AnnReps, 1957
22 BK, pp 101-2
23 AnnReps, 1961
24 Report and Valuation of Denman College by Cluttons, Oxford, 9 May 1985, Denman archives
25 Minutes of NFWI Executive Committee, 16/17 Jan. 1985
26 Interim Report, Jan. 1985, NFWI archives
27 ibid
28 Report by John Spicer, 4 July 1986, Denman archives
29 ibid
30 AnnReps, 1986
31 Ross Waller, *Learning to Live*, p 48, Art and Educational Publishers, 1946
32 Livingstone, RW, *Speech at the Fifth Birthday Party of the College*, Denman archives
33 AnnReps, 1986
34 Chairmen's questionnaire response (see Appendix 4)
35 Sylvia Foxton, North Yorkshire West, to the author (Questionnaire covering letter)
36 WD, p 261
37 HJInt
38 all quotes from completed questionnaires
39 Pauline Thompson, Coedpoeth WI, Lett.

Chapter 9 – "a Friendly Welcoming Place"

1 Appendix 1, p 246
2 Diana Trotter, Leicestershire, Lett.
3 Quest.
4 Quest.
5 from the report by the Chairman of the Management Committee to National Council, CCR, 1996
6 Quest.
7 Quest.
8 Report of the first Country Housewives course, 4–8 Oct. 1948, Denman archives File A 18
9 Lady Denman to Lady Albermarle, 4 March 1949, Denman archives File A 17
10 *Notes for Chairmen of Courses at Denman College*, dated 22 Feb. 1951, Denman archives File A 18
11 ibid
12 ibid
13 Quest.
14 Viola Williams, Wiltshire, "a WI member in various capacities since 1934", Lett.
15 EBInt
16 Quest.
17 Quest.
18 ibid
19 ibid
20 figures from questionnaire analysis
21 Prog. 1958
22 AnnReps, 1959
23 Quest.
24 Joyce Cormack, Avon Federation, letter to author
25 Joyce Cormack to Ann Evans, Avon Denman Rep. Letter now in Denman archives
26 Quest.
27 ibid
28 ibid
29 Quest.
30 Quest.
31 ibid
32 Joyce Cormack to author, *loc cit*
33 Gwen Paice, Cornwall, Lett.
34 Jeannie Peck, Lincolnshire, Lett.
35 Vera Rolph, a 92-year-old member from West Sussex, Lett.
36 AnnReps, 1966
37 Programme booklet for 1975 annotated by Hilda Jones, then Director of Studies, Denman archives

38 Vera Rolph, *loc cit*

39 Edna Norman, Lett. She enclosed copies of the Timetables for courses from 1957, 1958, 1963, 1965 and 1970, receipts and the programme for the Recital by Dennis Lee

40 Hazel Gaydon, Barcombe WI, in letter to author

41 Quest.

42 AnnReps, 1959

43 AnnReps, *passim*

44 HAHJTape

45 ibid

46 ibid

47 Avril Woolf, East Kent, Lett.

48 ibid

49 Quest.

50 Hazel Gaydon, Barcombe WI, East Sussex, to the author, 1996

Chapter 10 – "the Best in Liberal Adult Education"

This chapter derives almost entirely from the published programmes of the college (Prog.).

1 Denman College Syllabus, 7 May 1948, circulated to all WIs

2 Report of the first Country Housewives course, Denman College, 4–8 October 1948, unsigned but probably written for the Education Committee by the Warden, Denman archives File A 7

3 ibid

4 Lady Brunner to Pauline Brown (Principal 1987–89), 26 January, no year but probably 1988, Denman archives File A 53

5 Diary of a visit to Denman College, 4–8 Feb. 1952, by an unnamed WI member from Alphington WI, Devon, in that WI's archives. Photocopy provided by Christine Trigger.

6 Janet Moss, *Housewife,* Hulton Press, May 1949 (price 1/-). Lent to the author by Mary Clarke

7 Viola Williams, Wiltshire, Lett.

8 BK, p 55

9 *Agendas of A and A/B Courses.* Programme 13 (30 April 1956 – 26 April 1957), Denman archives

10 'Running the Country Home', *Reports on Courses,* 1955–57, Denman archives

11 BK, pp 70–71

12 'Puppets and Puppetry', *Reports on Courses,* 1955–57, Denman archives

13 'The Story of China and Glass', idem

14 'Local Government', idem

15 'Looking Your Best', idem

16 *Agendas of A and A/B Courses,* loc cit.

17 Edna Norman, Lett.

18 ibid

19 AnnReps, 1956

20 ibid

21 AnnReps, 1960

22 BK, p 80

23 Introduction, *List of Courses,* 1961 – 'Types of Courses and How to Apply for Them'

24 BK, p 97

25 Joyce Cormack, Lett.

26 AnnReps, 1961

27 ibid

28 Introduction, *List of Courses,* 1966

29 AnnReps, 1966

30 AnnReps, 1966

31 Introduction, *List of Courses,* 1974

32 CCR, autumn 1970

33 AnnReps, 1974

34 HJInt

35 AnnReps, 1971

36 AnnReps, 1980

37 AnnReps, 1980

38 AnnReps, 1981

39 Unless otherwise indicated, all the following quotations are from Quest.

40 Sylvia Foxton, North Yorkshire E, Lett.

41 *Ackrill Press* (local papers in North Yorkshire), 1 Nov. 1996. The author is indebted to Sylvia Foxton, North Yorkshire E, for this cutting

Chapter 11 – "the Very Best Lecturers and Teachers"

1 GJInt

2 Minutes of the meeting of all the subcommittees of the National Executive Committee to discuss the college programme, December 1947

3 Lady Anglesey in coversation with the author at Denman College, May 1997

4 HJInt

5 CMcCLB, p 94

6 'The Countryside in Autumn', *Reports on Courses*, 1955–57, Denman archives
7 HAHJTape
8 Jan Bateson to Helena Deneke, undated, Denman archives, 1959
9 Lady Brunner to Pauline Brown, 26 Jan. ca. 1988, Denman archives
10 Course programme, 'Genetics Now', 26–29 Oct. 1995
11 HAHJTape
12 H&C, Jan. 1970
13 H&C, April 1952
14 *The Country Housewife in the Garden*, NFWI August 1949 (printed by Oxford University Press and sold for 3d). No author mentioned but a copy was lent to the author by Mary Clarke who had written it
15 HJInt
16 Prog, 1975
17 Report from Conference of sucommittee chairmen organised by the General Education Subcommittee, 15 March 1956
18 Violet Hughes to Miss Bateson (acting Warden), 24 July 1959, Denman archives
19 Helen Anderson (Warden) to Miss Withall (NFWI General Secretary), 31 July 1972, NFWI archives
20 Erica Wooldridge to Miss Withall, 9 Aug. 1972, NFWI archives
21 Minutes of the General Education Subcommittee, 18 Nov. 1955
22 HJInt
23 GJInt
24 Prog, 1987
25 Pat Mann in coversation with the author
26 Quest.
27 Ernie Edwards, in conversation with the author
28 Margaret Merritt, in coversation with the author
29 Quest.
30 ibid
31 Quest.
32 Comment from a tutor to the author during a course, 1996
33 Quest.
34 Quest.

Chapter 12 – "Widen her Horizons"

1 Anne Stamper, *Education and the Women's Institutes*, Adult Education, 59, 33 (1986)
2 Graham Jones, Management Commitee Papers, Jan. 1997
3 Alan Pulford, *Survey of Existing Members and Potential Members Opinions,* Cheshire Federation of WIs, Sept. 1994, NFWI archives, or available from the Cheshire Federation office
4 ibid
5 NS
6 Sylvia Foxton, *Ackrill Press*, 1 Nov. 1996
7 Minutes of the Denman Management Committee, 31 July 1997
8 Rachel Root, Leicestershire, Lett.
9 Lett., but she wished to remain anonymous
10 Jose Loosemore, letter to author, 7 May 1997
11 Quest.
12 Rachel Root, loc. cit.
13 Rhiannon Bevan (Head of NFWI Wales Office) to author
14 Quest.
15 June Cox, East Sussex, Lett.
16 Gwen Richards, Caernarfonshire, Lett.
17 Joan Dean, Suffolk, in conversation with author, 13 Feb. 1997
18 *Slough and Langley Express*, 2 Jan. 1997 (provided by Sheila Gray)
19 Quest.
20 Rose Earl, Northamptonshire, Lett.
21 Jeannie Peck, Lincolnshire, Lett.
22 Quest.

Chapter 13 – "Focus for the Educational Work of the Organisation"

1 Both the Guide Association and the Scout Association have residential establishments but they are used for training leaders and for the use of the young people who belong to the Scout and Guide organisations.

    The Guide Association's Foxlease and Waddow Hall are both attractive old houses in their own grounds, and are used for adult leader training, for guiding activities and also for short holidays and leisure breaks for Guiders, Trefoil Guides and others. They are also available for hire for conferences for business, voluntary and public sector organisations.

    An Grianian, run by the Irish Country Women, and referred to in Chapter 15, is more like Denman, but it is for "all the people of Ireland", not just the ICA.

2 Minutes of the Office and Finance Subcommittee, 17 Nov. 1976. There was a suggestion that the registration in 1963 was not really required

3 ibid. The minutes report that "the only reference to the possibility on file [is] a letter to the Solicitor from Dame Frances Farrer [General Secretary] in 1946 to which there was no answer on file

4 Minutes of a conference of all subcommittee members, 3 Dec. 1947

5 BK, p 78

6 Minutes of Denman College Subcommittee, 1957

7 Minutes of Denman College Subcommittee, Nov. 1961

8 Minutes of Denman College Subcommittee, 15 Dec. 1973

9 Minutes of Denman College Subcommittee, 8 March 1974. Is the final conclusion of this matter the writing of this book?

10 AnnReps, 1978

11 Minutes of Denman College Management Subcommittee, 20 May 1977

12 *Consultative Paper on Future Educational Policy*, 2 Oct. 1977, NFWI archives

13 ibid

14 ibid

15 ibid

16 ibid

17 AnnReps, 1979

18 AnnReps, 1980

19 Kate Foss, telephone conversation with author

20 HAHJTape

21 HJInt

22 AnnReps, 1981

23 AnnReps, 1982

24 AnnReps, 1982

25 AnnReps, 1983

26 AnnReps, 1985

27 Minutes of the Working Party to consider the future of the Education Co-ordinating Group, 4 Nov. 1985

28 Mike Boice in JL p 152

29 AnnReps, 1994

30 1992 NFWI archives

31 comment made on one of the questionnaires returned from a tutor

32 Ross Waller, *Learning to Live*, Arts and Education, 1946, quoted in WD, p 102

33 *Report and Submissions from the Association of Wardens/Principals of Short-term Colleges of Residential Adult Education to the Committee of Enquiry on Adult Education*, Nov. 1969, quoted by WD, p 206

34 BK, p 41

35 CMcCLB, p 77

36 WD, p 168

37 BK, p 69

38 CMcCLB, p 91

39 BK, p 78

40 CMcCLB, p 85

41 CMcCLB, p 92

42 ibid, p 92

43 ibid, p 94

44 ibid, p 95

45 ibid, p 95

46 ibid, p 96

47 ibid, p 97

48 Minutes of Denman Subcommittee, 9 Jan. 1959

49 Private Session Minutes of Denman College Subcommittee, 9 Jan. 1959

50 Shirley Anglesey to Jan Bateson, 25 Sept. 1959, Denman archives

51 BK, p 77

52 Private Session Minutes of Denman College Subcommittee, 6 Nov. 1959

53 Minutes of the Office and Finance Subcommittee, March 1960

54 Private Session Minutes of Denman College Subcommittee, 6 May 1960

55 Private Session Minutes of Denman College Subcommittee, 16 Sept. 1960

56 HJInt

57 Private Session Minutes of Denman College Subcommittee, 4 Nov. 1960

58 ibid, Jan. 1961

59 Elizabeth Harris, Chairman of Denman Management Subcommittee, 1962–65, in conversation with author
60 H&C, July 1964
61 HAHJTape
62 HJInt
63 AnnReps, 1984
64 Minutes of Denman College Management Committee, 12 June 1986
65 AnnReps, 1989
66 Elizabeth Southey, Chairman of the Management Committee, 1991–94, National Chairman 1994–95, in conversation with author
67 AnnReps, 1994, where (unusually) all the staff are listed
68 VerbReps, 1945
69 Minutes of the Conference of General Education and chairmen of other subcommittees, 15 March 1956, NFWI archives, Folder Denman College Tutor Fees CHD3
70 Denman College, Proportion of costs borne by students 1949–58, figures provided by the college for Miss Gray, National Treasurer, 2 July 1959, NFWI archives, file Denman College Tutor Fees
71 Minutes of the meeting
72 Minutes of National Executive Committee, 22 Feb. 1960
73 Garner, Gwen, *Extraordinary Women*, WI Books, 1995, p 72
74 CCR, 1971
75 ibid
76 AnnReps, 1995
77 Prog, 1996/97
78 Minutes of conference of all subcommittee members, 3 Dec. 1947
79 Quest.

Chapter 14 – "Take Back Fresh Inspiration to Share with Others"

The case studies on accreditation and the development of science education draw largely on the author's personal experiences.

1 VerbReps, 1945
2 HD, p 177
3 BK, p 66
4 Denman archives, File A
5 AnnReps, 1956, p 16
6 AnnReps, 1959
7 AnnReps, 1963
8 East Sussex Fed. Annual Report, 1971
9 Anne Ballard, General Secretary NFWI, to all Federation Secretaries, Feb. 1973, NFWI archives
10 ibid
11 quoted in NFWI Newsletter 2 March 1973, NFWI archives
12 Elisabeth Harvey, account written for author, Denman archives. The plans for the conversion of the huts drawn up by Berkshire CC are in the NFWI archives
13 H&C, April 1952
14 Elisabeth Harvey, *loc. cit.*
15 AnnReps, 1956
16 AnnReps, 1988
17 Rachel Root, Leicestershire, Lett.
18 Keith Chandler and Derek Tatton to all participating in the ARCA Curriculum and Accreditation Study Course (3–4 Dec. 1996)
19 Prog, 1956
20 AnnReps, 1956
21 Lewis Wolpert (Chairman of COPUS), *Linking with Science and Everyday Life*, WI Science Newsletter, Spring 1996, available from NFWI
22 Mary Harris, *Denman Textiles Courses, Mathematics Skills Summary*, 28 Feb. 1995, Denman archives
23 VerbRep, AGM 1981

Chapter 15 – What is Special about Denman College?

1 Sir Richard Livingstone's 'Speech on the occasion of Denman College's fifth birthday', 22 Sept. 1953, Denman archives
2 RF, p 257
3 Walter Drews in conversation with author, 26 Nov. 1996
4 ibid
5 WD
6 unpublished; findings summarised in WD
7 Field, J, *Address to the Annual Conference of Principals in Short-term Residential Colleges at Horncastle College*, 1990, quoted in WD, p 274

8   Quest.

9   RF, p 258

10   Hopkinson DM, quoted in RF, p 258

11   Programmes of Urchfont Manor (1996), Missenden Abbey (1996) and Wansfell College (1997–98). Other information from *NIACE Year Book,* 1996–97, and *Time to Learn*, NIACE (published annually)

12   Legge, D, *The Education of Adults in Britain,* Open University, 1984

13   ibid

14   Quest.

15   WD, p 206

16   WD, p 263

17   Schacht, RH, *Week-End Learning in the United States*, Notes and Essays on Education for Adults, No 29, Chicago Centre for the Study of Liberal Education for Adults, 1960, quoted by RS

18   RWL

19   RS

20   Percy, K, et al, *Learning in Voluntary Organisations,* NIACE Unit for the Development of Adult Continuing Education, 1988, p vii

21   Elsdon, KT, Reynolds, J, and Stewart, S, *Voluntary Organisations Citizenship, Learning and Change,* NIACE, 1995, p 1

22   Elsdon, KT, et al, *Adult Learning in Voluntary Organisations, Case Studies,* University of Nottingham Department of Education, 1993

23   handwritten note in the Reports on Courses file 1956–57, Denman archives

24   figures provided by Tracey Strain, Programme planner, August 1997

25   Wedgwood Memorial College headed writing paper

26   Suzanne May, Vice-chairman of Denman Management Committee, 1986–88 and Acting Chairman after Agnes Salter was taken ill. Quest.

27   *Celebrating Eighty Years, 1910–1990,* Irish Countrywomen's Association, 1990

28   WDInt

29   WDInt

30   WD, p 236

31   Handy, C, *Understanding Voluntary Organis-ations,* Penguin Books, 1988, pp 79–81

32   WD, p 236

33   RF, p 259

34   Leighton, B, *Residential Education in a Hostile Environment* in *Residential Adult Education Trends and Prospects,* ed. by Field, J, and Normie, G, Warwick University, 1992

35   ibid

36   Quest.

37   NS, p vi

38   RS

39   Ernie Richards and Liz Colyer in discussion with author at Denman, 5 Dec. 1996

40   reported to author by Walter Drews who was a tutor at the same time

41   Margaret Merrit, art tutor at the college for 20 years, in discussion with author at Denman, May 1997

42   HJInt

43   Maggie Andrews (previously Morgan) MA pp 167–168

44   ibid, pp 219, 220

45   NS

46   RS

47   Carlton, S, and Soulsby, J, *It's never to late to learn*, Adults Learning, Vol. No 4, 1996, p 85

48   *Older and Bolder Newsletter*, 3rd Edition, NIACE, 1997, p 5

49   Carlton and Soulsby, *loc cit*

50   Burrell, M, *Faith in the Countryside,* 1990, p 11, distributed by The Arthur Rank Centre, National Agricultural Centre, Kenilworth, CV8 2LZ

51   Mike Boice in JL p 164

52   McGrath, S, *Adult Education and the Changing Roles of Women in Rural Communities,* ibid, p 185

53   Leonard, M, *The Women's Institutes with special reference to the East Kent Federation of Women's Institutes,* dissertation written for BA in Social History and Heritage Studies, University of Kent, 1996, p 36

54   Pugh, M, *Women and the Women's Movement in Britain, 1914–1959,* Macmillan, 1992, p 227. I am grateful to Monica Leonard for drawing this quotation to my attention

55 Roger Fieldhouse and Associates, *A History of Modern British Adult Education*, published by NIACE, 1966. The '2 pages' re 317–319 come in the chapter on 'Adult Education Auxiliaries and Informal Learning' by Peter Baynes and Harold Marks. In the same book, in the chapter on 'Women and Adult Education' by Roseanne Benn, the WI and Denman College get 5 lines

56 ibid, p 319

57 Quest.

Appendices

1 VerbReps, 1945

2 Field, John, *Residential Colleges Research Project*. This work, carried out at the University of Warwick Department of Continuing Education in 1990, remains unpublished. The findings are summarised in WD

3 WD

4 *The Swedish Folk High School*, Swedish National Board of Education, 1986

INDEX

ABOUT THE AUTHOR

Anne Stamper became a WI member in Ringmer, East Sussex, in 1964, and from 1978–81 she was Chairman of the East Sussex Federation of Women's Institutes. She was elected to the Executive Committee of the National Federation in 1981 and during the following ten years she served, in turn, as chairman of three subcommittees: Organisation, Public Affairs, and Education. She was a National Vice-Chairman from 1986–87, and has served on the Denman Management Committee as Vice-Chairman, and Education Adviser since 1991.

She represented NFWI on the NIACE Council and Executive Committee from 1983–86, and on the Women's Advisory Committee from 1985–88. She was a member of the Council again in 1990 and from 1994–96. She has also served on the IBA's Education Advisory Council (adult section) from 1985–92.

From the mid-1980s, she became a tutor on courses for training tutors of adults, and as a freelance trainer began to work with a variety of organisations. At the same time she started to work for the RSA Examinations Board to develop accreditation for those who organise and manage voluntary organisations. She chaired the working party that developed the qualification and she has been Chief Verifier for Community Schemes for ten years and a trainer and RSA External Verifier for Training and Development NVQs.

Anne Stamper is a member of the RSA Examination Board's Education Council and was elected a Fellow of the RSA in 1990.

She has also written materials for, and worked on training with, the Open University, the University of East London, Oxford Community Education, Gloucester TEC, Wealden District Council, East Sussex County Council, Southwark College, the Scouts Association, and Sussex Rural Community Council.

Her publications include: *Chemistry for Biologists* (jointly with her husband) (Allen and Unwin, 1971); Open Learning packs in 'A' Level Biology, 'A' Level Environmental Science, and *Organising in Voluntary and Community Groups* (National Extension College, various dates); *Education and Training Beyond School, Case Study – 'Environmentalism and Learning'* (Open University, 1993); *Accreditation in Voluntary Organisations and Community Groups* (RSA Exam Board, 1996).